MYTHS WE LIVE BY

RELIGIONS AND BELIEFS SERIES

The series includes books bearing on the religions of the Americas, the Bible in its relationship to cultures, and on ethics in relation to religion. The series welcomes manuscripts written in either English or French.

Editorial Committee

Robert Choquette, Director

Margaret Dufour-McDonald

David Jeffrey

Pierre Savard

In the Same Series

RELIGIONS AND BELIEFS SERIES, NO. 8

Myths We Live By

COLIN GRANT

University of Ottawa Press

University of Ottawa Press gratefully acknowledges the support extended to its publishing programme by the Canada Council, the Department of Canadian Heritage, and the University of Ottawa.

CANADIAN CATALOGUING IN PUBLICATION DATA

Grant, Colin

    Myths We Live By

(Religions and Beliefs Series; no. 8)
Includes bibliographical references.
ISBN 0-7766-0444-9

    1. Myth. 2. Civilization, Modern–20th century. I. Title. II. Series

BL304.G73 1998   291.1'3   C98-900333-7

Cover illustration after an original by Neil D. Grant

Typesetting: Infographie G.L.

ISBN 0-7766-0444-9

Printed in Canada

To Sheina, my mythus.

CONTENTS

PREFACE

Myth and religion have suffered similar fates in the modern Western world. Myth has been relegated to the naïvetés of the past, either as an expression of much simpler cultures or as the misunderstandings of the uninformed; religion escapes this fate only insofar as it retains some significance for individuals as a private option. However, as orphans of modernity, myth and religion may team up to challenge some of modernity's pretentions and, in the process, re-establish some of their credentials.

In its scholarly form as stories of gods, goddesses, and heroes, and in its popular form as a designation for falsehoods that have now been exposed and thus no longer deserve serious consideration, myth has recently come to have a fundamentally negative connotation. However, if the notion of myth is broadened to encompass perspectives and priorities that we take for granted, just as ancients took for granted the stories of gods, goddesses, and heroes and as people subscribed to exposed myths before their exposure, then we find ourselves facing a much more positive sense of myth—that of living myth, as unavoidable as it is elusive. It represents commitments in life that are so basic and assumed that we normally do not notice them, much less reflect on them.

Living myths represent a web of visions and loyalties that give life shape and meaning. Some of the more obvious are identifiable in terms of factors that enjoy widespread influence today, such as science, which provides the authoritative definition of reality for us; sport, which is so popular as a diversion that it can become an obsession; consumption, which readily changes means of living into ends; sex, which for feminists can be the defining category of life; ecology, which presents claims for total conversion in outlook and lifestyle; values, which turn out to reflect a nostalgic vacuity that allows us to think we are dealing with something significant when we are asserting preferences; and society, which readily replaces God as horizon of meaning.

The mythic dimensions of each of these areas become evident as the loyalty to it tends to assume proportions of totality. The sports fan who lives for sport is really living a sports myth; the person who lives to shop is living a consumer myth. When we are immersed in a life-threatening ecology crisis, the ecological challenge takes precedence over everything else; when sex is seen to determine opportunities in life, it can become the feature of central significance. The tendency for each of these living myths to assume dimensions of totality implies that they are performing functions of religion: they are defining our reality and establishing our priorities for living. Thus, the nature of our mythic involvement becomes evident when we approach it from the perspective of the totality that is peculiar to religion.

Myth becomes visible under the spotlight of religion, but this does not mean that myth and religion can be identified in any direct way. It is tempting, for example, to think of living myths as substitute religions; however, this is possible only if we have some direct awareness of religion itself. This would entail an involvement in a religion myth, but that presents difficulties because if each of these living myths reaches out toward religion, religion can hardly be just another myth, belonging somewhere beside the others. Religion must represent a distinctive kind of myth, and the most immediate way to think of this is to see religion as the myth that addresses the issue of totality explicitly. Thus, a religion myth, whatever its specific form, will represent a vision of what is ultimately real and worthwhile. Other living myths can then be seen as approximations to this, when they come to dominate life to the point of constituting sources of basic meaning and direction.

This means that religion represents the formal vantage point from which the reality of living myths is identified; it also constitutes a standard by which the religious pretentions of these myths stand exposed. Then the fact that they can take on religious proportions does not indicate a continuing significance for religion in secular culture, but suggests that we may be much further removed from genuine religious sensibility than we have supposed when we can allow interests and commitments such as science, sport, sex, and consumption to elicit the veneration appropriate to religion.

While religion provides a perspective on living myth, it is not without liabilities of its own. As the direct approach to the issue of totality, religion may be the most pretentious myth of all. A religion myth, taken seriously in its own right, is even more tragic than allowing other living myths to take on religious proportions. In exposing the religious pretentions of living myths, religion must include itself in that group, in spite of its distinctiveness, precisely in order to protect that distinctiveness. The transcendent reference of religion demands that religion be critical of itself as well as of the religious pretentions of other living myths.

Thus, while it is distinctive in addressing the issue of totality explicitly, religion shares with other living myths the danger of being taken too seriously in itself. Genuine religious sensibility involves a transcendent claim that is characterized by a simultaneous sense of having and not having. Consequently, myth represents the appropriate medium for expressing religious sensibility, just as religion provides the vantage point for recognizing our mythic involvements. The peculiar situation that we face today is the recognition that this is the case, that we are involved in myth and that our religion is mythic. This means that we are in the process of learning to live self-consciously with myth.

What makes this so challenging is that myth that is recognized is not functioning to full effect. For the prevailing understanding of myth, this amounts to dismissing it in the very act of recognizing it. Living myth is distinctive in presenting the challenge of living with broken myth, with myth that is recognized as myth. Such recognition affords an illuminating vantage point for reflecting on how we live today, and it also exposes the challenge of the significance of these perspectives and priorities in terms of religious visions in an age when there is a prevailing assumption that religion has been superseded as decisively as myth.

The material in this book has been tried out on Mount Allison students. I am grateful to them for their appreciation and challenge, and to colleagues and authors for insights and directives. I also appreciate the assistance of the editorial staff of the University of Ottawa Press. I am particularly grateful to Robert Choquette, director, Religions and Beliefs Series, Vicki Bennett, Editor-in-Chief, and Käthe Roth, Copy Editor. I am indebted to our ultracompetent department secretary, Robin Hamilton, for technical assistance in preparing the manuscript. Since myth is most recognizable in others, my most immediate experience of it comes from my two sons, a radio producer who exhibits an obsession with cars that is decidedly mythic and a graduate student who confirms the reality and influence of a sports myth, and of course from my main mythus, to whom the book is dedicated, my wife, Sheina.

1

THE MEANING OF MYTH

F<small>EW</small> endeavours would appear to be more useless than a consideration of myth, if myth is taken in the sense in which it is generally used. To refer to something as myth is to suggest that it is false, naïve, passé, a matter for the uninformed and the gullible. There may well be signifi- cance in the identification and examination of views and concepts that are seen to be false, but the study of myth becomes even more signifi- cant when myth is understood in more positive terms. If it is seen not as mistaken views but as comprehensive visions that give shape and direction to life, it moves from being dispensable misunderstandings to essential categories that we all take for granted. To appreciate myth in this comprehensive and engaging sense, we have to get away from the popular equation of myth with falsehood, and we must distinguish the personal sense of myth from the academic approach that has tended to characterize its scholarly treatment. Contrasts between these two prom- inent senses of myth should clarify the kind of understanding of myth that makes it a vital subject for study in the contemporary context.

Journalistic Myth

The clearest way to appreciate the popular pejorative connotation of myth is to cite some instances of its usage in this sense. A recent issue of *Business Horizons*[1] has an article with the title "The Mythical World of Workplace Violence—Or Is It?" The way "myth" is meant is given away in the subtitle, "Or Is It?" The title could be rewritten as

"Workplace Violence is Not a Subject for Serious Concern—Or Is It?" What the author is concerned with is that "a paucity of information on workplace violence, the suspect nature of some of it, and the perception that what data are available are being misinterpreted have led some researchers to conclude that the magnitude of the problem is not as serious as it is being represented." This leads to the title, the point of which is spelled out: "A series of myths has emerged from this controversy." This, in turn, identifies the point of the article, which is "to examine those myths" (31). People do not take workplace violence as seriously as they should because they accept certain misrepresentations of it, certain myths.

One myth is, "Research data on workplace violence include all physical acts of violence against employees, such as homicide, and rape, as well as against property, such as arson, robbery, and sabotage." This is a myth, because the truth is, "Annual information on workplace violence, derived from a consistent and valid methodology, is available only on workplace fatalities, notably homicides and suicides" (32). Another myth is, "The main perpetrators of workplace violence are employees." The truth is, "90 percent of homicides and 68 percent of assaults are committed by customers and strangers" (33). Who is most at risk for workplace violence? What is the most dangerous profession? The myth is, "The most dangerous occupation from a workplace violence perspective is law enforcement." But this is myth, not truth: "Although law enforcement is dangerous, the occupations with the highest risk of work-related homicides are taxi drivers and chauffeurs" (34). In terms of nonfatal assaults, it is health care workers who are most at risk—nurses' aids and nurses, especially those working in nursing homes (34). The message of the article is, "Perhaps the biggest myth of all is that there is a 'false crisis' in the concern over workplace violence." These myths have to be seen through before the seriousness of the situation can be appreciated. "A good starting point is obtaining better information about violent acts in the workplace" (35). There is the contrast—myth and better information. Myth is falsehood, the contrast to which is truth as accuracy.

In a lighter and briefer vein, Steve Martin contends in a *New Yorker* editorial that "Writing Is Easy!"[2] One reason for this is indicated in a paragraph heading: "Writer's Block: A Myth." The first line of that paragraph leaves no doubt about how the term is being used: "Writer's block is a fancy term made up by whiners so that they can have an excuse to drink alcohol."

These examples of the journalistic sense of myth reflect a common perspective, the connotation of falsehood. Lack of concern with workplace violence is unwarranted, and it is due to false ideas about the nature of the problem. It is a myth founded on myths, a false security based on misinformation. The idea that writing is a difficult activity, subject to dreaded writer's block is false; it is a myth.

Although this sense of myth carries the connotation of falsehood, and even of culpable falsehood, closer reflection on these typical examples might suggest that this view of myth is itself something of a myth, in its own sense of the term. That is, the suggestion that these views are simply false is itself false. The truth of the situation is much more subtle than this absolute designation of falsehood would allow. As the author of the article on workplace violence admits, how it is seen depends on how it is defined. This is more than a matter of information and statistics. It involves judgments: how serious does an attack have to be before it is considered violence? If we are to think of this as myth, then myth takes on a much wider connotation. The reference to writer's block may be frivolous, but it does reflect a clear assumption of the journalistic use of myth as connoting something that is simply false. To recognize that writer's block is a myth, assuming Martin means this seriously, does not discount the countless writers who have experienced this lull in creativity. They are living the myth, and for them it is not simply falsehood—or, if it is, it is one in which they are caught. In real life, truth is not so clear and unequivocal. Especially where significant issues are at stake, we are apt to discover that we are operating with fundamental visions and perspectives that are best understood as indispensable myths.

Besides ignoring these wider influences and allegiances that shape our vision of truth, the journalistic approach to myth has another curious feature in that, as falsehood, myth is really recognized only through exposure, and once exposed, it is no longer to be taken seriously. Something is identified as "myth" expressly for the purpose of dismissing it. Workplace violence is not a matter for general concern, but the claim that this is a mistake, and a mistake that is based on all sorts of confusion about the extent and seriousness of workplace violence, is meant to expose this lack of concern as a myth. It is wrong. If you get the point the author is trying to make, you will see that lack of concern is based on myth, and is itself a myth, and should be reconsidered. Myth is falsehood that is exposed as soon as its mythic nature is recognized. Writer's block is a myth, an excuse for getting drunk. If people take this tongue-in-cheek treatment seriously, they will not worry about writer's block again.

This curious situation, in which myth as falsehood really comes into existence though having its falsehood exposed indicates something about the nature of myth in general, and about this journalistic view in terms of falsehood in particular. The general point is that myth is functioning optimally when we are not aware of it. To identify something as myth is already to have stepped outside of its own perspective to some extent. This is the conundrum in which we shall continually find ourselves in this examination of contemporary myths. To identify something as myth is to have broken the spell to some extent. The further step that the journalistic sense of myth takes is to believe that this can be done directly and completely. To identify something as myth in this sense is tantamount to dismissal: myth is born and dies through exposure. As soon as something is recognized as myth—given life as myth, as it were—it dies.

The paradox of this identification of life and death is mitigated somewhat when we consider the perspective involved in the journalistic approach itself. The vehicles of journalism, the mass media, are in the information business. Their priority is to report what is happening as quickly and accurately as possible. From this perspective, falsehood is the enemy. It is not surprising, then, that the mass media should be intent on exposing and shattering myths, when myth is taken to be tantamount to falsehood, as in not taking workplace violence seriously enough, or in taking writer's block too seriously. The issue is the adequacy of this designation. And, as we have seen, what is at stake here is really the view of truth that is assumed. If truth is direct factuality, correct information, then myth can be dismissed as falsehood and misinformation. The question turns on how immediate or elusive we take truth to be. Another way to pose the issue would be to ask where journalists stand when they expose and shatter myths. Their assumption would be that they stand on evidence, on incontrovertible truth. The question this raises is whether their stand is so firm and assured, or whether they themselves are operating out of visions and priorities that shape their understanding just as surely as that of those who hold the myths they expose. Insofar as the truth is wider than their view allows, it could be said that they are operating out of an information myth.

Recognition that advocates of journalistic myth are making this kind of claim exposes another dimension of this sense of myth. Not only does it equate myth with falsehood on the basis of a view of truth as exact, correct information, but the myths it exposes are always those of other people. The exposer of the myth of workplace violence knows that it is a serious matter and wants to persuade those who are not concerned about it how wrong they are; Steve Martin knows that writer's block is just an excuse, and wants to make us aware of that (assuming that there is serious intent behind this playful piece).

Integral to the falsehood reading of myth is its association with other people, or at most, with the journalist's own past. The one thing that is totally precluded is any present ownership of myth. Who would want consciously and deliberately to embrace any aspect of falsehood? The issue, of course, is once again the adequacy of this reading of myth. What we are now seeing is that not only does this reading depend on a particularly narrow view of the nature of truth, but it also carries the implicit claim that the exposer of myth is in undisputed possession of that truth. If this is the case, there is nothing more to be said. The only recourse is to bow before the experts or to stake our own claim to expertise. If truth is more elusive, however, especially as the more significant issues of life come under consideration, it not only challenges this approach, but threatens to undermine the equation of myth with other people's falsehood. It opens up an alternative in which myth is seen as far less dispensable and our own situation changes from impersonal expertise to a more confessional recognition that we see life from the inside, drawing on all sorts of unrecognized and half-recognized myths.

Scholarly Myth

While myth is subject to dismissive treatment in the media, and tends to carry that connotation in popular usage, there is one place where it is taken very seriously: in academia. In anthropology, classics, folklore, philosophy, and religious studies departments, myth is often the subject of study and research. Perhaps its most prominent association in the scholarly sense is with classics courses. The myths of ancient Greece and Rome are standard academic fare, alongside the culture, history, architecture, and archaeology of those civilizations to which we are heir.

Mythology courses in classics departments identify the gods and goddesses of ancient Greece and Rome, and recount their exploits among themselves and in the world of mortals. So intertwined are these elements that the line between stories of the gods and goddesses and tales of human heroes is not always obvious: as a result, there is considerable ambiguity about the classical sense of myth. Tales of the immortals, sages, military heroes, and rulers who took on the aura of divinity obscure the line between the myths of the gods and folktales about extraordinary human exploits. Attempts are made to distinguish legends, sagas, fables, folktales, and other categories from myth in terms of differences in subject matter, scope, or intent. The fact that no generally accepted classification has emerged, however, testifies to the intricate and ambiguous reference of myth in this scholarly usage.

Perhaps the best that can be said is that while legendary accounts and great epic sagas are not always clearly distinguishable from myth in the context of classical cultures, as a general rule, myth may be identified in terms of its comprehensive focus and its interest in universal themes, such as those of origin, often bearing implicit, if not explicit, religious overtones.

One of the Greek myths that has resurfaced over the centuries down to our own times is that of Sisyphus. The gist of the myth is that Sisyphus, King of Corinth, angered Zeus, and as a result was condemned to spend eternity in Hades attempting to roll a rock up a hill, which inevitably rolled back down again. We can imagine that myth being told and retold in its original setting, conveying a vivid and immediate warning against offending the gods. The myth has come down to us in its more refined and elaborated literary form, and in the process has lost much of that immediate impact.

This scholarly approach takes myth very seriously, in contrast to the journalistic sense, in which myth is identified essentially to be dismissed. Here, myths are held to be interesting in themselves; they are catalogued and studied as clues to the beliefs and behaviours of ancient peoples. By that very fact, however, this approach bears a striking resemblance to the journalistic sense: in both cases, myths are from the past and, in a fundamental sense, belong to other people. If the journalistic usage refers to myths to which we subscribe ourselves, that subscription is over and done with to the point at which acknowledgment of our previous ownership is very unlikely. In the scholarly approach, our distance from the myths under consideration is integral to the study. In both cases, the myths are associated with other people, and our sense of dissociation has a great deal to do with the sense of falsehood connoted by this term.

Classical scholars do not devote their lives to the study of ancient civilizations without a profound fascination with, and respect for, the cultures they study; yet, as scholars, their approach is characterized by the detachment that befits academic endeavours. Nowhere is this detachment more evident than in the study of ancient myths. The foreignness of mythology from our own perspective on life is clearly indicated in the definition of myth provided by *The Oxford Classical Dictionary.*

> This may be defined as a pre-scientific and imaginative attempt to explain some phenomenon, real or supposed, which excites the curiosity of the myth-maker, or perhaps more accurately as an effort to reach a feeling of satisfaction in place of uneasy bewilderment concerning such phenomena. It often appeals to the emotions

rather than reason, and, indeed, in its most typical forms, seems to date from an age when rational explanations were not generally called for.[3]

Myths are pre-scientific, if not also pre-rational, attempts by people much more primitive than ourselves to account for and domesticate the bewildering and sometimes frightening world in which they lived. The parallel with the journalistic usage is clear. We are rational and scientific. We are informed. We know that gods do not exist, and so we are not going to take seriously stories that tell of the danger of offending them. We explain things by natural laws and statistical frequencies. Our interest in the mythology of the ancient Greeks and Romans is largely, if not exclusively, historical. As in the journalistic sense, so in the academic study of mythology, we look at myth from the superior vantage point of our own enlightenment.

In this century, the Sisyphus myth was revived by Albert Camus as a portrayal of the futility of life. In this usage, however, the myth is essentially illustrative of a perspective on life that is arrived at independently of the myth itself. In the myth's original function, the hearer identified with the plight of Sisyphus and was engaged by the myth directly and personally. This is not possible for us because the gods do not exercise this authority over our imaginations. If the myth still speaks to us, however, it may involve more than simply drawing on the myth for illustrative purposes. It may be indicative of the myth that defines reality for us, as the stories of the gods and their interactions with mortals did for ancient Greeks. The myth of Sisyphus speaks to Camus because deep down he sees life as pointless and futile. This basic vision could be regarded as the myth out of which he lives. Thus, the difference between a modern sophisticate such as Camus and devotees of ancient myths is not that Camus has left myth behind, as the classical definition would suggest, but that he is operating with a different type of myth.

The mythic immediacy of the ancient world and the scholarly detachment of the modern era are linked to some extent through the legacy of Western civilization. Greek philosophy and culture and Roman law and administration exert their influence across the centuries to this day. Greek and Roman religion, however, were eclipsed by the Judaeo-Christian traditions. As a result, we are apt to find myths that retain more direct connection with our understanding of life in these traditions studied by religious studies departments, than in the Greek and Roman focus of classics departments. One such possibility is the myth of the Fall recounted in the third chapter of Genesis. This is the story of how the first human pair, Adam and Eve, were enticed to eat the fruit of the forbidden tree, and in so doing, like Sisyphus, they offended God, and were ejected from their Garden of Eden paradise. Some Jewish and Christian believers would reject the application of the term "myth" to this account. For them, the veracity of the story depends on its having actually happened. "This is not myth, but a historic account of the origins of human life, and how it went wrong right from the start," some would assert.

There is a curious irony in this refusal to think of the account of the Fall as myth. The motivation for the refusal is essentially religious. The theological truth of the account is seen to depend on its historical accuracy. Either this is a true account of what really happened, or it is just a story. The irony is that behind this concern with the accuracy of the account lies the view of truth we saw implied in the journalistic sense of myth: truth is all or nothing, accurate information or falsehood. There is no consideration of a wider sense of truth that is more ambiguous and resistant to possession and display. For such an understanding, myth is a medium of truth, rather than its antithesis, and the more wide-ranging and significant the matter is, the more it is likely to be mythic truth that is at stake.

The Fall can be seen to be myth and truth at the same time because it is pointing to a perennial reality, and not to a distant historical event. From this perspective, the truth of the story does not depend upon the historical existence of Adam and Eve and their performing the actions attributed to them. The myth can be seen to be talking about you and me, and about life as we experience it today. It is about grasping at life out of our own narrow insecurity and the disastrous consequences that ensue when we try to displace God. A prominent example today is the environmental crisis. We have eaten the fruit of many trees through the ingenuity of modern technology, and it has often been very sweet. However, it is becoming increasingly difficult to avoid the negative side effects that were never anticipated in our enthusiasm for new power and control over life. Chemicals used to control insects ended up killing the songbirds that feed on those insects, and an early warning of environmental backlash was sounded in Rachel Carson's *Silent Spring*. Fossil fuels carry us around the world and make life more comfortable at home, but there are indications that we are in the process of transforming the atmospheric balance of the planet, with who knows what eventual consequences? Far from the account of the Fall losing its significance when it is detached from the historic accuracy of its details, it is only in this wider sense that it really takes on engaging meaning for us today. The limits on that meaning are set not by ancient events, but by our imagination and sensitivity.

A sense of truth as living engagement, in contrast to factual accuracy, gives myth a much more significant role in life generally, and challenges the tendency to exempt ourselves that goes with the equation of myth with falsehood or with beliefs and perspectives held by other people. But how wide can this sense of mythic truth be? Many Jews and Christians would have no difficulty with thinking of the Fall as myth, in the sense just described, but how many observant Jews would be ready to see the notion of the chosen people, or even the Torah, the sacred tradition of Jewish law that defines the shape of life for Jews, in similar terms? How many Christians would be comfortable thinking of the significance of Christ in terms of a redeemer myth? An answer to these questions will depend on how myth is understood. Insofar as myth stands in contrast to truth, the more significant a belief is, the more it must be distinguished from myth; conversely, the more myth is seen to embrace truth, the more it will be not only possible, but necessary, to think of our own basic perspectives, and not simply those of the naïve or the dead, in terms of myth.

Living Myth

In identifying myth with the past, journalistic and scholarly approaches, in their respective ways, reflect the dominant understanding of myth that has prevailed in the modern West. The shape of that understanding is articulated succinctly by the Dutch sociologist C.A. van Peursen, who describes our approach to life today as "functional," in contrast to the "ontological" focus that preceded it, and to the "mythic" outlook that preceded that.[4] The functional approach reflects the outlook and possibilities of the scientific era. Our inclination today is to try to figure out how things work and manipulate them so that they work as efficiently as possible. This approach differs from the more philosophical orientation of the ontological era that preceded the triumph of modern science. The inclination then was to try to understand and appreciate life, rather than to try to take control, as we have done in the functional era. If we go further back behind the search for wisdom, which is what "philosophy" really means (love of wisdom), that is where we find myth. The mythic approach to life is the earliest one of all, when human beings felt themselves to be surrounded by spirits, good and evil, and lived in terms of the stories of these gods, goddesses, and heroes, rather than trying to penetrate the mysteries of life rationally—much less through developing means of taking control.

A parallel schema is sketched by the pioneer anthropologist Sir James G. Frazer in *The Golden Bough*, where he identifies an animistic/mythological age, followed by a religious era, which has been succeeded by our own scientific epoch. An individualized version is given by Sigmund Freud in *Totem and Taboo*. The mythical age of animistic immediacy has its individual analogue in the narcissistic preoccupation with self. This is not self-consciousness in the modern sense, but almost the reverse, the undifferentiated sense in which there is little or no self-consciousness. Everything is self, and self is everything. Life is lived with an infantile immediacy. The self begins to emerge only when the individual begins to recognize the non-self—that is, that there is something, or, more likely, someone other than self. This recognition is usually evoked by the mother, as the other with whom the child has the earliest prolonged contact. This self–object differentiation corresponds roughly to the more reflective stage of rational speculation about the nature of reality that characterizes van Peursen's ontological era. The full development of this sense of external reality results in self-consciousness, corresponding to the functional approach of the modern era. To take charge of the world and shape it to our own requirements implies a sense of ourselves as distinct from the world and of the world as available to us in our distinctness.

One other version of this schema should be mentioned because it underlies van Peursen's sociological variation, and it has exerted considerable influence in its own right. It was proposed by the thinker who is generally regarded as the founder of sociology, Auguste Comte. He saw humanity progressing from the naïve projections of a "theological stage," in which people assumed that life was controlled by spirits that were really just enlarged versions of themselves, to the speculations of a "metaphysical stage," where they devised rational theories about reality, to the precision of the "positive stage" made possible by modern science. The terms vary to some extent, and some make explicit reference to myth while others do not, but the basic direction of the accounts is the same. Humanity has progressed from the naïveté of myth, through the reflection of philosophical speculation, to the precision of science. Thus, we are doubly removed from myth today, having moved from immediacy to the more sophisticated level of philosophical reflection, and from there to the more precise and rigorous methods of modern science.

The accuracy of this general characterization of the history of human consciousness can hardly be questioned. Myth in the immediate, living sense belongs to the directness of oral cultures. So different is this from life as we know it that it is difficult, if not impossible, for us really to appreciate what it involves. Our knowledge of ancient myths is mediated through the later development of writing. Thus, we have access to ancient Greek myths through the adventure stories of Homer or in plays and poems that reflect the shift from oral to written culture. Consequently, even in our earliest sources, the spell has been broken. Myths are identified in their own right, and so the authors stand outside them and treat them somewhat as artifacts, if not with a degree of detachment comparable to our own, at least with enough detachment to think of them in a way that is closer to our attitude than to that of the people who really embraced, and were embraced by, them in their engaging oral form.

This transition is given explicit statement in Plato, as rational reflection supplants the immediacy of story, and the new era of Christianity, with its priority given to the intellect, is moulded particularly by his legacy and that of his somewhat rebellious pupil, Aristotle. The immediacy of the gods, and of God, gives way to delineating correct beliefs about God and even to developing arguments to demonstrate that God exists. This kind of rational activity, even in theological form, is distinctly different from the immediacy of myth. The issue now has to do particularly with metaphysics, with determining what reality is really like.

The third stage is marked in particular by the scientific revolution. The first clear emergence of this era involves looking to the heavens, but the essence of the transition has to do with concentrating the human gaze on the earth. The scientific revolution became evident as a revolution in cosmology. The age-old sense of occupying the centre of the universe was shattered by the hypothesis, and its mathematical and observational confirmation, that we are on a planet orbiting the sun. Shattering though this demotion generally was, the impact of the scientific revolution was due even more to the method by which it had effected this transformation than to the substance of the change in the understanding of the universe itself, for with the passing of the long-accepted view of the universe went also the tendency to place confidence in any long-accepted views. The authority of tradition was replaced by the authority of evidence and experiment. The method of rational argument, drawing on the authority of Plato or Aristotle, or even on that of scripture, was replaced by the scientific method. Experimental evidence or, more recently statistical correlation, came to be the standard for truth.

This overall development helps to account for the tendency today to equate truth with accurate information, and for the tendency to see myth as the complete contrary of such accuracy. The connotation of story has receded, except perhaps in the sense of tall tale, and the connotation of superseded naïveté has become dominant. Myth is exposed falsehood. We have raised questions about this in terms of the view of truth assumed. If this equation of truth with accurate information is not totally adequate to deal with the issues life presents to us, then the absolute contrast between truth and myth may be overdrawn. We can now approach the same issue from the other side by considering changes that have taken place in the understanding of myth. The shift from oral to writing-based culture involves a basic shift from direct involvement in myth to a self-consciousness that stands apart from myth and categorizes and interprets it. When this is augmented by the emergence of the prizing of scientific accuracy, the distance from myth becomes so great that it is disowned completely. So myth changes from immediate truth in the stories of oral culture, to symbolic truth in the rational atmosphere of reflective self-consciousness, to complete fiction in the preoccupation with precise, scientific accuracy. In this third dispensation, we can hardly do anything but dismiss whatever is identified as myth.

The questions that emerged in glancing at this equation of myth with falsehood had to do with where the people who make the determination are standing when they make it. Myth, in this negative sense, is always what someone else accepts, or what was taken as true at some other time. The people who use myth in this way see themselves as myth-free, direct possessors of truth. This is what distinguishes what Comte called the "positive stage." The strange thing is that this is also precisely what characterizes naïve believers in myth, for whom myth is absolute truth. Could it be, then, that, far from having left myth behind entirely, the person who looks out from within the modern scientific perspective is really operating out of a different form of myth? This is not the myth of story, or even the interpreted myth of rational explanation, but a myth of total mastery and control. We have moved from narrative myth, in either the immediate stories of oral cultures or the more deliberate literary accounts, to what has been called "ideological myth."[5] Thus, the myth we are involved with is decidedly rationalistic. It involves forms of consciousness, rather than stories, and that shift carries a momentum of its own by which the consciousness tends to take more precise forms. Where the story myth of oral cultures operates with pictures, and the literary myth of the succeeding literary phase operates with words, contemporary ideological myth can be seen to concentrate on numbers. Its goal is to plot every speck in space and every instant of time. We shall see that twentieth-century physics has created complications for this ideal, but in spite of this, the goal of a complete blueprint of reality retains strong mythic power.

Thus, to see contemporary approaches that profess to have left myth far behind as being "still involved in myth" does not mean that we have to deny the direction of development outlined. The myth to which the devotee of the modern scientific outlook subscribes is very different from the stories of gods, goddesses, and heroes that character-ized myth in its earliest form. As humanity has moved from that im-mediacy of story, through philosophical reflection, to the quest of scientific accuracy, the nature of myth itself has changed. "If the cul-ture of science locates its highest values not in mystic symbol or ritual or epic tales of faraway lands and times, but in a mode of conscious-ness, why should we hesitate to call this a myth?"[6] The modern scien-tific era operates with a vision of reality and of our own place and significance in it just as surely as any metaphysical or mythical vision. In this sense, myth has been transformed rather than transcended.

Thus, when I refer to contemporary myth I do not intend to equate myth with falsehood, as in the popular, journalistic sense; nor do I mean simply to transplant the ancient story myths to the present. The claim being made is that there are unavoidable perspectives and priorities that give shape to life today, and that these represent the mythic horizons that define reality for us. As we shall see, the scientific outlook itself is one, if not the, fundamental ingredient in that mix.

Not only can we be seen to operate with our own myths today, even though our approach to life is very different from the era we associ-ate particularly with myth, but the function of our myths might not be as different from that of those ancient stories as we might be inclined to think. The move to more rational forms does not necessarily mean that story has been left behind. What is going on may be indicated by the structural approach to myth developed by Claude Lévi-Strauss, who attempted to get behind specific myths to the common structures implied in them. This might seem to confirm the rationalization of myth, but the intent and result are quite the opposite. Identifying myth in terms of modes of consciousness may involve not intellectualizing myth so much as reclaiming its basic story form. For these modes are not seen as intellectual options that we can pick and choose from the remote stance of rational reflection; they are, rather, basic perspectives that enable us to see in the first place. They are the stories that we live, in an age that thinks it has relegated stories to the periphery of enter-tainment. People in the arts know that stories and entertainment are not at all peripheral. A structural approach to myth seeks to identify some of the basic stories we live.

This identification of myth with formative perspectives means that particular myths will tend to be especially elusive. Used in this sense, myth refers to perspectives we look through, rather than at. What we are attempting to do is to look at the glasses we normally wear. But, of course, we have to do that without the benefit of the glasses themselves. It might seem that we are really seeing with our own eyes, but what we are looking at, of course, is the glasses through which we normally see. What is more, the question that myth poses is whether we can see anything at all without glasses. Or perhaps a better analogy is that our eyes themselves are the lenses through which we look out on life. We are always looking out from some perspective and vantage point. When we try to ask what that is, we may identify some perspectives that are crucial for our view of life, but these will always be identified from some other perspective that we cannot get at directly. We cannot look at glasses and through them at the same time; or, at least, that kind of looking is not the kind we normally do. We certainly cannot look at our own eyes. In fact, those who do look at eyes and seek to understand how they work tell us that there is more to their functioning than the understanding of them as lenses that give us a perspective on what is before us would suggest. Apparently there is a blind spot between the lines of vision of our two eyes. We are not aware of this because the brain compensates for it, aligning the signals that come in from the range of each of our eyes so that it appears that we have uniform access to what is before us. This elaborate mechanism for the physical act of seeing may give some indication of what goes on on the mental and spiritual sides. In taking certain meanings and priorities in life for granted, we draw on fundamental myths that represent the eyes of the soul. As we cannot see the mechanism through which we are seeing, so these basic myths that shape life for us can be expected to resist our attempts to take possession of them in any direct and thorough way.

A further complication, which might actually ease the situation somewhat, is that any myth we identify will be only one of several that inform our outlook on life. It may be a prominent or a decidedly secondary influence, and it may be in the ascendancy or in decline as a formative factor in our lives. This ebb and flow of myths is true of cultures and eras, as well as of our own experience as individuals. What is prominent for us is likely to be strongly influenced by what is prominent in our culture. Thus, to have some sense of this wider situation provides useful clues to the myths we take for granted.

One characterization of this process from the 1970s identifies it in terms of three stages of myth—compelling, supplemental, and rationalized.[7] Compelling myth refers to the emerging myth that grips some people, and may or may not grow and thrive to exert wider influence. Supplemental myth is the kind that is so established that it is simply taken for granted. Rationalized myth has reached the stage where it is seen to require interpretation and explanation. The American situation in the 1970s is seen to be characterized by the compelling myth of "the hips," the awakened young people who dropped out of the rat race and were intent on replacing the impersonal bureaucratic world they had inherited with a world of mutual concern and respect, a world of peace and love. They were confident that they could implement the Beatles' summons to "Give Peace a Chance." The supplemental myth of the 1970s is "scientism," the generally unquestioned acceptance of the modern scientific view of the universe and confidence in the methods of science to solve the problems that we encounter. The rationalized myth is identified as Christianity. Institutionally, as well as ideologically, Christianity has dominated Western culture, and its legacy continues to exert an influence in spite of the increasing secularity of the modern era. However, in the 1970s secularity edged Christianity from the supplemental situation, where it was taken for granted, to the rationalized phase, where it was seen to be in need of defence and explanation.

We may well have different ideas about the best candidates for these categories today. We are generally influenced by the Judaeo-Christian heritage more than we are inclined to recognize in the contemporary secular atmosphere, but this atmosphere means that there is not as much interest in rationalizing the Christian myth as there was in the 1970s; fewer people have enough direct interest to feel the need to interpret and defend it today. It may even be that science itself has become the rationalized myth, given its need for defence in the wake of the environmental devastation to which it is seen to contribute. The former role of science as supplemental myth may be seen to be occupied today by the culture of business. Economic priorities have a major claim to be among the most prominent assumed in the contemporary context. The compelling myth that is championed by some people with the fervour of the new vision of the hips of the 1970s, which raises questions about its prospect for achieving supplemental status, is the ecology myth. These candidates are certainly not beyond debate, and we might even question the categories themselves. It might be necessary to recognize more kinds of myth, for instance—perhaps a broader category that would acknowledge the lingering influence of Christian visions along with those of science and economics. What does seem clear is that some kind of scheme is necessary to recognize both that we are subject to several myths of different scope at the same time, and that the scope and influence of each myth is subject to change in our own experience as well as in the general cultural atmosphere.

One solution to this fluidity of myth is to seek to identify bits and pieces of contemporary experience that seem to serve mythic functions. In this vein, Roland Barthes takes all sorts of elements of French life as having mythological significance—"The World of Wrestling," "Soap-powders and Detergents," "Toys," "Steak and Chips," "Striptease,"

"The New Citroen."[8] This has the merit of focusing on concrete elements of contemporary life, but the fragmentary nature of this plethora of mythic themes can also appear diffuse and pointless. A fellow Frenchman, Jacques Ellul, castigates Barthes's "piecemeal" approach.[9] If everything can be myth, this could amount to saying that myth has no distinctive meaning at all. While the localized elements of life that Barthes identifies may well carry associations and meanings that go far beyond the particular item itself, they are too specific and limited to warrant the designation of myth. They might be indications of what are compelling myths for some people. How significant these compelling myths will turn out to be remains to be seen; thus, these fragments in themselves are doubly problematic.

One of the basic reasons for reserving the myth label for more comprehensive visions is indicated by Barthes himself in his insistence that "the form of myth is not a symbol."[10] In this self-conscious treatment of myth on which we are embarking, there will probably be a tendency to think of myth as though it were symbol. A symbol is something that stands for something else. A flag is the symbol of a country. When soldiers salute the flag, they are not saluting a piece of cloth. All that the flag stands for is implied through its symbolic role. It might seem natural to think of myth in this same way. The myths we will identify stand for all sorts of associations. That is implied in Barthes's identification of fragments of daily life as carrying wider significance beyond the immediate activity itself. But myth is at once less conspicuous than symbols and more immediate. Symbols are recognized as such, even though we may not be particularly aware of their symbolic nature much of the time. Myths tend to be so taken for granted that they are not identified directly at all. We cannot point to them the way we can point to an object such as a flag or a crucifix. Yet, at the same time, we may be more directly in touch with active myths than we are with symbols. We move toward and away from symbols, but myths stay with us. They are the visual, intellectual, and spiritual atmosphere in which we live.

Identification of the myths that are most influential in our lives is complicated by the fact that there is an oscillating web of myths that support and compete with one another. When to this we add the elusive nature of myth itself, we begin to sense something of the magnitude of the task that is involved, for, by its very nature, where myth is functioning at its fullest, it is most difficult to detect. Thus, in setting out to identify and examine our own myths, we are in some ways attempting the impossible. We cannot look at our own glasses and see through them at the same time. But we can take our glasses off, look at them, even clean them, and put them on again. We might decide that it is time we had our eyes checked, and perhaps try on a new pair of glasses. This is the type of thing we shall attempt to do with myths. The goal is to identify some of the central myths that shape life for us today. Some of us will buy into some of these more than others, but as citizens of the late-twentieth-century West, it is unlikely that any of us are untouched by any of the myths we shall consider.

Notes

1. Donald W. Meyers, "The Mythical World of Workplace Violence—Or Is It?" *Business Horizons.* 39(4) (Jul–Aug 1996): 31–36.

2. Steve Martin, "Writing Is Easy!" *New Yorker.* 72(17) (24 Jun–1Jul 1996): 156.

3. "Mythology," in *The Oxford Classical Dictionary,* ed. N.G.L. Hammond and H.H. Sculland, 2nd ed. (Oxford: Clarendon Press, 1979), p. 718.

4. C.A. van Peursen, "Man and Reality—the History of Human Thought," *The Student World.* 56(1) (1963), 13.

5. Martin S. Day, *The Many Meanings of Myth* (Lanham: University Press of America, 1984), pp. 3ff.

6. Theodore Roszak, *The Making of a Counter Culture* (New York: Doubleday Anchor Book, 1969), p. 214.

7. Richard E. Moore, *Myth America 2001* (Philadelphia: Westminster Press, 1972), pp. 26ff.

8. Roland Barthes, *Mythologies,* trans. Annette Lavers (London: Jonathan Cape, 1972).

9. Jacques Ellul, *The New Demons,* trans. C. Edward Hopkin (New York: The Seabury Press, 1975), p. 96.

10. Barthes, *Mythologies,* p. 18.

2

A SCIENCE MYTH

Sᴄɪᴇɴᴄᴇ has few rivals for primacy among the influences that shape modern Western sensibilities. The distinction between the modern era and previous ages can be attributed in large measure to the emergence of science. In terms of the stages of myth considered above, science appeared as the supplemental myth that was taken for granted as the reigning Christian myth became problematic and required rationalization. As I suggested in glancing at this development, science itself may now be somewhat facing this problematic fate because of the ecologically destructive side effects of technological processes. Developments such as the depletion of natural resources, the possible hazards of synthesized chemicals and genetic manipulation, and the worrisome potentially deleterious effects of nuclear radiation raise questions about the essentially positive evaluation of science that has hitherto been assumed. Thus, the science myth may be in the process of being overtaken by the ecology myth. Yet as official definer of reality, there is nothing in the modern era to rival science as former of our mythic consciousness in this broad sense. However, the mythic nature of science is more apparent now than it was when science functioned with full mythic power.

The emergence of popular concern about the impact of science has an internal counterpart in developments within science itself. In retrospect, we can see that the single-minded adulation of science reached a climax in the nineteenth century and has been rendered increasingly problematic by developments in this century, especially in the most material branch of science, physics. These developments suggest that the world out there is not as fixed and our grasp of it not as direct as the view of science as providing clear and certain information has been inclined to suppose.

The search for the basic building blocks of the universe has been a long preoccupation of humanity, dating back at least to ancient Greece and Democritus's idea of atoms as the fundamental, indivisible elements of matter. It seemed that this ideal was realized in the last century as chemists set about identifying and cataloguing the different varieties of atoms and it was only a matter of time before the whole substance of the universe would be explained in terms of different combinations of these basic atoms. This project was fatally undermined in the early part of this century as physicists proceeded to break the atom down into yet smaller components. Largely due to the work of Lord Rutherford, the atom was seen to consist of a nucleus surrounded by orbiting electrons. The nucleus is positively charged, and tiny in comparison to the whole atom. The cloud of electrons circling it are negatively charged, so that the atomic structure is made possible by the presence of electromagnetic force, which keeps the electrons orbiting the nucleus. The nucleus itself also turns out to be composite, consisting of protons, which carry the positive charge, and electrically neutral neutrons.[1]

A visual representation of the Rutherford atom suggests that if the nucleus is thought of as the size of a pea, the whole atom would have a radius of three hundred feet, roughly the size of six squared football fields.[2] Although there are a host of electrons whirling around this tiny nucleus, there is a lot of empty space in this atomic arrangement. In fact, in this view, contrary to our common-sense assumption about the solidity of material objects, matter is composed largely of empty space.

That physicists have been able to identify the tiny nucleus of the already tiny atom is thus an amazing feat. However, through the course of this century they have gone much further, moving to an even more minute level. Matter was seen to be composed of two more minute types of particles—quarks and leptons. There are six types of each, and they represent the basic building blocks of matter; along with the twelve messenger particles of the three forces (electromagnetism, which holds the atom together, the strong nuclear force, which holds the nucleus together, and the weak nuclear force, which accounts for the decay of some nuclear particles), they constitute the Standard Model that contains the "secret of the universe."[3] Physics has brought us to the most minute particles that exist. Even a vague sense of just how minute indicates how astounding this accomplishment is. The atom itself is one ten-billionth of a centimetre in radius and weighs one millionth of a billion-billionth of a gramme.[4] Dimensions of this scale defy visualization, and physics has now moved two levels further down, beyond the nucleus and electron components, to the ultra-minute quarks and leptons. Quarks are ten to the fifteenth power smaller than the atomic nucleus.[5]

Physicists operate with such small items that they have to identify them in terms of powers of a whole number. What makes this particularly dramatic is that the increase at each stage is an exponential one. Each previous answer is multiplied by itself to the number of times indicated by the power. The effect is illustrated by the following consideration: ten seconds raised to the seventh power equals a little more than two months, ten seconds raised to the ninth power equals thirty years, and ten seconds raised to the eighteenth power is equivalent to the fifteen billion years the universe has been around.[6] The items physicists are dealing with involve executing this operation in reverse. Thus the power to which the prime is to be lowered is indicated with a minus sign. The size of quarks, ten to the minus fifteenth power smaller than the atomic nucleus, gets us to a level of reality that is approaching the vanishing point.

If we recall that this is not the first time physics has claimed to have discovered the smallest components of matter, we might wonder if even this astoundingly small range might still be exceeded. There are indications that this is already happening, not through identification of still more minute particles, but through the notion that at its most fundamental level, matter is not composed of particles at all: along with the penetration to ultra-minute components of matter, there has been a parallel development that suggests that what we are really dealing with at this level can be thought of as waves as well as as particles. At the beginning of this century, Max Planck demonstrated that light can be thought of as waves. It moves not in constant beams, as common sense suggests, but in clumps or bundles that he called by the Greek term quanta. This idea was applied to the atom by Niels Bohr, who found that the orbit of electrons around the nucleus was more understandable if allowance was made for changing paths, rather than the fixed orbits that had been assumed. Thus subatomic activity has an element of randomness: minute particles jump around in unexpected ways that defy the expectations of classical physics.

That this minute level lends itself to these two kinds of models, particles and waves, some aspects suggesting particle-like substance, however minuscule, and others being understandable only in terms of wavelike movements, creates a complication in claims to have arrived at the basic building blocks of matter. What is it that has been identified—particles or waves, or both? Have we reached the point where the whole notion of matter has been dissolved into what classically has been the parallel notion of energy? Not only does the search for atoms, for the indivisible building blocks of matter take us into more elementary subatomic levels, but we seem to be reaching a point where this whole notion of primary building blocks is itself dissolving. It might even appear that we are reaching "the end of physics":

> The most recent speculation of the theoretical physicists is that elementary particles are not particles at all but vibrations of tiny loops of quantum-mechanical string, wriggling around in twenty-six-dimensional space. This is the modern equivalent of the classical physicist's hope that all matter could be understood in terms of atoms that behave essentially like little billiard balls.[7]

Besides this basic ontological question, the quantum revolution represents a transformation in the methods of physics. The elusiveness of quanta of energy means that physicists cannot hope to locate subatomic particles in isolation; the best they can do is to locate a large number of particles and then plot these on a probability curve. As a result, post-quantum-theory physics makes it clear that the most we can expect from science is statistical probability. The ideal of a completely accurate picture of reality in itself is shattered by the quantum barrier.

Post-quantum-theory physics is characterized by what Werner Heisenberg called "the uncertainty principle." At this minute level of investigation there is an element of uncertainty that we cannot expect to eliminate. It is a feature of reality itself, and not something that will yield to improvements in measuring devices or better theories. What is more, this elusiveness is aggravated by our very attempts at measurement. If physicists want to determine the position of an electron, for example, they do this by focusing a beam of light composed of photons on it. The problem is that the photons have an impact on the electron, so that the measurement process becomes part of what they are seeking to measure.[8] When we reach into the most minute dimensions of reality, we find ourselves staring back. The ideal of discrete, objective knowledge is compromised through the unavoidability of our own impact on what we are trying to understand. Thus we can see why, from the inside, as well as through the popular public concern with its possible deleterious effects, the obviousness of science that gave it mythic status is becoming problematic. Yet consideration that science may now be entering a phase of rationalized myth, in which its obviousness is being superseded by rationalization and defence, does not mean that it has ceased to exert major influence on our understanding of reality. Even as rationalized myth, science probably has no rival as definer of what is real for late-twentieth-century Westerners. If science is destined to experience the kinds of challenges that have undermined the hegemony of Christianity in the Western world, that process is still in its early stages.

Science and God

Science displaced Christianity in the modern era by offering an equally comprehensive vision of reality. If its vision did not extend as far in terms of offering supranatural explanations, this was more than compensated for by the clarity and certainty of the vision it did present. In place of beliefs, it offered facts. Rather than truth being handed down from above, in a divine revelation, science was engaged in assembling particular facts in an ever-expanding edifice of established truth. This distinguished what Comte called the "positive" era from previous metaphysical speculation and mythological immediacy.

In replacing Christianity as the dominant myth of Western culture, science displaced God by scientific explanation. Science was in the business of providing natural explanations; to look to God as explanation for any phenomenon would simply be bad science. There is a famous story about the French astronomer Laplace being confronted by Napoleon in these terms. Napoleon is supposed to have said something like, "Monsieur Laplace, I understand that you have written a book about the universe and never once mention God." Laplace is reported to have replied, "Sire, I have no need of that hypothesis!" Science is in the business of explaining the universe in its own terms. For the intricate, interlocking system of facts it is accumulating, God is an extraneous hypothesis. The scientist who says, "God did it!" is a poor scientist.

This retirement of God did not occur instantaneously. In fact, some of the most prominent early scientists were staunch believers. In spite of the difficulties some had with organized religion, they tended to see themselves as reading God's handiwork in nature. The general solution was to locate God back at the beginning of the process, rather than to dismiss God completely. For this outlook, known as deism, God is the first cause, the final explanation for the existence of the universe, but is not particularly involved in its workings now. It is sometimes referred to as the absentee landlord view of creation. The most influential early modern scientist Sir Isaac Newton actually found a place for God in the ongoing life of the universe. Newton, more than anyone else, was responsible for solidifying the new heliocentric, in contrast to the traditional geocentric, view of the universe. Through concepts such as mass and motion, and particularly gravity, Newton depicted the universe as a great machine, with planets moving in appointed orbits, like intermeshing cogs. The problem was that the observed movement of the planets did not quite correspond to his calculations. His solution was to conclude that God steps in from time to time to readjust the orbits to keep things running smoothly. It is not clear whether he reflected on what this implied about the competence of God as creator of the machine, but, in any case, the need for recourse to God as adjuster was later eliminated by improved calculations.

This has been the general pattern of scientific development. And the response from religion has been equally consistent. As science has developed more and more elaborate explanations, the room for recourse to God has progressively diminished. But religion has still been able to point to the beginning itself. If the planets move in regular orbits that require no adjustment, how did those regular orbits come about? Where did the planets themselves, and the stars they orbit, come from in the first place? The question of origin is the point where science and religion continue to encounter one another most directly. The issue has been most contentious in the area of biology, where the origins of life, and in particular of human life, raise especially sensitive questions. However, the question of where the line is to be drawn between religion and science has emerged in dramatic ways in this century in the same place it appeared originally, in physics and astronomy.

The traditional Western view of the universe sees it as the creation of God. The dominant myth is the one derived from the first chapter of Genesis, in which the world is fashioned, level by level, over a period of six days. There is also the more homey version of the second chapter of Genesis, which dwells particularly on the origin of human beings, with the depiction of God, like a potter, fashioning Adam from the ground. The view that tended to prevail, and probably still does for many of us, is likely to be a conflation of these two accounts. We have this vague sense that the universe, and our own species, got started at some point, launched by the creative, intelligent power that we call God. The curious situation created by physical science in this century is that it continues the threat to that explanation by seeking to develop ever more comprehensive accounts of the origins of the universe that do not look beyond the universe itself and, at the same time, through the intricacy and apparent design that it discloses, provides more and more evidence for creative intelligence underlying the whole process.

The scientific parallel to this traditional understanding of creation is what is called the big bang. According to this explanation, the universe originated from a gigantic explosion. The gases and dust particles condensed into stars and planets as they shot out from this dramatic bang. We find ourselves living in the expansion of this explosion, on a tiny planet, orbiting an only relatively bright star, the sun, in a galaxy, the Milky Way, that is only one of some one hundred billion galaxies. If we raise the question that religion has been inclined to raise since the emergence of modern science, "What exploded?" or "Where did that original nucleus come from?" the assumption that the obvious answer is "God!" encounters various obstacles. The most immediate is the claim that there was no big bang at all. The universe did not begin; it has always existed. This explanation is known as the steady state theory; its best known and most ardent exponent is Fred Hoyle.[9] Its basic contention is that the universe is in a constant process of renewal, with hydrogen atoms, the basic building blocks of the universe, emerging at a constant rate that is too low to be detected, but significant enough to account for a continual renewal of the whole process. One account sets the rate at about one hundred hydrogen atoms per cubic metre every 300,000 years. These atoms condense into stars, and move off at the speed of light, so that the stars, too, defy detection.

The steady-state explanation represents a truly scientific account. The universe is explained in terms of itself. It is understood as an ongoing process that does not point to an initial cause as the big bang theory can appear to do. In fact, Hoyle resisted the big bang account precisely because it was not really scientific—it left room for extraneous factors. The steady state provided a neat, self-contained explanation that accounted for the universe in completely scientific terms. Unfortunately for Hoyle's position, an event took place in 1965 that all but banished the steady state theory, and virtually confirmed the big bang. This was the discovery by two physicists working for Bell Telephone Company of mysterious radiation coming from space. It turns out that this radiation is the fading glow of the big bang that launched the universe.[10] This suggests a vindication of the religious answer: the universe did have a dramatic beginning, for which God was required. As Robert Jastrow suggests in *God and the Astronomers*, it looks as though science has discovered what religion has been claiming all along.

> For the scientist who has lived by his faith in the power of reason, the story ends like a bad dream. He has scaled the mountains of ignorance; he is about to conquer the highest peak; as he pulls himself over the final rock, he is greeted by a band of theologians who have been sitting there for centuries.[11]

It would be a nice irony if Hoyle's strictly scientific explanation turned out to be the dogmatism, while the scientific evidence supports the creation affirmed by religious believers for centuries.

Believers will relish this prospect, not least because of the beating that their convictions have taken from the impact of science. However, closer examination reveals further obstacles to identifying the hand of God behind scientific evidence. Even though the evidence confirms the big bang, we still have to ask what preceded it and what will result for the universe that emerged from that explosion. Are we to think there was nothing before the big bang except, perhaps, God alone in a solitary state of divine self-sufficiency? Does confirmation of the big bang support the reading of people like Steven Weinberg and Bertrand Russell, who accept that the universe had a dramatic beginning, but see this not as evidence of God but of the prospect of an equally dramatic end, with the implication of an attendant futility attaching to the whole process? The picture that results is vividly drawn by Steven Weinberg, in *The First Three Minutes: A Modern View of the Origins of the Universe*:

> As I write this I happen to be in an airplane at 30,000 feet, flying over Wyoming en route home from San Francisco to Boston. Below the earth looks very soft and comfortable—fluffy clouds here and there, snow turning pink as the sun sets, roads stretching straight across the country from one town to another. It is very hard to realize that this all is just a tiny part of an overwhelmingly hostile universe. It is even harder to realize that this present universe has evolved from an unspeakably unfamiliar early condition, and faces a future extinction of endless cold or intolerable heat. The more the universe seems comprehensible, the more it also seems pointless.[12]

The significance that we so casually appropriate withers not only because we are dwarfed by the immensity of what appear to be vast empty reaches of space, but because of the transitory nature of terrestrial life in this vast cosmic panorama.

This depiction of our situation has been given mythic power by the photographs of the blue planet from space. The image we are left with is that our home is a strange anomaly in the vast emptiness of space, and equally precarious in the dimension of time. But this is an understanding that has been reinforced, and not originated, by the view from space. Back at the dawn of the space age, Bertrand Russell was issuing equally dire assessments of human destiny in this precarious universe.

> That man is the product of causes which had no prevision of the end they were achieving; that his origin, his growth, his hopes and fears, his loves and his beliefs, are but the outcome of accidental collocations of atoms; that no fear, no heroism, no intensity of thought and feeling, can preserve an individual beyond the grave; that all the labours of the ages, all the devotion, all the inspiration, all the noon-day brightness of human genius are destined to extinction in

the vast death of the solar system, and that the whole temple of man's achievement must inevitably be buried beneath the debris of a universe in ruins—all these things, if not quite beyond dispute, are yet so nearly certain that no philosophy which rejects them can hope to stand.[13]

Acceptance that the universe had a beginning is no more guarantee of the hand of God behind it than the steady state view that finds the explanation for the universe within the universe itself.

Indeed, these questions bring us back in a curious way to something like the steady state alternative. Although the universe as we know it emerged from a gigantic explosion, rather than being in a state of eternal gradual generation, that explosion may have been one of a series. The big bang may be followed eventually by the big crunch, and the big bang that accounts for the present universe may have been the result of the big crunch of a previous universe. Thus, while not in a steady state, the universe would involve an inclusive process that is closer to the outlook of steady state than to the originality implied in the idea of big bang taken on its own. This is known as the oscillating universe view.

Confirmation of this direction has come from the Cambridge physicist who has been referred to as the new Einstein, Stephen Hawking, in his work on black holes. Black holes are the dense nuclei thought to result from the collapse of burnt-out stars. They are the dense nucleus that remains when a star implodes. Their density is what accounts for the name "black," the basic assumption being that they exclude light completely. The prevailing understanding was that anything that falls into a black hole disappears, entrapped in this total darkness, until Stephen Hawking began investigating the phenomenon. In 1973 he began asking what would happen to particles around black holes in light of Heisenberg's uncertainty principle and Einstein's general theory of relativity regarding the curvature of space.[14] What Hawking found was that particles can escape from black holes. While it is generally true that particles cannot exceed the speed of light, and so those caught in black holes would remain forever trapped there, the uncertainty principle allows for occasional exceptions to this. Along with the curvature of space, this could allow particles to exceed the speed of light just long enough to escape black holes.

The significance of this discovery is that "the particles in a black hole need not have an end of their history at a singularity."[15] That is, black holes are not final, as they were assumed to be. They are implicated in creation as well as destruction; rather than representing the end of matter, they might be a transition point, the collapse that becomes the nucleus for a new eruption. This could be how the universe itself is to be accounted for. "The big bang resembles a black-hole explosion but on a vastly larger scale."[16] Thus, black hole research qualifies the big bang understanding of the origins of the universe in the direction of the steady state explanation. The explosion that accounts for the universe as we know it may well have been the result of a previous collapse, and rather than pointing to God, the big bang would point to an earlier stage of the process of which it is a component.

Hawking's combination of astronomical phenomena such as black holes and particle physics is indicative of the direction that modern physics has taken. The interconnection of astronomy and physics evident in the origins of these modern disciplines has been reaffirmed in this century as particle physics, which not only reaches down into the most minute layers of matter, but in so doing is also reaching back to the origins of the universe. In the big bang reading of the origin of the universe, it all began from a nucleus that was so dense that it was no larger than a fraction of the size of a pinhead. That ultra-dense state accounts for the ultra-strong explosion that was the big bang, and it also means that at this stage quantum theory applied to the whole universe. Particles were bouncing off each other at enormous velocities in the early stages. In fact, they would not be able to begin to adhere to form the components of atoms, and then atoms themselves, until the expansion had progressed to a state at which the temperature had cooled down enough to permit this. What particle physicists are attempting to do today is to get back to those original conditions by building ever larger particle accelerators that whirl particles around at speeds approaching those of the origins of the universe and seeing what happens when they crash into one another. The largest accelerator in operation, the Tevatron at Fermilab in Illinois, can get back to within a millionth of a millionth of a second of the big bang at the instant when particles in the accelerator reach maximum collision impact.[17] The Tevatron is four miles in circumference, a huge donut buried in the ground. The next generation, the on-again-off-again Superconducting Super Collider proposed for Texas, is to be fifty-four miles in circumference. Perhaps it will disclose the final secrets of the universe.

Besides the inability to emulate the very high particle speeds that would have characterized the intense heat of the universe in its initial explosive state, one obstinate problem in particular prevents physicists from combining the understanding that has been achieved into one coherent account of the universe: what to do with gravity. The quantum approach explains the other three basic forces—the electromagnetic force, the strong nuclear force, and the weak nuclear force. So far, however, nobody has been able to reconcile quantum theory with the most far-reaching force of all, gravity. As the exploding universe expanded, gravity emerged, and it continues to account for the long-distance connections of stars and planets. But where does it belong in that dense initial stage of the universe that is explained in terms of quantum theory?

The object of this attempt to encompass gravity in quantum theory is known as the grand unified theory (GUT) or the theory of everything (TOE). Some think that there is a missing particle or field that will tie it all together, the Higgs particle, referred to for the purpose of selling books as the "God Particle."[18] This is the view of an experimental physicist who hopes that a big enough accelerator can be built to identify the tiny elusive key to it all. Theoretical physicists talk in terms of "superstrings," interconnected waves of particles that intertwine and separate.[19] One of the most ardent theoretical searchers for a theory of everything is Stephen Hawking, who thinks that "both time and space are finite in extent, but they don't have any boundary or edge."[20] This builds on Einstein's theory about the curvature of space. It means that one can have virtually a finite infinite; one can continue to travel around the world without coming to an end, even though the earth itself is finite. If this same reasoning applies to time, it is possible that the universe is finite, and so subject to complete understanding by science, as Hoyle's steady state explanation attempted to assure. The feasibility of this result depends on the prospects for a theory of everything that would explain the universe in its own terms and on how adequate any explanation would be for the universe as we know it.

Science and Humanity

The question of the prospects for a theory of everything poses the issue of where the line is to be drawn between science and religion in a particularly fundamental way. Can science be expected to provide a theory of everything that would answer all outstanding questions? The phrase "theory of everything" suggests this, and it would be required for science to have the truly mythic scope that has been associated with it. It would have to be comprehensive and final. What is at stake is really whether science can displace religion totally and adequately. This question could be considered directly, in terms of the respective interests and methods of the two approaches, but the answer will be clearer if we consider the more specific content that a scientific account would involve. Physics seeks to explain the universe in terms of its most elemental units. But this universe contains more than physical reality. It has also produced conscious beings, who inquire about the universe. Can science account for this dimension?

The issue of consciousness is two steps removed from the concerns of physics. In between is the distinction between the inorganic and the organic, the emergence of life as opposed to objects. This is the subject of biology, which is really the science of life. Modern biology was shaped decisively by Charles Darwin's theory of natural selection, or, as it is more popularly known, the theory of evolution. Darwin's account of the origins of life completed the displacement of God initiated by modern physics. As God was no longer needed to account for the movements of the planets, so, after Darwin, God was not needed to account for the emergence of life. Species developed through a process of trial and error, as individuals with advantages in the struggle for survival passed on their advantages, so that gradually species were transformed. There was no need for external reference to God to account for the diversity of nature; the different species were selected naturally.

This consolidation of the displacement of God was reinforced by the more precise procedures of genetics, in a combination with evolutionary theory that Julian Huxley, in the 1940s, called "the modern synthesis." In some ways, genetics represents the biological counterpart of particle physics. It moves from the level of species, through cells and the chromosomes that comprise them, down to genes as the basic biological particles. However, the central development of this direction does not display a counterpart to the revolution that physics experienced through quantum theory. Geneticists continue to depict DNA (deoxyribonucleic acid), the basic building block of life, with the spiral peg-and-ball model of the double helix that is a counterpart to the atomic-energy symbol of the atom as a ball being circled by other balls that physicists have long abandoned in their recognition of the elusiveness of primary forces.[21] Geneticists thus remain loyal to Darwin's roots in the Newtonian perspective.[22] As a result, their depictions and projections are characterized by a fundamental determinism.

A prominent example of this direction is to be seen in sociobiology's treatment of altruism. The leading pioneer of sociobiology, E.O. Wilson, sees the social sciences and the humanities being embraced by "the Modern Synthesis."[23] The aim is to produce a biological explanation for what is now dealt with in the social sciences and the humanities. This aim is realized in an explanation of what appears to be altruistic behaviour in terms of what Richard Dawkins calls *The Selfish Gene*. On the surface, a bird issuing a warning call to a flock when a predator is spotted and a mother bird feigning a broken wing to lead a hungry fox away from her vulnerable brood and leaping into the air at the last possible moment to escape the fox's jaws certainly appear to be behaving altruistically. The sentry bird and the mother bird are putting themselves at risk for the sake of the other birds. From the genetic point of view of sociobiology, however, this is not altruistic behaviour at all. On the contrary, it is decidedly selfish. The sentry bird shares genes with the birds it warns, and the mother bird shares genes with her offspring. The source of the apparently altruistic behaviour in each case is the genetic makeup of the bird. Half of a mother's genes are represented in her offspring, and siblings too share half their genes because they get their genes from the same two parents. As the relation becomes more distant, the gene ratio drops; one quarter is shared between uncles and aunts and their nephews and nieces and between grandparents and grandchildren, and one eighth between first cousins and between great-grandparents and great-grandchildren. Thus, if the sentry bird has two siblings or eight first cousins in the flock, nothing is being sacrificed at the gene level. If the mother bird saves two of her brood, her genes will come out even.

If this sounds strange and callous, it is only because we romanticize nature. If we saw it as the sociobiologist does, we would see that genes are what it is all about. "They are in you and me; they created us, body and mind; and their preservation is the ultimate rationale for our existence."[24] Not only birds and animals, but we too, are programmed by genes. "We are survival machines—robot vehicles blindly programmed to preserve the selfish molecules known as genes."[25] We exist only because genes need us to replicate themselves. Dawkins is not as extreme in his determinism as are some sociobiologists. He ends *The Selfish Gene* with a plea for us to rebel against the tyranny of genes and chart our own course. The implication is that we have achieved a level of evolution that allows us to interfere with the evolutionary process though our critical consciousness. Yet that call is precarious because any such possibility finally derives from the genetic base. Thus, even when human distinctiveness is recognized, the underlying sociobiological perspective carries the implication that this too is programmed.

Genes represent bedrock for sociobiology. They are the clue to the whole process of life. "What are DNA molecules for?" Dawkins asks, and then he answers in his own uncompromising terms.

> If we accept the view of life that I wish to espouse, it is the forbidden question. DNA is not "for anything." If we want to speak teleologically, all adaptations are for the preservation of DNA; DNA itself just *is*.[26]

DNA is the great "I AM," the ultimate source that accounts for life itself. Yet Dawkins recognizes that DNA is not finally self-explanatory. Its very complexity seems to presuppose an originating process that would involve something like itself being available to produce DNA in the first place. "Cumulative selection cannot work unless there is some minimal machinery of replication and replicatory power, and the only machinery of replication that we know seems too complicated to have come into existence by means of anything less than many generations of cumulative selection."[27] Natural selection is such a complicated process, particularly when it is seen at the intricacy of the gene level, that it seems to presuppose itself. In other words, the complexity poses the question of how this involved process ever got started.

The only answer that Dawkins can suggest to this nagging question is one that would not seem to be particularly compatible with the canons of science itself. He concludes that it all started by sheer accident. "At some point a particularly remarkable molecule was formed by accident. We call it the replicator."[28] The barren, lifeless universe suddenly and miraculously threw up a molecule that could reproduce itself, and life began. Do you hear violins? Dawkins attempts to give this tale a scientific veneer by presenting it in numerical terms. Even the most venturesome biochemists are reluctant to pronounce on the odds of a self-replicating molecule suddenly emerging, but Dawkins puts a number on it. He asks us to consider the possibility that there is only one chance of this happening in a billion billion years. This would seem to rule out the possibility of life on earth happening by chance because it seems that the earth has only been around for some four and a half billion years, and life processes seem to have been under way for all but about the first billion years. But, says Dawkins, if we assume that the earth is the only planet on which life has emerged, and if there are enough planets in the universe to account for the rest of the numbers in these high odds, then the probability criterion is met and the self-replicating molecule can be regarded as a credible occurrence; a very unlikely, but not impossible, novelty. Thus, for Dawkins, the problem is solved. "A miracle is translated into practical politics by a multiplication sum."[29] This is the scientific explanation for the origins of life. Sheer accident is seen as a probability, however slight, by postulating a sufficient number of planets to meet what are purely speculative odds to begin with.

The best-known version of this recourse to chance as the ultimate scientific explanation is probably Jacques Monod's *Chance and Necessity*, in which Monod likens the emergence of life to the proceedings of a casino.

> The universe was not pregnant with life, nor the biosphere with man. Our number came up in the Monte Carlo game. Is it surprising that, like the person who has just made a million in the casino, we might feel strange and a little unreal?[30]

Although the odds against a big gambling win are such that there would be far fewer gamblers if they really stopped to consider these odds, even the slim chances of a big win that gambling involves are good compared with the odds against life emerging in the universe. Monod's casino analogy obscures the difficulty of establishing odds that is apparent in Dawkins's treatment. Fred Hoyle, whom we have already encountered as the advocate of the steady state theory, has likened the odds against the first cell emerging by chance to a Boeing 747 being assembled by a tornado swirling through a junk yard filled with airplane parts.[31]

This suggests quite a different situation from Monod's casino analogy. Big casino wins may be rare, but they are be no means unknown. Can you imagine a modern jetliner being assembled by a tornado? A tornado might tear one apart, but to create one strains the bounds of credibility. As Mary Midgely points out, Monod overlooks his reliance on the presence of the casino itself as the humanly designed context that makes the chance possible.[32] If we take Monod's analogy seriously, does it end up pointing to the originators of casinos as the sponsors of the chance these establishments make possible? The emergence of casinos is not a particularly striking phenomenon. The odds against their appearance, given human beings and their proclivities, cannot be thought to be very great. In fact, they might even be seen as inevitable in some form or other. When the analogy is transferred to the cosmic level, however, extremely high odds emerge—not against the emergence of any particular form of life, but against the appearance of life itself. If the emergence of life is to be attributed to chance, although we have no way of determining what the odds against this might be, clearly they are in a totally different league from casino odds. One depiction suggests that the chances of chaos rather than order characterizing any particular arrangement are so great that if we were to think of a creator selecting from among all possibilities "to find an ordered universe, the creator would have to scour a selection of 'models' that is so vast its numbers could not be written down on a sheet of paper as big as the entire observable universe."[33] Some casino!

The arbitrariness of the recourse to accident and chance tends to be confirmed even more strongly when we consider the range of odds that are reflected in the composition of the universe as we are coming to know it. It turns out that this life-giving universe has emerged only because of an array of very precise developments. The immense pressure exerted by the big bang was very quickly countered by the force of gravity, which pulled stars and planets together into galaxies. If the force of the initial explosion had been just slightly stronger, the particles would have moved off too quickly to coalesce into galaxies. If the force had been slightly less, it would have been counteracted by gravity, and the whole thing would have collapsed in upon itself in a short time. Stephen Hawking reckons that "if the rate of expansion one second after the Big Bang had been smaller by even one part in a hundred thousand million million it would have collapsed before it reached its present size."[34]

A similar situation holds at the subatomic level: "if the proton-neutron mass difference were not about twice the mass of the electron, one would not obtain the couple of hundred or so stable nucleides that make up the elements and are the basis of chemistry and biology."[35] The simplest chemical element is hydrogen, with a nucleus consisting of a single proton circled by a single electron. Helium is next, with each nucleus containing two protons and two neutrons, with two electrons circling the nucleus. About 75 per cent of a star consists of hydrogen and roughly 25 per cent of helium, with only about 1 per cent consisting of heavier metals. Hydrogen is transformed into helium through a process of radioactive decay. If the force of that decay were slightly stronger, no helium would be produced, and if only slightly weaker, all of the hydrogen would be converted into helium. In order to achieve the seventy-five/twenty-five ratio, the forces had to be within a very precise range. The heavier elements emerge through high-speed, high-temperature collisions that occur in stars. Here again, the forces of those collisions had to be just right. A 1 per cent variation could mean that an element like carbon would not have been produced, and since all life forms depend on carbon, life in the universe would have been impossible. The heavy elements are spread across the galaxy by the explosion of stars known as supernova, and this, too, depends on precise forces. If the force is too strong the neutrinos become involved in reactions within the nucleus of the star; if too weak, the elements are not transported by the neutrinos being propelled from the exploding nucleus through the outer layers of the star. The fundamental forces and the basic masses of particles and planets occupy a very narrow range of possibility. Slightly more or slightly less in any of these areas, and we would not be here.[36]

These amazing coincidences not only challenge the view that the universe is a product of sheer chance, they answer Weinberg's concern about our own apparent insignificance in the vast emptiness of space. The spatial and temporal vastness of the universe is not unrelated to us, because without the developments that this scope has made possible, we would not be here. If the universe was just the size of our own galaxy, it would have collapsed back upon itself within one year.[37] The hundred billion galaxies that are seen to constitute the universe are needed to assure the right proportions of forces and masses that have made life possible. Similar considerations apply to the vast age of the universe. "The total time of fifteen billion years is really the minimum we could have gotten for making all the elements, putting them into the dust of the cosmos, and getting it all swept up eventually in our solar system which does have all the essential elements of life."[38]

So striking is this relation between our understanding of the processes by which the universe came to be and the ingredients essential to our existence that our emergence is seen as an explanation for the existence of the universe. The explanation is known as the anthropic principle. On the surface, it might seem that once again we are seeing science coming full circle, and ending up where religion has always been. One of the most disturbing things about the new Copernican view of the universe was that it removed humanity from the centre, and as the immensity of space came to be recognized, this demotion came more and more to carry the connotation of insignificance. Darwin's association of humanity with other life forms confirmed this impression of the demotion of humanity. Now it turns out that it appears that the universe has been geared to producing life, and ultimately conscious life represented most fully by human beings. Take that, Copernicus!

This reversal is not exactly what the anthropic principle involves, however. Rather than explaining the universe as existing to produce us, it contends that our existence explains the universe.[39] We do not know the origins of the universe. We do know that it has produced conscious life. The most ardent exponents of the anthropic principle contend that the universe exists because we are conscious of it.[40] Behind this lies quantum theory, which suggests that our own observations influence the results we achieve. The contention that this is an explanation for the universe, however, is a highly idealistic and anthropocentric proposal. It might even be regarded as an inverted theological rationale. Science cannot look to God as explanation; so the amazing coincidences between the dimensions of the universe and the presence of intelligent life are explained in terms of humanity.

In thus bordering on theological rationale, the anthropic principle departs from the strict canons of science. In contrast to hypothetical explanations, which are testable by observation and experiment, the explanation of the anthropic principle is after the fact. It explains the universe once human beings are known to inhabit it, but it does not account for the presence of human beings in the first place.[41] Yet while science has difficulty embracing the anthropic principle, the amazing coincidences on which it is based remain, and, even if science comes up with more specific explanations for these, their very existence remains significant: "Even if all apparently anthropic coincidences could be explained . . . it would still be remarkable that the relationships dictated by physical theory happened also to be those propitious for life."[42] These coincidences suggest that physics and biology are moving together out of the divergent specialities they have attempted to develop. The anthropic principle pushes this unification to the point where theological echoes may begin to be heard. In this quest for ultimate explanation, the mythic nature of science is inescapable.

Science and Myth

Through its own accomplishments, science has burst the bounds of its conventional depiction. Recognition of the complexity and creativity of modern science resulted in an expanded view of its methods, which, in retrospect, can be seen to expose something of its implication in myth. The revision to the understanding of scientific method has been the work of philosophers of science more than of scientists themselves. The latter tend to focus on the immediate problems presented in their own areas of research, while the former look at science from the outside and consider its wider implications. Thus, there is a time lag between developments in science and recognition of their implications, and so it was only in the second half of this century that the impact of the revolutionary developments that took place in physics in the early part of this century really began to be appreciated.

While physicists were establishing relativity and quantum theory, in the early part of this century, philosophers were insisting on the precision and accuracy of science as the only reliable avenue to knowledge. The Vienna Circle on the Continent and A.J. Ayer in England promoted a standard of knowledge based on science as establisher of sure and certain facts. The central concept of this view of the methods of science was the verification principle. Nothing was to qualify as knowledge that was not subject to strict verification exemplified by scientific experiment. In this view, there are only two kinds of knowledge: the sure but purely formal knowledge of reason exemplified in logic and mathematics, and the particular and verified knowledge of empirical facts established by observation and experiment. The knowledge that two times two equals four is absolutely certain, because it is true by definition. That truth is not going to change, but it does not tell us anything about the real world. It tells us that if someone has two apples, and another person has twice as many, that that other person will have four apples, but it cannot tell us whether or not anyone has apples at all. That is something that can be determined only by investigation, and that is the method that science exemplifies. Real knowledge is the hard knowledge of science, verifiable in principle, if not actually verified already. Anything that is not subject to such verification cannot be taken seriously as knowledge.

This reading of science was seen to capture the widespread understanding of science, affording it the veneration that has elevated it to mythic status as definer of reality for modern Westerners, and increasingly for most other inhabitants of the planet as well. However, this positivistic approach was not without its critics. Other philosophers pointed out, for example, that the verification principle could not pass its own test. On its own terms, it did not qualify as knowledge. It was not purely formal, like mathematics or logic; it was more a regulative principle than a formal one. At the same time, it was not subject to the empirical verification that it required of factual knowledge. In addition to this internal contradiction, the verification principle just did not fit the complexities that increasingly were recognized to characterize science.

Around the middle of this century, Karl Popper proposed an alternative to the verification principle. He recognized that the requirements it placed on scientific knowledge were too stringent, yet he wanted to preserve the distinctive knowledge that science can attain. His solution was to substitute a falsification principle for the verification principle. Science offers reliable knowledge, such as is to be found nowhere else, not because everything it affirms has been, or even necessarily can be, proven, but because it is constantly subject to being disproved. Scientific knowledge is distinguished by the fact that it is in principle subject to falsification. If we cannot say what would falsify a particular claim, we know that we have moved beyond the bounds of science. Thus, while claims to constitute the only source of firmly established knowledge are abandoned, science is still seen to represent the best avenue we have to firm knowledge because its commitment to truth is so great that its affirmations are constantly subject to refutation. Knowledge that withstands this openness is the best we can have or want.

The falsification criterion sounds more realistic than do the stringent requirements of the verification principle. However, further developments in philosophy of science saw Popper's solution as an unsatisfactory compromise. The falsification approach suggests that science operates with a pervasive tentativeness. It is constantly ready to see its conclusions and affirmations challenged and refuted. Consideration of how science actually operates suggests that it is much less tentative than this. The notion that science raises hypotheses that are constantly subject to falsification in light of experimental evidence is contradicted by the determinative role that theoretical visions play in shaping expectations of, and providing regulative principles for, scientific research. "A theory of great generality is usually abandoned only in favor of an alternative theory, not just because of conflicting data."[43] Falsification of theories is as difficult as verification. Theories tend to come with a certain inertia, especially when they have a relatively wide range of application. Max Planck went so far as to suggest that "a new scientific truth does not triumph by convincing its opponents . . . [but] . . . because its opponents die, and a new generation grows up that is familiar with it."[44] Indeed, the wider the range covered by a theory, the more resistant it is likely to be to displacement.

Far from constituting tentative, hypothetical guesses that await the verification or falsification of experiment, theories can themselves be the source of discovery. Even allowing for the professional competition between theoretical and experimental physicists, the testimony of theoretical physicist Stephen Hawking has to be taken seriously: "In theoretical physics, the search for logical self-consistency has always been more important in making advances than experimental results."[45] Planets and particles have been discovered because theories said they must be there. Physicists discovered the top quark because it was needed to complete the theoretical explanation. What is more, the progressive sophistication of modern physics and the practical limitations on replicating conditions progressively closer to the singularity of the big bang suggest that the theoretical dimension is likely to become even more significant. "In cosmology, as in particle physics, experimental or observational evidence is becoming scarce, and theory is increasingly removed from what can be measured or detected; cosmology may come to be ruled more by aesthetic preferences than by the traditional principles of science."[46] Verification and falsification readings seem less and less viable as indicators of what science really involves.

At most, these views of science, which still enjoy wide popular appeal, can be associated only with the more prosaic activities of science, with what Thomas Kuhn calls normal science. In his seminal work *The Structure of Scientific Revolutions*,[47] Kuhn distinguishes between normal science, which is highly conservative, and revolutionary science, which takes place only when the established way of doing things breaks down, so that there is what Kuhn calls a paradigm shift. A dramatic example of a paradigm shift in modern science is the move from the mechanistic approach of Newtonian physics to the uncertainty of relativity and quantum physics of this century. This transition, and especially others of less dramatic scope and intensity, should be routine on Popper's falsification reading. The reality is, however, that change is resisted in science as in other human activities. Rare individuals pioneer the revolutions; the majority resist. In fact, Kuhn found science to be more like religion than the verification or falsification views would suggest. Far from taking possession of reality in the direct way of the verification principle, or in the tentative probings of the falsification approach, scientists reflect the loyalties that come with indoctrination into a legacy of concepts and methodologies that can be likened to the training of initiates in religious communities. Science is very much a social operation. The knowledge of reality it makes possible is attainable only after prolonged exposure to perspectives and practices that provide initiation into ways of seeing and measuring that are foreign to the uninitiated.

The sophistication and complexity of science suggest that far from functioning as a collector and cataloguer of facts, it is much more accurately understood as a creator and adjuster of elaborate visions. This means that, at least on its cutting edge, in the areas of what Kuhn calls revolutionary science, science itself is a very imaginative and creative activity. Thus the line between the sciences and the arts begins to blur. So much is this the case that another prominent recent philosopher of science has insisted on this kind of parallel. Around the middle of this century, Michael Polanyi became so dissatisfied with the positivistic portrayal of science that he gave up a promising career as a research chemist to promote better understanding of what science really involves. His best-known book, *Personal Knowledge*,[48] is not about psychology or religion, but about natural science. He contends, in contrast to the popular, positivistic view, which understands science as an impersonal accumulation of objective factual data, that science is really a very human enterprise from the proposal of tentative theories to the recording of instrument readings. Furthermore, it all takes place under the auspices of fundamental visions and expectations that are taken to define reality and to support the specific approaches that science employs.

In terms of basic method, then, the understanding of how science operates has changed dramatically over the course of this century. From the insistence on verification that reflected expectations aroused by nineteenth-century successes, it was necessary to shift to the more tentative criterion of falsification, until, in the latter half of the century, philosophers such as Polanyi and Kuhn gained increasing recognition for their contention that science has more in common with other human approaches to life than we have been inclined to recognize.

The increasing expansiveness in the understanding of scientific method provides a convenient basis for recognizing the mythic dimensions implicit in science. The move from verification to falsification to paradigm reflects the need to acknowledge how science is implicated in fundamental and total visions regarding the nature of reality. The verification approach represents the narrowest view of science, depicting it as the careful amasser of isolated facts. Even here, however, surreptitious recourse to total visions can be detected in the assumption that these isolated facts can be expected to add up to and constitute a coherent picture. Falsification is less restrictive, but it still reflects a piecemeal approach in that scientific theories are seen to stand or fall on their own. With recognition of the governing role of paradigms, we approach a much more explicit recognition of the necessity of mythic vision.

The verification view of science represents a positivistic reading according to which science is seen to be in the business of erecting a totally reliable platform of fact, continually and infallibly, extending its reach from this secure factual foundation. This not only gives science the advantage of building on a secure foundation; it also means that its range of claims is much more modest than religious and philosophical visions that try to take in everything. This is what exposes religion and philosophy to affirmations of mythic proportions; science, in contrast, is modestly and carefully extending its secure base of operations within the range of established knowledge. Science deals with facts. It is at the other extreme from myth.

When the verification reading of science has to yield to a falsification approach, and this in turn becomes overshadowed by the recognition that science involves fundamental paradigms, the modest tenor of the verificationist agenda is shattered by the realization that science operates with a vision that is as total as any other, and that this may even be inescapably so. If the area of fact, which science is seen to represent in the positivistic, verificationist reading, is really tentative and preliminary, then the devotee of science will look to other areas for explanations of the wider reaches of reality. But this is not what tends to happen. The factual understanding that science is seen to provide is preliminary and tentative only in the sense that it is not yet able to explain everything. The limitation is a practical one, and does not seem to hold at the level of theory. In theory, the tenacious confidence in science is accompanied by an expectation that eventually its factual base will be extended to encompass everything that is worth knowing. This means that in the present, science is operating with a totality of vision that is of mythic proportions. Far from representing a limited foray into the range of what can be established as factual, it sees the whole of reality as subject, in principle, to its mastery. The apparent humility of science in this most positivistic mode thus really conceals a massive imperialism of vision that subordinates or dismisses every other kind of vision. This recognition might be indicative of a generic inevitability of myth. It may well be the case that in order to deal with any particular, some view of the whole is assumed. At least in the present case, it seems clear that even in this most narrow form, science is very much a mythic enterprise.

Thus, far from representing tentative forays into a vast unknown, the dominant approaches of contemporary science imply total visions of reality that place us, at least in the person of the researchers, at the centre of a reality that is assumed to be finally and totally compliant to our, or their, ingenuity. That this is not seen as a transcendent vision, comparable to those that centre in stories of gods, goddesses, or God, may be due only to the fact that it is we ourselves who are at the centre of this science myth. This should not be taken to imply that the scientist explicitly or deliberately subscribes to this type of mythic vision; it is more likely the case that it comes with the territory. Scientists are apt to become what Arthur Peacocke refers to as "unreflective and implicit 'reductionists'"—"they undergo a very natural psychological transition from the methodological necessity of the way they work to an unanalyzed philosophical position."[49] In attempting to get to the small identifiable units, whether in physics or biology, it is easy to assume that reality is simply the total aggregate of these units, and not to recognize not only that there is more to life than this reductionistic perspective can allow, but also that the reductionists themselves are involved in assumptions and perspectives about what is finally real and worthwhile. Because of this implication in a fundamental vision about the nature of reality, the legitimacy of, and necessity for, referring to science as myth is evident.

Those who recognize that science works from paradigms are not likely to be particularly troubled by the suggestion that science involves myth. For advocates of the falsification approach, and especially for any who remain under the influence of the stricter verification outlook, such an alliance can only seem utter heresy. Advocates of the positivistic approach to science would be horrified at having their position characterized as myth. They have nothing to do with things like myth; they are operating with pure fact. As they see it, that is what distinguishes science and makes it the only reliable avenue to truth. The irony is that it is precisely this insistence that reveals just how mythic science really is.

The mythic nature of the narrowest, most positivistic version of science is indicative of one of the most distinctive characteristics of myth, the dimension of immediacy. The tenacity with which the claims for science as the only source of reliable knowledge are advanced betray a commitment of mythic proportions. This sense of having direct and conclusive access to truth is precisely what characterizes myth when it is operating with full effect. The contemporary person who places total confidence in science is doing the same kind of thing that ancient believers in the gods and goddesses were doing when they heard the ancient myths as immediately relevant. Thus, ironically, the stronger the insistence on the authority of science, the clearer the mythic nature of this confidence becomes.

Science is implicated in myth not only because, in spite of its profession of naturalistic intent, it reflects total visions of the nature of reality that are of transcendent proportions, and because it constitutes an immediate horizon of meaning for all of us to some extent, especially for those who take it for granted without any inclination to recognize that they are doing so, but also because it inevitably and inescapably involves a corresponding vision of ourselves. This constitutes a third characteristic of myth that is implicit in modern science. The view that reality is composed of minute bits that we should be able to master sees us as masters. Stephen Hawking puts it bluntly: "We may break through to a complete theory of the universe. In that case, we would indeed be Masters of the Universe."[50] He is equally blunt about how this applies to himself. He tells of how in his youth he built models and invented games that he could control, and speculates that this is the motivation that underlies his researches in physics: "If you understand how the universe operates, you control it in a way."[51] The motivation of science is to control; this means that to the extent to which we embrace the science myth, we see ourselves as controllers, ideally, if not in reality. We are in the business of extending our control; what we do not control now is assumed to be a target for our future expertise.

There is also a curious irony in this reflexive implication of the science myth. A reflective scientist like Hawking can recognize this characterization of himself to be implied in the basic intent of the scientific enterprise, but the mastery and control he pursues cannot really take him into account. The problem is illustrated by the early-nineteenth-century German philosopher Hegel, who attempted a philosophical version of a theory of everything, a rational vision that would account for the whole of reality. Søren Kierkegaard, the Danish philosopher who, in spite of popular perceptions, is really the progenitor of existentialism, pointed out that Hegel's grand scheme lacked one crucial factor, Hegel himself. Kierkegaard likened Hegel to someone who builds a magnificent palace, and then lives in a hut on the grounds. Any scheme, philosophical or scientific, that purports to explain reality in objective terms leaves us out. When sociobiologists propose to extend the objective explanation to include ourselves by attributing our behaviour to our genetic make-up, they are including our species in the scientific account, but they themselves remain exceptions. They stand on the outside, masters not only of the natural order and of other life forms, but also of the human being. The control orientation of the science myth assumes our own characterization as controllers, and so, by definition, cannot include us.

This exclusion of us can also be seen from the other side as our total assertion. While we remain outside the scientific picture, as its creators, and alien to the universe we understand, as its controllers, this picture and this understanding are ours. The self that is excluded from the explanation is master of the universe. The import of this assumption is not lost on science-fiction writers. The vision of humanity generally reflected in science fiction not only sets humanity at centre stage but assumes that humanity constitutes the horizon of meaning. It is completely natural for us to seek to take in the universe in godlike fashion, because we are God. "The quasi-mythology of modern times, unlike the ancient myths, makes no reference to God or to any power more ultimate than man himself."[52] The attempt to take it all in does not simply leave us out of the picture, then; it assumes that there is nothing but our picturing. This reflexive dimension further identifies and assures the mythic nature of science.

That science reflects a total vision of reality, one that is assumed authoritative and that carries inescapable implications about ourselves, clearly establishes the mythic proportions of the outlook that is often held to represent the antithesis of myth. To appreciate the full mythic scope of science, however, we have to return to the substance of the vision itself, to the aspiration to provide a theory of everything, which, as we saw, really represents the question of whether science can be expected to displace religion completely. In *A Brief History of Time*, Hawking speculated not only about achieving a theory of everything, but about knowing "the mind of God."[53] In his later *Black Holes and Baby Universes*, he confesses that he considered not including this phrase, but muses that its inclusion might have doubled the sales of the book, just as, conversely, he had been warned that every equation included could be expected to cut sales in half.[54] Yet the phrase is more than a throwaway line, or a sales gimmick, for Hawking. In one sense, the unified theory he seeks would amount to knowing the mind of God. He resists the suggestion that the question of ultimate origin should be left to religion. "I think that the initial conditions of the universe are as suitable a subject for scientific study and theory as are the local physical laws."[55] Yet he also acknowledges that the knowledge of the mind of God that could be expected from his theory of everything has inherent limitations. "Although science may solve the problem of how the universe began, it cannot answer the question: why does the universe bother to exist? I don't know the answer to that one."[56] The result is that we have conflicting claims. In some ways, Hawking does not recognize any source of knowledge other than science; in another sense, he recognizes that science cannot be expected to explain the ultimate why of life.

The resolution that is usually reached over this dilemma is to declare a division of territory. The how questions, having to do with the mechanics and processes, are assigned to science, and the why questions, having to do with purpose and meaning, are assigned to religion. While this would accord with the differences in Hawking's statements, and reflects a general distinction between the kinds of interests of science and of religion, the real interests and preoccupations of human beings are not likely to fit so neatly into such a division. For each of us, one or the other of these perspectives will almost certainly be more primary and determinative. We have seen that science represents a total vision of life, and that its aim is control, so that it assumes a view of ourselves as controllers. This is directly contrary to the religious inclination to acknowledge a reality greater than ourselves to whom we are ultimately answerable. This difference in basic orientation suggests that what is at stake is ultimately of mythic proportions. To expect science to answer all questions, eventually, and to think that we can leave the questions it cannot answer open, is to adopt the science myth without reservation. The alternative is to recognize that science, too, ultimately represents a mythic perspective, that anticipations of a final unified theory must also bear the marks of mythic limitations.

> This theory of everything will be, in precise terms, a myth. A myth is a story that makes sense within its own terms, offers explanations for everything we can see around us, but can neither be tested nor disproved. . . . This theory of everything, this myth, will indeed spell the end of physics. It will be the end not because physics has at last been able to explain everything in the universe, but because physics has reached the end of all the things it has the power to explain.[57]

The difference between the expectation that physics will eventually be able to explain everything in the universe and the expectation that physics may one day reach its own limits represent the two main approaches involved in the science myth. The expectation that physics may eventually explain everything represents a naïve inside endorsement of the science myth; the view that physics may achieve a theory of everything which would represent the exhaustion of its own powers of explanation is possible only for one who recognizes the mythic nature of science itself.

Notes

1. Paul Davies, *God and the New Physics* (New York: Simon and Schuster, 1983), p. 146.

2. Leon Lederman, with Dick Teresi, *The God Particle* (New York: Delta, 1993), pp. 154ff.

3. Lederman, *The God Particle*, p. 338.

4. Lederman, *The God Particle*, p. 176.

5. Davies, *God and the New Physics*, p. 159.

6. Lederman, *The God Particle*, p. 20.

7. David Lindley, *The End of Physics, The Myth of a Unified Theory* (New York: Harper and Collins Basic Books, 1993), p. 18.

8. Lederman, *The God Particle*, p. 176.

9. Ernan McMullin, "How Should Cosmology Relate to Theology?" in A.R. Peacocke, ed., *The Sciences and Theology in the Twentieth Century* (Notre Dame, IN: University of Notre Dame Press, 1981), pp. 32ff.

10. Davies, *God and the New Physics*, p. 21.

11. Robert Jastrow, *God and the Astronomers* (New York: W.W. Norton, 1978), p. 116.

12. Steven Weinberg, *The First Three Minutes: A Modern View of the Origins of the Universe* (London: Andre Deutsch, 1977), p. 154.

13. Bertrand Russell, "A Free Man's Worship," in *Why I Am Not a Christian* (New York: Simon and Schuster, 1957), p. 106.

14. Stephen Hawking, *Black Holes and Baby Universes, and Other Essays* (New York: Bantam Books, 1993), pp. 80ff.

15. Ibid., p. 81.

16. Ibid., p. 111.

17. Lederman, *The God Particle*, p. 253.

18. Lederman, *The God Particle*, pp. 56, 368ff.

19. Ian Stewart and Martin Golubitsky, *Fearful Symmetry, Is God a Geometer?* (Oxford: Blackwell, 1992), p. 255.

20. Hawking, *Black Holes and Baby Universes*, p. 19.

21. Mary Midgley, *Science and Salvation: A Modern Myth and Its Meaning* (London and New York: Routledge, 1992), p. 174.

22. Wolfgang Smith, "The Universe Is Ultimately to Be Explained in Terms of a Metacosmic Reality," in Henry Margenau and Roy Abraham Varghese, eds., *COSMOS, BIOS, THEOS* (LaSalle, IL: Open Court, 1992), pp. 113ff.

23. E.O. Wilson, *Sociobiology, The New Synthesis* (Cambridge, MA: Harvard University Press, 1975), p. 4.

24. Richard Dawkins, *The Selfish Gene* (London: Granada, A Paladin Book, 1978), p. 21.

25. Ibid., p. x.

26. Richard Dawkins, "Replicators and Vehicles," in *Current Problems in Sociobiology*, ed. King's College Sociobiology Group (Cambridge: Cambridge University Press, 1982), p. 45.

27. Richard Dawkins, *The Blind Watchmaker* (Burnt Mill: Longman Scientific and Technical, 1986), p. 141.

28. Dawkins, *The Selfish Gene*, p. 16.

29. Dawkins, *The Blind Watchmaker*, p. 145.

30. Jacques Monod, *Chance and Necessity*, trans. Austryn Wainhouse (London: Collins Fount Books, 1977), p. 137.

31. Henry Margenau, "The Laws of Nature Are Created by God," in Margenau and Varghese, *COSMOS, BIOS, THEOS*, p. 63.

32. Midgley, *Science as Salvation*, p. 42.

33. Davies, *God and the New Physics*, p. 168.

34. Stephen W. Hawking, *A Brief History of Time* (New York: Bantam Books, 1988), p. 121.

35. Hawking, *Black Holes and Baby Universes*, p. 2.

36. For a compact treatment of these narrow ranges, see John Gribbin and Martin Rees, "Cosmic Coincidences," *New Scientist*. 125 (1699) (3 Jan 1990): 51–54.

37. Sir John Eccles, "A Divine Design: Some Questions on Origins," in Margenau and Vargese, *COSMOS, BIOS, THEOS*, p. 161.

38. Ibid.

39. George Gale, "The Anthropic Principle," *Scientific American*. 245 (Dec 1981): 154.

40. John D. Barrow and Frank J. Tipler, *The Anthropic Cosmological Principle* (Oxford and New York: Oxford University Press, 1986).

41. Ernan McMullin, "How Should Cosmology Relate to Theory?" in Peacocke, *The Sciences and Theology*, p. 43.

42. B.J. Carr and M.J. Rees, "The Anthropic Principle and the Structure of the Physical World," *Nature*. 278 (12 Apr 1979): 612.

43. Ian G. Barbour, *Myths, Models and Paradigms: A Comparative Study in Science and Religion* (New York: Harper & Row, 1976), p. 100.

44. Max Planck, *Scientific Autobiography and Other Papers* (New York: Philosophical Library, 1949), pp. 33ff.

45. Hawking, *Black Holes and Baby Universes*, p. 42.

46. Lindley, *The End of Physics*, p. 131.

47. Thomas S. Kuhn, *The Structure of Scientific Revolutions* (Chicago: University of Chicago Press, 1970).

48. Michael Polanyi, *Personal Knowledge, Towards a Post-Critical Philosophy* (London: Routledge and Kegan Paul, 1962).

49. Arthur Peacocke, *God and the New Biology* (San Francisco: Harper & Row, 1986), p. 1.

50. Hawking, *Black Holes and Baby Universes*, p. ix.

51. Ibid., p. 5.

52. John Macquarrie, *The Scope of Demythologizing* (Gloucester, MA: Peter Smith, 1969), p. 235.

53. Hawking, *A Brief History of Time*, p. 175.

54. Hawking, *Black Holes and Baby Universes*, pp. 37 and 29.

55. Ibid., p. 51.

56. Ibid., p. 99.

57. Lindley, *The End of Physics*, p. 255.

3

A SPORTS MYTH

Newspapers devote pages, if not complete sections, to sport. Radio stations feel obliged to include updates on sport along with hourly bulletins on news and weather. A significant amount of television time, especially on weekends, is taken up with sport, not to mention a specialized cable channel devoted exclusively to it. Any area of life that gets this much media attention has to have a significant impact, perhaps even on those who might not consider themselves sports fans. The most dedicated fans can be seen to be totally captivated by a sports myth.

The Play of Sport

An American study[1] indicates that as many as 96.3 per cent of the population express significant interest in sport in terms of participating in, watching, or reading about it somewhat regularly or following particular teams or players. Almost 70 per cent check sports scores daily, and 42 per cent take part in sports themselves. There is hardly any other optional area of life that can come close to commanding this level of attention, with the exception of entertainment, of which sport would in fact represent a significant component. Why has sport attained such a dominant place in modern Western culture? What are the sources of its appeal?

Social-science research identifies seven categories of explanation for direct participation in sport.[2] Much involvement is simply instinctual, representing a natural inclination for play and activity. Second, there may be a deliberate attempt to develop skills; third, an attempt to achieve mastery. Social motives account for the fourth, fifth, and sixth reasons: using sport as a means of fitting into a social milieu or to make contacts, perhaps for business purposes; as a more direct means of social contact for its own sake; and as a means of effecting social control, since sport offers an acceptable way of releasing excess energy and exhibiting aggressive behaviour that would not be tolerated in other contexts. Finally, sport affords the opportunity for individuals to express themselves.

The spectator appeal of sport involves different motives. A survey of two American cities showed that a clearly leading reason for watching sports was to follow one's favourite team. Three other reasons formed a second, closely related group of motives. The drama and tension of televised sport afford a welcome contrast to the scripted and prerecorded format of most other programming. An interest in learning the game, either the basics for novices or the subtleties for veteran viewers, was almost as prominent, followed closely by the third component of this group of reasons, watching sport simply to relax. At the low end of the scale were three further motives that reflect little interest in sport itself. These ranged from "letting off steam," which presumably involves something more dramatic than simply relaxing, to being attracted by the sportscasters, to seeing a sportscast as an excuse for drinking, reflecting the success of the close association between professional sports and breweries. A survey of students' motives[3] showed basically similar results, with one interesting difference. The main motive is similar, following their team and enjoying the thrill of victory, but the second and third groups of motives are essentially reversed: an opportunity to let loose and break out the beer was in second place, while motives having to do with learning or just passing the time came in last. The cynical conclusion apt to be reached by university professors is that it should be no surprise that partying and drinking should outrank learning for students. Such a suggestion evokes the students' response that learning does not represent a form of relaxation for them.

These sources of the appeal of sport are well summed up in James Michener's three criteria.[4] For participants, first and foremost, sport should be fun; second, as a bonus, sport should promote health. For spectators, sport should be entertaining. Fun, health, and entertainment go a long way toward accounting for the appeal of sport, but sport can be seen to hold these attractions only because of certain intrinsic qualities that it possesses.[5] Sport is fun and entertaining because particular games are carefully structured so that they provide optimum levels of competition, which makes the drama possible. The number of downs allowed in football to attempt to advance the ball ten yards, the distance between bases in baseball, and the size of the net in soccer are all carefully calculated to assure the maximum level of competition between offence and defence. Rules committees and annual meetings of professional sports organizations are constantly concerned with fine-tuning the rules and regulations to assure that this optimal level is maintained. The carefully constructed nature of games suggests another underlying source of attraction. This heightening of competition elicits ever new heights of athletic prowess on the part of players. It is an element more evident in the careers of individual athletes, as with Olympic competitors, for example, but it is not absent from team sports, as fans of sufficient interest to be connoisseurs of records well know. Thus, the refinements that make the thrill of victory particularly significant also elicit almost superhuman performances from individual athletes, providing added incentive for the discriminating viewer.

Viewers who get the most out of televised sport, who really appreciate what goes into an outstanding performance in team or individual contexts, are those who have participated in sport themselves. "Sport is popular in part because it showcases forms of human accomplishment that most of us can appreciate precisely because we have first-hand experience of how difficult they are."[6] A punt returner carrying the ball almost the length of the football field, while barely eluding the pursuit of defending tacklers, is much more meaningful for someone who has played football, or even someone who has done some running, and can feel that second wind that comes when you think you can't take another step. Others may find viewing sports entertaining, but the depths of the struggle and the levels of skill exhibited will elude them. Yet in a curious way, the participant viewer and the casual viewer each reflect the basic thrust of sports—the absorption that takes us out of our ordinary routine, the enjoyment of play.

The most basic contrast is not between participant viewers and casual viewers, or even between viewers and participants, but between those who enjoy sport, at whatever level, and those who take it so seriously that it ceases to be play. The most obvious candidate for the latter category is the professional athlete, for whom sport is work. In one sense, the professional athlete might achieve intense enjoyment in honing his or her talents to the peak of perfection and savouring the results of victory, but the total involvement that this demands is also an occupation. This gives sport an added dimension for the professional athlete, and one that can change the significance of sport for the viewer. In fact, the meaning and significance of sport can be seen to depend on how far it is identified in terms either of play or of athletics.

Our modern English word "sport" derives from the Middle English *desport* or *disport*, which in turn derive from the Old French *desporter*, "which literally meant to carry away from work."[7] Thus, "sport" has as its direct meaning an activity that constitutes an alternative to work. In contrast, "athletics" derives from the Greek verb *athlein*, which means "to contend for a prize," or from the nouns *athlos*, "contest," or *athlon*, "a prize awarded for the successful completion of the contest."[8] Thus athletics is much more deliberate and goal oriented than sport. In fact, if words were used carefully, most of what claims our attention as sport in contemporary culture would really be called athletics. Newspapers would have "Athletics" sections and Saturday and Sunday sportscasts would be called "Athletics Weekend."

What we have come to think of as sport has developed through a shift from the spontaneity of play to the deliberate focus of athletics. As a matter of classification, it is possible to identify stages by which the meaning of sport can be seen to extend further and further from the equation with play. The first stage in this progression involves a distinction in the sense of play itself in terms of which play can be either spontaneous or organized. When it is organized, play becomes a game. Games, in turn, can be distinguished as noncompetitive or competitive. Competitive games, then, are really contests. Contests can be of either the intellectual or the physical variety. Physical contests are sports.[9] This departs from the literal meaning of sport, which equates it with play, but that departure is not so much a violation of the literal definition of sport as a reflection of historical development that has changed its meaning.

It is easy to imagine a playful form of sport prevailing prior to the contests and athletics of the modern West. Peasants wrestled and kicked around a homemade predecessor of the soccer ball, while the nobility hunted, fished, and hawked.[10] In fact, books on sport before the middle of the nineteenth century equate sport with hunting, fishing, and shooting—the sport of the gentry. The antecedents of sport as games, as we have come to think of it, were the uncouth pursuits of the drinking, brawling peasantry.[11] However, both forms were characterized essentially by play. It is true, though, that there was a dimension of pre-modern sport that we are apt to overlook today. While it lacked the organizational sophistication of its modern successor, the idea that it represented the total diversion of play may reflect an element of romanticism as well as an overlooking of the importance of religion in pre-secular culture. Not only did monks play soccer at Easter, but Shrove Tuesday was actually known as "football-day."[12] Of course, the ancient Olympic games were dedicated to the gods of Mount Olympus. Thus, while earlier sport might seem virtually identical to play, in comparison with the athleticism of contemporary sport, it may have had its own external sources of motivation in terms of seeking or celebrating the divine.

The assumed religious context and the spontaneity of play that characterized sport in its earlier forms were displaced in the last century by the deliberate isolation and structuring of particular athletic activities. "Modern sports were born in England and spread from their birthplace to the United States, to Western Europe, and to the world beyond."[13] The birthplace was English public schools, which on this side of the Atlantic would be thought of as private schools, institutions such as Eton and Rugby and Harrow, as well as the universities of Oxford and Cambridge. "The Public School not only standardized popular collective sports, and invented new ones. They placed them in an arena to be viewed, marrying participatory with spectatorial dimensions in such a way as to cement the bond of player with the represented institution."[14] Traditional religious connotations, as well as diversion from the serious business of maintaining life, were replaced by a concentration on sport for its own sake. It did serve external functions, such as promoting school spirit, and, Marxists in particular would contend, solidifying class loyalties: soccer, for example, became the working-class sport, while rugby was played at the better schools. However, sport was venerated in its own right, with sportsmanship being virtually synonymous with the human ideal. The classic depiction of this phenomenon, Thomas Hughes's *Tom Brown's Schooldays* (1857), indicates how "the pursuit of excellence is, by becoming a team thing, moralized into a microcosm of communal virtue."[15]

The organizational dimension involved in the emergence of sport in its own right was furthered by the development of associations for the various sports and the gradual professionalization of some of these. This last phase was accomplished by a complementary process of commercialization that has extended so far that even so-called amateur athletes are involved in an athletic-commercial complex that rivals the military-industrial complex so prominent during the cold war period. The shift from play to athletics, culminating in the athletic-commercial complex, goes a long way toward accounting for the prominence of sport on the contemporary scene, and it is central to the mythic power that sport exercises today.

The Purpose of Sport

The move from play to athletics not only goes a long way toward accounting for the prominence of sport today, it also suggests that the mythic influence that results might not be peculiar to sport. Commercialized athletics can be seen to represent an imposition of extraneous goals and interests on sport. Christopher Lasch describes what he calls "the degradation of sport," and he sees this as being due not, as many think, to sport being taken too seriously, but, on the contrary, to its not being taken seriously enough.[16] Sport has been co-opted and transformed to serve purposes that are different from, and perhaps even antithetical to, the play that is the purpose peculiar to sport itself. At the heart of this development lies a strange transformation. "As sport is bureaucratized, it loses its attachment to specific substantive ends—its intrinsic gratification—and becomes important in its own right. Ironically, this then makes sport a deployable tool, available for use for a variety of different purposes."[17] Thus the issue of the mythic power of sport concerns not only the present predominance of sport, but also the possibility that this predominance is being co-opted by extraneous interests.

The development that effected the shift from play to athletics involves various dimensions. In some ways, it can be seen to reflect the effect of the formative influences that have shaped the modern world as such. Organized, commercial sport, like every other modern phenomenon, would be inconceivable without the development that has been most instrumental in shaping the modern West, the emergence of science. It is no accident that modern sport emerged in the land that also produced Sir Isaac Newton, the major synthesizer of the new view of the universe produced by the new science.[18] The direct impact of science on sport is evident today. Through improvements in sports equipment and the perfecting of training techniques, including the possibility of improving performance through drugs, science makes its presence felt to the point where questions arise as to how far the competition has shifted from the athletes to the scientific experts behind them. Beyond these technical applications, however, there is a more pervasive influence in terms of the outlook instigated by science. The importance of results and the expectation of their realization through devotion to detail and patient application are qualities that have been promoted through the success of modern science. Ultimately, the formative influence is a change in the understanding of measurement. Where "measure" used to refer to a sense of moderation and balance, as in Aristotle's advocacy of the golden mean (courage being the golden mean between cowardice and foolhardiness), in the modern scientific era, it has become quantified, taking on the connotation of comparison, of "more or less." The calculations that produce victory and the importance of records in modern sports are inconceivable without this modern sense of measurement and the assumption of its foundational importance.

The application of the pursuit of constant improvement to sport involves another central element of the modern world, one emphasized particularly by sociologist Max Weber. The Weberian approach puts emphasis on the importance of bureaucracy and organization in accounting for the peculiar developments of the modern era. In its application to sport, six characteristics are seen to distinguish modern sport from its more playful predecessor: secularism, equality, specialization, rationalism, bureaucratic organization, and quantification.[19] First, sport is secular. When the wide receiver promptly kneels in the endzone after scoring a touchdown, this is an individual expression of personal piety, in contrast to the runner in the ancient Olympics, who was understood to be running for the honour of the gods. Second, sport is based on equality. Modern sports are above all competitive. Native cultures retain games that reflect communal participation across lines of age, sex, or social status; in the modern West, sport is essentially for individuals who occupy a similar level in terms of age, size, and skills. Competition for membership on professional teams is as intense as competition against other teams. Third, sport involves specialization. The competition is not just for a place on the team, but for particular specialized roles. Major-league teams are really two teams to begin with, an offensive team with the task of scoring points, and a defensive team with the task of preventing other teams from scoring on it. Within these specialities, there are particular spots on the field, court, or ice. An outfielder would probably be incompetent as a catcher; a goalie would probably make a poor right-winger. Fourth, sport is rationalized. We have seen how rules are fine-tuned to assure maximum competition and drama. Leagues are expanded, and schedules arranged, to make the sport as extensive and accessible as possible. Fifth, sport epitomizes bureaucratic organization. The logistics of professional sports leagues and teams demands massive and precise organization. The modern Olympics involves an elaborate process through which cities compete to host the games. When a city is finally chosen by an elaborately wined and dined Olympic selection committee, a local organization faces the challenge of arranging, and usually constructing, facilities and assuring availability of accommodation, transportation, and other essential services for participants and spectators. All of this, of course, is supervised by the bureaucracy of the International Olympic Committee. Sixth, sport is subject to quantification. The central point of hourly sportscasts is to provide scores, but this is just the most obvious index of the importance of numbers in modern sport. Occasionally, sportscasts will indicate the more extensive role of numbers by reference to a record-breaking performance—most career goals, a new home run record. Baseball is particularly obsessed with records; however, the use of numbers is pervasive in professional sports, to the point where one thorough survey of the transformation that has characterized modern sport is called *From Ritual to Record*.[20]

Another essential factor in modern sport is its commercialization. The modern analysis that emphasizes the significance of the economic dimension most distinctly is the one that follows the direction set by Karl Marx. In the Marxist analysis, there is a general and a more specific thesis. The more specific thesis is the anti-capitalist one, which sees a basic division in society between oppressed workers and exploitive owners and looks for the revolution that will eliminate this injustice and usher in the classless society. The general thesis is that ultimately economics is at the bottom of everything. Whatever relevance the specific Marxist position might have in its application to sport, the insistence on the importance of economic considerations finds an obvious candidate for confirmation in the progressive commercialization of sports in the recent past. Publicity about multi-million-dollar signings by major-league athletes gives the commercial focus of contemporary sport particular prominence. Closer consideration of the whole process quickly indicates that this represents a late catching-up on the part of players who have finally organized in players' associations and employ personal agents to claim their share of the income that owners formerly reserved largely for themselves. This difference of interests between owners and players, who in this context are the workers, could be seen as confirmation of a specific Marxist reading of contemporary sport, if millionaire players can be thought of as the proletariat.

Whatever the merits or problems of a strictly Marxist, class-oriented reading of the situation, there can be no doubt about the commercialization of sport. The multi-million-dollar salaries and hundreds of millions of dollars return on owners' investments reflect not only the operations of large, often domed, stadia, but especially the lucrative television contracts that disseminate the game across the nation and around the world. Sportswear and items bearing team logos represent major commercial enterprises. "Sport, television, and advertising all seemed to have focused into a single promotional entity,"[21] Richard Gruneau observes of CBC coverage of a World Cup downhill ski race at Whistler, British Columbia, in March 1986, but that impression reflects a more pervasive symbiosis between sport and the mass media. "Sport events are relatively easy to cover and inexpensive to produce and admirably meet the media's need for the dramatic and sensational. They also deliver better than any other kind of programming an audience of the more affluent male members of the population."[22] Sport, media, and business coalesce in a mutually supportive and domineering athletic-commercial complex that constitutes one of the most prominent and influential dimensions of contemporary life.

If the shift from play to athletics were explained by these wider movements of the modern era, then sport would be little more than a reflection of the wider society. "Sport is the symbolic expression of the values of the larger political and social milieu."[23] This would mean that what characterizes sport in itself has been totally submerged in professionalization and commercialization. Defenders of the continuing integrity of sport regard this as an unacceptably reductionistic view precisely because of its "reducing the values in sports to those of the wider society."[24] This issue is of far more than academic significance, because when it is posed from the other direction, it is the question of the effect that the athletic-commercial complex has on us. How much is sport an enjoyable escape from the routine demands of life, and how much does it represent a further immersion in the priorities that we think we are escaping? Almost certainly, both dimensions are present; "media sports serve in a dialectic role as both a socializer and an escape."[25] The difficulty is in knowing where to draw the line, if, indeed, a line can be drawn at all.

In itself, sport should provide fun and entertainment. But fun and entertainment are among the dimensions of life that most readily lend themselves to commercial exploitation. It is not possible to have fun unless you have the right sports equipment and the proper clothing, which will almost certainly come with substantial price tags. Entertainment is packaged by the media, which depend on the sponsorship of commercial interests that not only insert commercials in the media presentation but plaster their names and logos over boards and fences surrounding sports surfaces and ingrain them in the playing surfaces themselves. In this setting, where is the line between sport and commerce to be drawn, or can it be drawn at all? A clear-cut division that would require that sport be entirely commerce-free would rule out all professional sport. Indeed, serious competitive amateur sport would also be ruled out because of the deferred income from endorsements, if not from the subsidization of training and the allowances that would hardly differ in principle, however much they may differ in amount, from professional remuneration.

To see all external rewards as illegitimate would essentially eliminate the entertainment dimension of sport. Indeed, if sport is characterized primarily by play, then not only tangible rewards but concern with winning might represent a compromise of the playful spirit of true sport. The game itself, rather than any result, should be the focus. Playing should be its own reward. The irony is that it is precisely those who become totally absorbed in the game who turn out to be most successful at it. This demand for total concentration leads Adam Smith to refer to sport as "a Western Yoga."[26] The concentration of Jack Nicklaus is cited in illustration of this complete absorption in the game, where the club becomes an extension of his being, and everything but the challenge of the present hole is obliterated. A Western version of this might be Michael Polanyi's emphasis on the importance of context for achieving a true focus, so that in this case the game itself constitutes the defining framework that makes the concentration possible.[27] The implication, then, is that the best players, in the internal sense of those who can lose themselves completely in the game, turn out to be the best players, in the external sense of qualifying for the rewards that good play affords.

Internal goods and external gains are connected through the prominence of winning. Games would lose their point if we were to take such an idealistic view of sport that winning was disregarded. Yet it is possible to allow winning to take on a centrality and connotations that render the impact of sport decidedly negative: "To overemphasize the value of winning is to diminish the numerous other internal goods of sports, and it is to point in a direction in which it becomes *more* difficult, not less, to be a good person."[28] How the achievement of personal-best performances and the thrill of winning that is intrinsic to sport are compromised when external goals make winning the only point of competing is evident in drug scandals in individual and team sports. For viewers, an indication that winning is acquiring disproportionate prominence is at hand in the increasing acceptance and expectation of violence in sport.

In Canada, the escalating violence in hockey is hyped by the guru of guts and gore, former marginal NHL player and ex-coach of the Boston Bruins, Don Cherry, who augments his career in sports broadcasting with a chain of sports bars, the promotion of *Rock 'em Sock 'em* videos featuring the most violent hits in games, and fronting for Pro-Line sports gambling. A promotion for Pro-Line features Cherry standing over prostrate football players on whom he sneeringly drops a football, saying, "Hey buddy, are ya lookin' for this?" Anyone who questions his glorification of violence is a wimp. Cherry has an ally in American theologian Michael Novak, who sees the violence of football as a reflection of the real violence in all of us, which liberals would like to pretend does not exist.[29] This is Novak's answer to charges such as the claim that football gained popularity over the essentially non-contact baseball in the Vietnam-era 1960s because of its appeal of violence.[30] Novak claims for sport the innocence of neutrality that artists, reporters, and advertisers claim when they are charged with being implicated in promoting less than savory features of life, and he contends that, like other prominent dimensions of contemporary life, sport simply reflects what is out there in the wider society and in no way bears any responsibility for promoting violence. Ironically, this is tantamount to acceptance of the reductionistic thesis that sport simply reflects the values of the wider society; a curious position for people who are promoters of sport.

A more realistic reading would see the prominence of media sport today not only as reflecting the values of the wider society, but as actually promoting some of the more questionable ones. Sports academics who have studied the Canadian scene conclude that violence is promoted by the athletic-commercial complex. "Our belief is that hockey violence persists in North America almost solely because NHL executives believe that violence helps to sell tickets, especially in American cities where fans are less attuned to the subtleties of the game."[31] The selling of ice hockey in the American south has entailed considerable marketing ingenuity, which has found the encouragement and publicizing of violence much more effective than instruction in the fine points of the game. When subjects viewed different segments from a hockey game (one with and the other without rough play) with commentary on each that either emphasized or downplayed rough play, the viewers perceived rough play when commentators suggested it, even when it was not present, and were not particularly aware of it when commentators did not draw attention to it, even when it was present.[32] Such evidence confirms the fear that the prominent and influential media presentation of contact sports promotes, and does not simply reflect, the violence that increasingly characterizes contemporary life.

The concern that sport is being used to promote violence in the interest of attracting viewers and increasing revenues can be countered by the defence of advertisers, reporters, and artistic creators that they are simply reflecting what is out there or are meeting popular demand. If people did not want to see violence in sport, it would not be so popular. The same argument can be used to justify the sale of hard drugs, child pornography, or any other commodity. It begs the question of the value of the commodity by attributing that choice to the consumer. That question cannot be begged by either those who are concerned with the presence of violence in contemporary life or those who care about sport. "If we accept the cliché that hockey is a reflection of our national character, what does it say about us? Are we bloodthirsty yahoos who prefer watching mayhem to slick passing and fancy stickhandling?"[33]

Insofar as violence is being encouraged to sell sport and the products behind it, the mythic power of sport is being used to the detriment of sport itself. Beyond its culpability in encouraging the violence that has become all too common, this crass use of sport shows contempt for sport itself. *New York Times* columnist Robert Lipsyte is particularly pessimistic about the future of sport because of the way it has been exploited:

> Sports are over because they no longer have any moral resonance. They are merely entertainment, bread and circuses of a New Rome, nothing makes this more chillingly real than our current Babes [counterparts of Babe Ruth]: Mike Tyson and Tonya Harding. Two of the neediest, most troubled and misguided young people in athletic history, they are the archetypal extremes of this frenzied, confused sports endgame.[34]

Through its commercialization, sport has sold its soul. "Casey [of "Casey at the Bat" fame] is just out for himself, and the owners can be counted on to betray him, us, and all of Mudville."[35] Not only has sport changed to athletics, but athletics has come to be commercialized sport. In the process, sport itself has become a totally disposable commodity.

The Perspective of Sport

By nature, sport should not have a purpose; it is supposed to be a diversion. However, the playfulness of sport leaves it vulnerable to imposed purposes, allowing it to be packaged and commercialized for interests that might have little to do with sport itself. That this has been possible may be due not only to the absence of deliberate purpose in sport itself, but also to the loss of the wider context that sustained that carefreeness of sport in the past. It may be that the playfulness of sport was made possible by a sense of being involved in a play of life in a wider religious sense, and that the loss of that sense has deprived sport of its playfulness through its becoming subject to other visions as well as other interests.

In becoming a commercial showcase, sport is reflecting a comprehensive vision of life represented by the athletic-commercial complex. "The effect on the audience of this mode of representation is often an unquestioned acceptance of the cultural meanings and myths that are set forth in the mass media sports coverage."[36] When the inherent attraction of sport is combined with the expertise of modern commercial packaging, sport can be seen to take on a new version of its ancient role as vehicle for religious veneration. This is a cause for concern, because while the playful nature of sport suggests that it should be all-absorbing, it does not follow that it should be allowed to absorb all. When sport does absorb all, it ceases to be a diversion and becomes an obsession. This may well be the significance of the massive prominence of sport in contemporary secular culture; it can be seen to have become the focus for the veneration formerly reserved for religion. This situation would be particularly ironic, for it would mean that not only have we lost the playfulness of sport itself, but we have even gone beyond the ancient use of sport as a vehicle for veneration of the gods to allow it to become the substance of religious devotion itself.

Contemporary sport is so intimately associated with modern secular culture that it is probably difficult to realize how in another culture sport can be just as intimately associated with religion. The original Olympic Games, for example, were not at all simply athletic contests in our modern sense. They were staged to honour the gods, and athletes participated on these terms.[37] In fact, the ancient Olympics also ended for religious reasons. When Christianity became the official religion of the Roman Empire in the fourth century, it could hardly permit athletic festivals honouring the gods of ancient Greece, even though by this time the seriousness of the religious foundation had been significantly eroded. Consequently, the most prominent form of ancient sport familiar to us was begun and ended in the name of religion.[38]

The modern Olympics, revived in 1896, are as resolutely secular as their ancient counterparts were religious. Their symbol is rings representing the five continents. They afford an opportunity for the best athletes in the world to compete, through the sponsorship of their countries, to determine who is truly best. In this way, the games can be seen to be truly athletic contests. They reflect the results of years of intensely dedicated training and provide a showcase for the zenith of athletic prowess. At least, this is the official view. The reality, as we all know, is that Olympic athletes are far from being amateurs, with the top ones receiving remuneration that rivals that of their professional counterparts. If this income from endorsements and personal appearances is to be held in trust to preserve the appearance of amateur status, the tactic is severely undermined by the luxury cars and ostentatious jewellery these athletes manage to acquire while still competing. In this regard, contemporary Olympians might not differ so much from their ancient counterparts, for while they competed to honour the gods, the athletes of old too had their material rewards, sometimes shifting their allegiance to another town as present athletes might shift to a corporation that came up with a more lucrative advertising deal.[39] This

shift of geographic loyalties might also suggest a wider similarity between ancient and modern Olympics. Even the fundamentally secular
orientation of the modern games might not stand in complete contrast
to the religious context of the original Olympics. When the first-,
second-, and third-place winners stand on the medals podium, with
gold, silver, and bronze medallions hanging around their necks, listen-
ing to the national anthem of the winner's country being played, might
this not represent for them, and for many of those looking on, a modern
counterpart to the veneration of the gods? Insofar as this is the case,
modern sport should be seen not simply as an expression of the secular
outlook of the modern world, but as a substitute for the religious veneration that is officially relinquished.

The singing of national anthems prior to the beginning of professional games is a further indication of the link between sport and the
modern religion of nationalism. There is probably no more vivid version of this than in the United States, and within American professional sports, there is probably no more vivid example of this link than
the annual championship game of professional football, the Super
Bowl. An analysis of a Super Bowl pregame show on NBC concludes
that it amounted to the development of a nationalistic fantasy focused
on themes of the American Dream. "Among the more prevalent of
these were themes concerning racial and ethnic integration, national
and family unity, due process of law, rugged individualism in the form
of the maverick, hard work, family businesses, patriotism, heroism,
simplicity in the form of the common man, equality, the multifaceted
character of great leaders, commitment and pride, and last, but not
least, the relation of sports to American character."[40] The result, this
analysis concludes, is "a chain link fence through which professional
football, and perhaps all media portrayals of sports in America may be
better understood."[41] This is a chain-link fence of images that create a
mythic world. The *New York Times* columnist who was so discouraged
about the direction sport has taken, Robert Lipsyte, calls this world
"SportsWorld" and sees it functioning as "socializer, pacifier, safety
valve; as a concentration camp for adolescents and an emotional
Disneyland for their parents."[42] Media sport creates an alternate world
that may be more compelling and formative than the world of day-to-
day experience.

This alternate world of sport readily takes on religious dimensions. One enthusiast claims to speak for millions in suggesting that
Lipsyte's "SportsWorld is on sacred ground and the chapel to which we
come to worship."[43] Another says of his collection of baseball books
that "they help me contemplate the mystical meeting of sport and life,
the way rosary beads help some Catholics touch the relation between

God and man."[44] This author also refers to "the high holy days of the World Series."[45]

Sport can provide ways of orienting ourselves in time. Where religious cultures define the passage of time in terms of sacred seasons, sport can fulfil this function in a secular culture. The Christian year, for example, centres around the celebration of Christmas and Easter and involves a liturgical calendar that has preparations for these seasons and special days that follow on from them. Christmas and Easter have been secularized and commercialized, perhaps even more thoroughly than professional sport. As occasions for family gatherings and festivals of consumer culture, they continue to provide some points of orientation for a secular age, but their usefulness in this regard is greatly diminished from their full range of intrinsic meaning when every Sunday was a reflection and anticipation of Easter, for example. Sport provides a more detailed liturgical calendar for a secular culture. Without realizing it, many of us measure the passing seasons in terms of the sports that are associated with them. Spring means the return of baseball, which, along with golf and tennis, sees us through the summer. Autumn brings football, hockey, and basketball, and these get us through the winter months, until the promise of spring returns with spring training for a new baseball season. This may be seen not only as a replacement for the Christian pattern that shaped the pre-modern West, but even as a return to nature-based religions that were more directly aligned with the changing seasons. Ancient worshippers who placated the gods of fertility to assure good crops in the spring may find a contemporary counterpart in baseball fans who delight in the warmth of the strengthening sun on the plastic seats in their favourite stadium.

A whole array of parallels can be drawn between sport and religion.[46] The training of the athlete and the faithfulness of the sports fan emulate the devotion of the religious believer. The dedication of the fitness fanatic rivals any discipline undertaken by medieval monks. People sweating regularly in fitness classes, health clubs, and gyms are a secular equivalent of the monk's faithful saying of the offices, with the incentive of achieving the body beautiful rather than eternal salvation. In professional sports, it might not be too far-fetched to suggest that, for some, the players are seen as priests who celebrate a sacred tradition for them. The celebrations have their rituals, sacred places, and special days. These have nothing to do with the superstitions players might go through before a game or before coming to bat; they have to do with the routines of the game itself, the atmosphere of the stadium or rink, and the sacred associations of special days such as "Monday Night Football" or "Hockey Night in Canada." There might even be a counterpart to the ecclesiastical organist, rousing the worshippers in the stands. Anyone who has ever watched the opening salvo of the northern hemisphere's men's professional golf tour, the Masters, and heard the hushed and reverent tones with which the commentators describe the traditions and atmosphere of the Golf and Country Club of Augusta, Georgia, where the Masters is held, and noticed the liturgical green jacket with which the winner is robed, usually by the winner from the previous year, can hardly miss the message that this is sacred ground and sacred tradition. A new bishop is being consecrated in this cathedral of golf. These associations lend credibility to the contention that "it is not just a parallel that is emerging between sport and religion, but rather a *complete* identity."[47] For the truly serious sports fan, sport does not simply take on the trappings of religion; it is religion. It reflects a devotion that precludes any other religious allegiance.

The proselytizing of the religion of sports is much more subtle than are more traditional varieties. Appeals for converts are not common, mainly because they are not necessary. Children are so automatically institutionalized into sport, and sport is so prominent through media representation, that there is less need to seek converts than there was for the medieval church when it held the monopoly on Christendom. Nor is the ubiquity of sport simply a reflection of the hegemony of the athletic-commercial complex. When it elicits depths of devotion of religious proportions, we can expect that it is exerting significant mythic powers.

A dramatic depiction of how sport can constitute the controlling myth that drives a person is presented in the film *Field of Dreams*, based on W.P. Kinsella's short story "Shoeless Joe Jackson Comes to Iowa." An obsessive Iowa baseball fan (he speaks of "The great god Baseball," and says that his birthstone is a diamond and his astrological sign is hit and run!)[48] has a dream (or is it a vision?) of Shoeless Joe (the legendary left-fielder of the Chicago White Sox, who, along with seven other players, was suspended from major-league baseball for life because he was involved in throwing the 1919 World Series. It was Shoeless Joe who was asked by the pleading kid after the story broke, "Say it ain't so, Joe."), which assures him that if he builds a baseball diamond in his cornfield, Shoeless Joe will come to play on it. The film shows the shadowy figures of Shoeless Joe and the other baseball immortals materializing from between the tall corn stalks. "If you build it, he will come," is the assurance that the farmer is given. He builds it, and they come. His wife Annie goes along with her husband's obsession, but she is not really a fan.

> She attends ballgames with me and squeezes my arm when there's a hit, but her heart isn't in it and she would just as soon be at home.

She loses interest if the score isn't close, or the weather's not warm, or the pace isn't fast enough. To me it is baseball, and that is all that matters. It's the game that's important—the tension, the strategy, the ballet of the fielders, the angle of the bat.[49]

Kinsella writes of baseball with a note of the mythic bordering on the mystical, in which it has a sacred aura that rightly demands devotion.

Another of Kinsella's stories tells of dedicated fans conspiring to replace the AstroTurf of their stadium with real sod during a baseball strike. Night after night they sneak out of their houses, arm themselves with rakes and hoses and the other equipment required for laying sod, and foot by foot they restore the natural grass surface. More is going on here than a plot on the part of traditionalists to harken back to the kind of field they played on. The spacious, well-maintained grass surface of a baseball diamond, with its expansive outfield, may well have maintained a sense of the pastoral era as the modern world became increasingly urbanized.[50] Baseball may thus carry mythic overtones of rural innocence and simplicity.

Connoisseurs of baseball find even more intrinsic hints of even wider significance. In its setting and structure, baseball can be seen to transcend time and open out into eternity. While most sports run by the clock, with a specified ending time and division into periods or halves or quarters, baseball has no time restrictions. Each inning ends only when both teams have had three outs.[51] In theory, a game could go on forever. Similarly, where other sports take place in bounded areas, with each team defending one end and attempting to score at the other end, in baseball one team occupies the whole field when the other team is at bat. Even more telling is the fact that the foul lines beginning at home plate and running out through first and third bases are open-ended, getting wider as they extend into the outfield, and, in theory, reach into eternity.[52] Baseball does not have a monopoly on such imagery. If football is not quite so suggestive of the contrast of the eternal in the temporal, it does reach out temporally in both directions. The heavily padded, helmeted figure of the football player may appear similar to the swaggering primitive of the early stages of the race and also like a space dweller of a future civilization, carrying his breathing apparatus around with him.[53] The point is not that the fan sitting in the stadium, or watching the game on television, is thinking in these terms. Myth is most effective where it is not noticed. Sport affords ways of transcending the limits of time in a secular culture bereft of overt approaches to eternity.

Insofar as sport operates with these mythic perspectives, providing a way of orienting ourselves in time and even offering hints of eternity, it clearly functions with mythic overtones of religious proportions. It is refreshing in an age of secular boredom to find someone like Kinsella, who can depict people absorbed with such enthusiasm. There is something exhilarating about a person who lives his dreams to the extent of building a baseball diamond in a cornfield so that players excluded from the game they loved because they got caught up in its corruption can play again. But it is a dream. Consequently, exhilarating though it is, there is also something sad about intelligent adults investing sports with religious significance. As the play that offers an alternative to the claims and responsibilities of everyday life, sport has a crucial diversionary role in contemporary life. When it takes on the trappings of religion and elicits the devotion of the sacred, it can only be an indication of the barrenness of the secular atmosphere in which we live. There is no shortage of capitalizers ready to take advantage of this devotion, to sell violence or whatever it takes to profit from this vacuum. Not that the strategy is so blatant or deliberate; those who seek to profit from sports violence may well occupy this vacuum themselves. One of the wisest assessments of the place of sport in our mythic horizons was probably that offered by the legendary former voice of the Montreal Canadiens, an ardent lover of sport, hockey, and the Canadiens, Danny Gallivan, when he said of the sport he loved, "In the grand scheme of things, it's only a game!"

Notes

1. George Vecsey, "A Nation of Sports Fans," *New York Times* (16 Mar 1983): B11.

2. Lawrence A. Wenner, "Media, Sports, and Society: The Research Agenda," in Lawrence A. Wenner, ed. *Media, Sports, and Society* (Newbury Park, CA.: Sage Publications, 1989), p. 19.

3. W. Gantz, "An Exploration of Viewing Motives and Behaviors Associated with Television Sports," *Journal of Broadcasting.* 25 (1981): 263–75.

4. James A. Michener, *Sports in America* (New York: Fawcett Crest, 1976), pp. 24ff.

5. Frank B. Ryan, "Sports and the Humanities: Friends or Foes?" in William J. Baker and James A. Rog, eds. *Sports and the Humanities: A Symposium* (Orono: University of Maine at Orono Press, 1983), pp. 18ff, suggests three sources of appeal that bear some similarity to the conclusions proposed here.

6. Ann Hall, Trevor Slack, Garry Smith, and David Whitson, *Sport in Canadian Society* (Toronto: McClelland & Stewart, 1991), p. 35.

7. James W. Keating, "Sportsmanship as a Moral Category," *Ethics.* 75 (1964): 27.

8. Ibid., p. 28.

9. Allen Guttmann, *From Ritual to Record, The Nature of Modern Sports* (New York: Columbia University Press, 1978), p. 9.

10. Ibid., p. 58.

11. John Wilson, *Playing by the Rules: Sport, Society, and the State* (Detroit: Wayne State University Press, 1994), pp. 15–16.

12. Carl Diem, *Weltgeschichtedes Sports*, 3rd ed., (Frankfurt: Cotta, 1971), Vol. 1, p. 513, in Guttmann, *From Ritual to Record*, p. 126.

13. Guttmann, *From Ritual to Record*, p. 57.

14. Anthony Skillen, "Sport: An Historical Phenomenology," *Philosophy*. 68 (1993): 359.

15. Ibid.

16. Christopher Lasch, *The Culture of Narcissism* (New York: Warner Books, 1979), p. 195.

17. Wilson, *Playing by the Rules*, p. 18.

18. Guttmann, *From Ritual to Record*, p. 85.

19. Ibid., pp. 80–81.

20. Ibid.

21. Richard Gruneau, "Making Spectacle: A Case Study in Television Sports Production," in Wenner, *Media, Sports, and Society*, p. 136.

22. Wilson, *Playing by the Rules*, p. 296.

23. Robert Lipsyte, *SportsWorld: An American Dreamland* (New York: Quadrangle Books, 1975), p. 351.

24. Robert L. Simon, *Fair Play: Sports, Values and Society* (Boulder: Westview Press, 1991), pp. 187–88.

25. Michael R. Real, "Super Bowl Football Versus World Cup Soccer: A Cultural-Structural Comparison," in Wenner, *Media, Sports, and Society*, p. 201.

26. Adam Smith, "Sport is a Western Yoga," cited in Joseph C. Mihalich, "Existentialism and the Athlete," in Pasquale J. Galasso, ed., *Philosophy of Sport and Physical Activity* (Toronto: Canadian Scholars' Press, 1988), p. 106.

27. See Margaret Steel, "What We Know When We know a Game," in Galasso, *Philosophy of Sport and Physical Activity*, p. 119.

28. Randolph Freezell, "Sport, Character, and Virtue," *Philosophy Today*. 33 (Fall 1989): 212.

29. Michael Novak, *The Joy of Sports* (New York: Basic Books,1976), pp. 84ff.

30. P. Gardner, *Nice Guys Finish Last: Sport and American Life* (New York: Universe Books, 1975), p. 115; Paul Hoch, *Ripoff the Big Game* (New York: Doubleday Anchor Books, 1972), p. 7.

31. Hall et al., *Sport in Canadian Society*, p. 217.

32. P. Cominsky, J. Bryant, and D. Zillmann, "Commentary on a Substitute for Action," *Journal of Communication*. 23 (1977): 150ff.

33. Hall et al., *Sport in Canadian Society*, p. 214.

34. Robert Lipsyte, "The Emasculation of Sport," *New York Times Magazine* (2 Ap 1995): 56.

35. Ibid.

36. Hall et al., *Sport in Canadian Society*, p. 143.

37. See Guttmann, *From Ritual to Record*, p. 21.

38. Robert J. Higgs, "Sports and the Humanities: The State of the Union," Baker and Rog, *Sports and the Humanities*, p. 96.

39. Lawrence A. Wenner, "The Super Bowl Pregame Show: Cultural Fantasies and Political Subtext," in Wenner, *Media, Sports, and Society*, pp. 175ff.

40. Ibid.

41. Ibid., p. 176.

42. Robert Lipsyte, *SportsWorld*, preface.

43. Lawrence A. Wenner, *Media, Sports, and Society*, p. 7.

44. Peter H. Wood, "Sports and American Values," in Baker and Rog, *Sports and the Humanities*, p. 32.

45. Ibid., p. 33.

46. Charles S. Prebish, "Heavenly Father, Divine Goalie: Sport and Religion," *The Antioch Review*. 42 (Summer 1984).

47. Ibid., p. 312.

48. W.P. Kinsella, "Shoeless Joe Jackson Comes to Iowa," in *Shoeless Joe* (New York: Ballantine Books, 1982), p. 6.

49. Ibid., p. 10.

50. Guttmann, *From Ritual to Record*, pp. 115ff.

51. Leon H. Warshay, "Baseball in Its Social Context," in Robert M. Pankin, *Social Approaches to Sport* (Rutherford: Fairleigh Dickinson University Press; London and Toronto: Associated University Presses, 1982), p. 227.

52. Guttmann, *From Ritual to Record*, p. 107.

53. Michael R. Real, "Super Bowl Football," p. 199; Guttmann, *From Ritual to Record*, p. 125.

4

A CONSUMER MYTH

ALTHOUGH sport designates a relatively specific area of human activity, it can exert a mythic influence comparable to that of the wider reaches of science. A more natural ally for the science myth, however, and one prominent in the sport myth itself, is to be found in the pervasive presence of commercial considerations in contemporary life. Indeed, if, as definer of reality, science can be seen to provide the theology of secular culture, commercial interests can be seen to shape the liturgy. While science tells us what we can believe, business in its manifold forms provides the means for practising and reinforcing these beliefs.

The Emergence of Consumer Culture

It is difficult to imagine a more apt designation for the dominant form of life that we are embraced by and pursue today than "consumer culture." Over the course of the modern period, and particularly since the Second World War, we have moved "to a commercialized or an economized culture in which the common denominators which unify and dominate all areas of activity are business-related or business-grounded considerations such as dollar-value, profitability, marketability, efficiency, contribution to the gross national product, etc."[1] Consumerism is virtually synonymous with citizenship in modern technological civilization. Even back-to-nature romantics and isolationist hermits find it difficult, if not impossible, to avoid the grip of commodity culture completely. For the rest of us, who pass our days in the direct embrace of that culture, the impact is so pervasive and routine that we are apt to notice only a very small fraction of its constant reinforcement. Its pervasiveness gives it a prominent claim to the status of dominant contemporary supplemental myth, the stage at which a myth is almost totally taken for granted. Its persistent thrust moulds our values and shapes our visions, constituting an encompassing mythic perspective that tells us what is worthwhile and how we should be living.

This picture of a monolithic commercial environment defining goodness through the appeal of its promotion of acquisition and consumption, while widely acknowledged, is by no means universally endorsed. For example, Andrew Greeley, a Roman Catholic sociologist, takes issue with this type of characterization as presented by Daniel Bell in *The Cultural Contradictions of Capitalism* and by Alvin Toffler in his warnings regarding *Future Shock*: "Are we really all that different in our sensibilities than our predecessors? Or do we merely know a little more, talk a little more, and move about a little more freely?"[2] Greeley shares Bell's suspicion of modern culture, but he wonders if people have really bought into it as fully as analysts such as Bell would seem to think.[3] Myths are not only elusive because of their pervasiveness, but are also readily subject to caricature. We must beware of the element of arbitrariness in references as broad as those referring to modern or contemporary consumer culture. "There is no single point in history before which we were all nature's children, after which we became the sons and daughters of commerce."[4] And yet, allowing for the simplification of such generalizations, it is surely undeniable that the modern era has been characterized by the development of pervasive commercial enterprises and that this trend has intensified in recent years.

Not to recognize a fundamental difference between the modern world and previous ages is, at the very least, to ignore the reality and impact of the industrial revolution. This technological transformation in methods of production, and its attendant shifts in economic and social organization, results in ways of living that were inconceivable in previous ages. Not only is production impersonalized, as factories replace craft guilds and wider circles of trade broaden the range of available supplies of goods, but the form of life itself is changed in the process. There is a transition from what economists call a use economy to an exchange economy.[5] Self-sufficiency, when people produced food, clothing, and other items for their own use, or, at least, for the use of the nobility with a remainder left for themselves, gradually gave way to an exchange economy in which people were increasingly likely to be engaged in production of items for the market, to be exchanged for items produced by other people. In this way, exchange itself, and the market through which it was arranged, became an increasingly prominent dimension of life.

The mass production made possible by modern industry has resulted in an abundance of consumer goods that far exceeds what would have been available to the nobility in pre-modern times, in variety if not in quality. This abundance has escalated particularly since the Second World War. Alvin Toffler points out that if the last fifty thousand years of human existence were to be divided into lifetimes of approximately sixty-two years each, there would be approximately eight hundred lifetimes, and within this expanse, "the overwhelming majority of all the material goods we use in daily life today have been developed within the present, the eight hundredth lifetime."[6] It is obvious that the electronic world, and especially the much-touted information highway, constitutes a new development. Every year, if not every month, there are significant new possibilities in electronic communication. Beyond this obvious novelty, however, there are what have become more mundane novelties that represented revolutions in comparison with previous methods. The lowly ballpoint pen, for example, provided portability for written communication that, in its own way, bears some resemblance to the electronic possibilities that are presently so impressive. So much of what we take for granted is revolutionary by the standards of other human lifetimes.

As new products have become available, it has become necessary to persuade people that they need them, whether it is a detergent with a secret ingredient that guarantees still brighter washes, or a labour-saving device that further reduces the amount we have to exert ourselves. We have tended to accept our need for such advances, but that acceptance has probably been less automatic than we are likely to assume today. The eager embrace of the way of consumption that we tend to take for granted today was forged against considerable resistance. There is general merit in Max Weber's thesis that the modern industrial era grew out of the atmosphere of the Protestant work ethic. The primary values were diligence and thrift. Those virtues on the part of the captains of industry who pioneered the new ventures, and of the workers who did the actual manufacturing, assured the production that made the increasing abundance of new goods possible. But diligence and thrift do not easily embrace consumption and spending. The clash between these stances was postponed throughout the first half of this century by the sacrifices demanded by two world wars and the intervening economic depression. With the recovery and rebuilding that followed the Second World War, the shift got under way in earnest. Social policy steered a new course in the direction of an ethic of consumption, in contrast to the previous ethic of production and saving.[7]

In the present atmosphere of easy credit, it takes some imagination to appreciate the outlook of people who had lived through the depression, and the shortages of wartime, not to mention an absence of the abundance of goods we have come to take for granted, along with the assumption that these should be accessible to us. In the middle of this century, expectations and outlooks were very different from what we take to be so obvious. The difference is perhaps nowhere more evident than in the attitude toward credit. The credit card that has become the standard mode of operation for many contemporary consumers was generally unheard of in the 1950s, when personal and family indebtedness might extend to a mortgage loan for a house and a bank loan for a car, although in the latter case many would forgo purchasing a new car, or any car, until they had saved enough to pay for it. The guiding assumption was that consumption should follow income; we are entitled to what we can afford now.

Even with the obvious appeal of the cornucopia of consumer goods that began appearing as industry moved from wartime production to consumer durables (if that combination of words is not too obviously oxymoronic), people had to be re-educated out of their conservative economic mind-set and into an acceptance of consumption. This was accomplished particularly by what Ralph Glasser has called "Ad-ucation,"[8] education by advertising. What is particularly insidious about this, according to Glasser, is that it involves much more than changing economic attitudes, convincing thrifty spenders to embrace future indebtedness in the interests of present consumption; it extends to basic visions about the nature and purpose of human life. So profound is this influence that Glasser identifies the advertisers as the new high priests and sees them as having replaced religious and political leaders in defining not only social priorities, but the basic meaning and purpose of human life.[9] Consumption has not only been made attractive; it has been rendered sacred. It stands near the top of the list of myths that can be identified as definitive for contemporary life.

Like all myths, the consumer myth is difficult to see from inside. The more we are moulded by it, the more difficult it is likely to be for us to appreciate that this is the case. It can be identified as myth only from the vantage point of some other perspective. The conservative economic outlook that it has replaced provides some perspective, but to appreciate the depths of the contrast we have to look further back. Although consumerism proper really only got underway after the Second World War, the basic direction was established through the industrial revolution and with the shift to a market economy that helped to make this revolution possible. That shift involved what Karl Polanyi has called "the great transformation."[10] The market approach transformed nature into land in the sense of real estate, life into labour as a person's marketable value, and livelihood in the sense of a place and sustaining role in life into capital. While it may be salutary to recall here the warning against romanticizing past ages so that we do not assume that our consumer culture was preceded by perfect harmony with nature, there can be little doubt that this culture has involved a basic transformation in fundamental attitudes toward nature and to ourselves. Seen in these terms, consumption does not refer simply to the availability and attractiveness of consumer goods, but to the commodification of life itself. The natural world changes from a sustaining order to a commodity to be owned and exchanged for profit; a person's life is judged by the rate that he or she can command in the labour market; a person's security in life is determined by the capital that he or she owns as an individual. The intense promotion and acceptance of consumption as a way of life that has characterized our recent past can be seen to be the working out of this commodification of life that began centuries ago. The resulting consumer myth has become so pervasive that we can only look back in pity on those who lacked the abundance of goods that we enjoy. But it may also mean that we are unable to appreciate the rich possibilities that were present before nature became real estate, life became measured by market value, and our security and status were determined by the assets we can claim individually.

Consumerism as Materialism

If we recognize that our lives are shaped significantly by a consumer myth, we are then faced with the question of what that myth involves. The most obvious feature of consumer culture is its material focus. Many would say that the central difference between our way of life today and that of previous ages is that we are intensely materialistic, and many see this as a fundamental source of concern with consumer culture. It makes things the object of its veneration, and in so doing it reduces persons and the personal to the status of things. This concern is often voiced in the name of religion. Consumer materialism is seen as a prominent foe of Christian concern with the primacy of the personal, in both Catholic and Protestant forms. One Catholic theologian presents his summation of the problem with consumer society in the following terms: "We no longer see persons, we see *things*. And things, like idols, are dead."[11] The Catholic economist E.F. Schumacher subtitles his influential book *Small Is Beautiful* with the descriptive phrase

"A Study of Economics as if People Mattered." A century ago, Ralph Waldo Emerson complained of Protestant America that "things are in the saddle, and ride mankind!"[12] This contrast also was prominent in Erich Fromm's characterization of the modern West as fixated on having to the detriment of its appreciation of being. What is at stake, he contends, is the difference between "a society centered around persons and one centered around things. The having orientation is characteristic of Western industrial society, in which greed for money, fame, and power has become the dominant theme of life."[13]

The remedy prescribed for this diagnosed ailment consists of an "Up with people! Down with things!" type of revolution in attitude and practice. So John Francis Kavanaugh developed an elaborate scheme in which what he calls the Commodity Form is contrasted with the Personal Form as two antithetical modes of life. "The Commodity Form sustains and legitimates the entire fabric of dehumanization."[14] It does this by constituting a basis for valuing, knowing, willing, behaving, loving, and perceiving reality that is the contrary of personal versions of these activities.[15] The remedy is to be found in the promotion of a renewed vision and a venture of humanization through the pursuit of the personal mode of these fundamental activities that have been taken over by the tyranny of the Commodity Form.

The promotion of the personal is an understandable reaction to the determinative position accorded the commodity in consumer society, but whether it is an adequate response, even in terms of this society, is another matter. It can be argued that consumer society is not finally explicable in terms of an obsession with things, but represents contempt for things. Things are consumed, not respected. To treat things as commodities, then, is precisely an expression of our personal tyranny over things rather than of their tyranny over us. Ironically, the Commodity Form is thus itself an expression of the Personal Form. It is the separation of ourselves from other creatures in what Peter Singer has called "speciesism"[16] that has allowed us to treat other species as commodities. In this sense, there may even be some justification for Lynn White's suggestion that the Judaeo-Christian emphasis on human domination over creation must share some of the blame for the ecological crisis.[17] The sense of our own superiority over nature, and of a mandate to dominate nature through our superior wisdom, is certainly consistent with the consumption of nature that has been particularly characteristic of modern industrial society.

Recognition that the problem with consumer culture is more contempt for things than concern for things has resulted in proposals to correct this balance. Thus, Christopher D. Stone proposes that the doctrine of rights be extended to things, although he acknowledges that a substantial sales job would be required before people would be willing to take this seriously. "There is something of a seamless web involved: there will be resistance to giving the 'thing' rights until it can be seen and valued for itself; yet it is hard to see it and value it for itself until we can bring ourselves to give it 'rights'—which is almost inevitably going to sound inconceivable to a large group of people."[18] It is a significant step to recognize that the heart of our difficulty as we struggle under the sway of the consumption imperative is not that we put things ahead of people but that we do not really care about things either. The driving force of consumption is not appreciation but use. The consumer society is the throw-away society. This is what makes it so destructive environmentally and spiritually. That this can be corrected by according rights to things, however, is not entirely obvious or problem-free.

Far from offering promise as a solution to our devastating consumption ethic, to develop a "bill of rights" for things could be seen as an extension of the problem: if the Judaeo-Christian tradition bears some responsibility for a sense of the natural order being at our disposal, that sense became acutely problematic only in the wake of the repudiation of that tradition through modern secularism. This suggests that environmental destruction has been due not so much to a repudiated Judaeo-Christian legacy, or even to the continuing influence of that legacy facilitated by the massive escalation in the human impact on nature made possible through modern technology, but to the anthropocentric and egocentric outlook that characterized secularism. One expression of that mentality is the claiming of rights. While this is a significant development politically, and is especially important in situations of oppression, its mythic horizon would seem to be precisely the one of assertion and aggression that is so evident in environmental consumption.

Asserting rights of things might thus represent a further entrenchment of the mentality that lies behind the worst excesses of consumerism. But this is not the only irony that seems to be involved in this direction. While the basic mythic horizon of rights language is modern anthropocentrism, the extension of this to things also results in obscuring the distinctiveness of the human and the personal. There is not much point in proposing any course of action for human beings unless there is a fundamental difference between human beings and other life forms and things. Thus, emphasizing our affinity with things, as an antidote to our contempt for things, may be doubly problematic. What seems to be required is a more subtle approach that acknowledges the importance and integrity of things, while also preserving the distinctiveness of the personal.

An alternative to tendencies to oppose or to identify persons and things is suggested in Abraham Maslow's very influential characterization of human beings in terms of a hierarchy of needs, which acknowledges our fundamental dependence on the material order but also recognizes the distinctiveness of human life as reaching beyond those primary needs.[19] According to this scheme, we experience five ascending levels of needs. The most basic is the physical, our requirement for the essentials of life such as air, water, and food. Second is the level of safety, which includes all that goes to make up a secure and dependable environment. Third is the need for acceptance, to be loved, to belong. Fourth, we need to feel good about ourselves, to have a solid sense of self-esteem. Fifth, we need to reach beyond ourselves for spiritual fulfilment, for what Maslow called self-actualization. As a hierarchy, these needs must be met in this ascending order of significance. Only when we have the basic necessities do we, and can we, become concerned about security. Having achieved a basic sense of security, we then look for more human fulfilment in social relations. From there we move on to a mature sense of self, and we are then in a position to move toward the fullest reaches of self-fulfilment.

Here, material and nonmaterial needs are combined so that our dependence on the material order cannot be ignored, but the importance of the distinctively personal is also affirmed. Yet, while Maslow's hierarchy preserves both sides of the spectrum, in contrast to the tendency to allow either the material or the personal to take over, there is concern that it still keeps these dimensions too far apart. The problem can be seen in two ways. From one perspective, it appears in the tendency to assume that human beings exist essentially as individuals and develop social connections only at a later stage. Primary physical needs, and even security needs, are presented essentially in individualistic terms; only when these needs are met do individuals begin to address their social needs for community and communion. In fact, the whole scheme is premised on the assumption that life can be understood adequately from the perspective of the needs of the individual. The other way in which the problem is viewed is in the strict progression and irreversibility of the hierarchical order. Physical needs must be met before social or spiritual needs can be addressed, with the concomitant assumption that physical needs are subject to satiation and, on this basis, are essentially distinct from social and spiritual needs. Thus, Maslow's recognition of material and personal dimensions can be seen to render these dimensions fundamentally distinct.

A more organic recognition of the mutual interaction and reinforcement of material and personal dimensions is proposed by William
Leiss in *The Limits to Satisfaction*. "In industrialized as well as in
other societies the ensemble of needs constitutes a uniform sphere of activity, each segment of which mirrors the common characteristics of
the whole."[20] Even the most primary physical needs are met differently
in different cultures. How we deal with the physical order is permeated
with symbolic meanings. This is particularly significant in consumer
culture. "The sphere of material exchanges is not transcended, but
rather is extended ever more deeply into the 'psychological' domains."[21] Far from moving on to social and spiritual needs once our
physical needs are satisfied, we address our physical needs through
social, and perhaps even spiritual, dimensions. It is not sufficient that
a jacket should protect us from the cold; it must also carry a socially
approved label, thus addressing what for Maslow is the more peculiarly
human need of belonging. How material needs might be used to address
spiritual needs brings us to the heart of the consumer myth.

Consumerism as Spirituality

Consumerism cannot simply be equated with materialism because it
consumes, rather than cares for, material things. It is no solution to the
contempt for things to elevate the material to the point where the distinctiveness of the personal is obscured. Maslow's recognition of a
spectrum running from the physical to the personal is more promising,
but his hierarchical scheme may leave these dimensions essentially
separate. The most promising avenue for understanding what consumerism involves would seem to be a variation of William Leiss's organic
approach, which sees material and symbolic dimensions as constituting a flowing web of meanings that characterize all human attempts to
achieve satisfaction. However, Leiss's explanation may be a little too
good. It heals the breach left by Maslow so thoroughly that there would
seem to be no way of distinguishing between good and bad ways of sat-
isfying needs, except in terms of anticipated consequences. The limit
that Leiss sees to consumer satisfaction is the one posed by the environment. The natural order will not sustain continually expansive consumption indefinitely. However, the web of Leiss's organic alternative
is so tight that there would seem to be no basis for relative judgments
about the respective merits of the satisfactions identified in Maslow's
hierarchy of needs. This reduces the usefulness of Leiss's organic
approach for getting at the thrust of consumer culture, insofar as that
thrust may involve the attempt to satisfy personal and, ultimately,
spiritual needs by material means. Leiss helps us to see that this may

well be what is happening, but he tends to see it as something of an inevitability.

The issue of how organic or artificial the association of material satisfactions with spiritual needs really is is posed most vividly in consumer culture by the phenomenon of advertising. So central to consumer culture is advertising that it tends to be as difficult to identify and assess as consumer culture itself. An entry point into consideration of what advertising involves is to be found in the debate over whether it is primarily an instrument of selling or of marketing. Here, selling refers to the attempt to convince people that they need the product being advertised to the point of actually creating a want for it; marketing, on the other hand, determines what people really do want, so that advertising plays the more innocent role of reminding people of their wants and of the availability of particular products to meet them. Each of these views of advertising has had a prominent advocate, with the distinguished economist John Kenneth Galbraith defending the selling thesis, and the influential business academic Theodore Levitt advocating the marketing thesis.

The central thesis of Galbraith's *The Affluent Society* is, "The affluent society increases its wants and therewith its consumption *pari passu* with its production."[22] As the productive ability of society has increased through modern technology, advertising has emerged to create the demand for the goods produced. Thus, rather than telling the public what is available, advertising functions to create the demand for what is available. This artificial creation of wants Galbraith calls "the dependence effect," by which he means "the way wants depend on the process by which they are satisfied."[23] This process assures Galbraith that these wants are not urgent. People are susceptible to the manipulations of advertising because, as members of the affluent society, they have passed the stage of having their needs satisfied, and do not know what they want. This is the central function of modern advertising— "to bring into being wants that previously did not exist."[24]

From the perspective of modern business practice, Levitt accuses Galbraith of overlooking the difference between selling and marketing. "Selling focusses on the need of the seller, marketing on the needs of the buyer."[25] What Galbraith fails to appreciate, according to Levitt, is that sales and advertising can continue only because customers are satisfied. The smart seller is the marketer who does not simply promote a product but researches and addresses the needs of the potential buyer. "The view that an industry is a customer-satisfying process, not a goods-producing process, is vital for all businessmen to understand."[26] The distinction between the product orientation of the seller and the purchaser orientation of the marketer cannot be drawn more clearly. However, as Levitt expands on its significance this contrast begins to blur, and selling does not seem to be totally banished from the sight of the enlightened marketer. We find him saying things such as: "Management must think of itself not as producing products but as providing customer-creating value satisfactions."[27] It seems that the goal of the marketer is not to satisfy customers but to create them. Management's job is not only to produce satisfactions, rather than simply products, but to produce satisfactions that are "customer-creating."

That something like this has to be involved with new products would seem to be especially evident. Even Levitt acknowledges that "generally, demand has to be 'created' during the product's initial *marketing development stage*."[28] At this point, it is difficult to see where Levitt's marketing view of advertising differs from Galbraith's selling view. It may not be insignificant that Levitt puts "created" in quotation marks. It is an intrusion into his official position, for the creation of demand is all Galbraith's thesis requires. Advertising, then, is responsible for creating desire to match the products that modern technology makes available.

Vindication for this conclusion is forthcoming from no less an authority than Levitt himself. In spite of his vaunted distinction between selling and marketing, Levitt castigated the Hoover Corporation precisely for applying this distinction. In market surveys of European consumers, Hoover discovered wide national differences in preferences for washing-machine features in Sweden, Britain, Italy, Germany, and France. Some preferred top-loading machines, others front-loaders. There were wide differences in the size of machine preferred. Italians opted for enamel drums, while Swedes liked stainless steel. But rather than applaud this marketing orientation, Levitt ridiculed Hoover for catering to consumer taste. "The message for Hoover should have been obvious: produce only the simple, high-quality machine preferred by the British and sell that same machine aggressively on the Continent."[29] The marketer castigates marketing and promotes selling—so much for the distinction between selling and marketing!

Yet the apparent totality of Galbraith's victory does not answer the question of how a thinker of Levitt's calibre can end up endorsing the position he explicitly denounces. It would seem that Levitt's position is not as contradictory as it first appears. The directness of the contradiction depends on ambiguity over the notion of wants. When he challenges Galbraith's contention that advertising creates wants in the consumer, and when he later contends that advertising should tell people what they want in a washing machine, he is addressing different levels of wants. The particular wants that involve features of washing machines are secondary and can be safely ignored by advertising. This would apply as well to wants for new products, which people cannot possibly have in specific form until they come to know the product. Beneath these secondary wants for specific products or features, however, there are more primary wants, which advertising must take very seriously, and must engage in extensive market research in an attempt to address. Thus, what Hoover should have done, according to Levitt, was pitch its machines through an appeal to what buyers of washing machines want out of life. "The media message should have been that *this* is the machine that 'you,' the homemaker, *deserve* to have, and by means of which your relentlessly repetitive heavy daily household burdens are reduced, so that *you* may spend more constructive time for more elevating attention to your children and more loving attention to your husband."[30] While the specific tone of Levitt's tactic might not prove particularly effective today, the level at which it aims, that of our most basic aims and desires, remains crucial for contemporary advertising.

Advertising convinces us that we need products by appealing to our most fundamental wants. We will want a new computer because we want to be in touch and not to be left standing at the side of the information highway. "Marketing does not sell a product—it sells a dream; a dream of beauty, of health, of success, of power,"[31] Ralph Glasser contends, pointing out that lipstick is presented not as coloured grease but as a source of beauty, sexual fulfilment, and happiness, and that alcohol is presented not as a relaxant but as a badge of manhood and assurance of social acceptance. Sophisticated sellers are marketers, marketing not to our particular needs and wants but to our deeper and more pervasive needs for security, acceptance, and fulfilment. "In this sense alone is it true to say that 'demand' can be created."[32] But this sense is a very fundamental one.

Far from targeting consumers with particular messages, either promoting a product or seeking to elicit an isolated response, in its modern sophisticated form the central thrust of advertising involves a total, inclusive process that seeks to enfold the consumer in a world of its own creation. The renowned literary critic Northrop Frye likens this subtle working of advertising to the experience of an extended train trip.

> As one's eyes are passively pulled along a rapidly moving landscape, it turns darker and one begins to realize that many of the objects that appear to be outside are actually reflections of what is in the carriage. As it becomes entirely dark one enters a narcissistic world,

where except for a few lights here and there, we can see only the reflection of where we are. A little study of the working of advertising and propaganda in the modern world, with the magic lantern techniques of projected images, will show us how successful they are in creating a world of pure illusion. The illusion of the world itself is reinforced by the more explicit illusions of movies and television, and the imitation world of sports.[33]

The mythic dimensions of advertising begin to emerge clearly. Far from simply hyping particular products, advertising is creating a world for us. It not only tells us that a certain brand of toothpaste will give us whiter teeth, it does so through pictures and settings that imply that it will also give us richer lives. Beer is not only an enjoyable drink; it comes with attractive, jovial friends. Cars are not simply means of transportation; they are symbols of freedom, status, and power. Advertising speaks not to the immediate needs that products might be expected to meet as food, clothing, transportation, and so on, but to the wider social and spiritual needs for belonging and meaning. This is the mythic dimension of advertising that is really interesting and worrisome.

In these terms, advertising effects the combination of Maslow's hierarchy of needs that Leiss advocates. However, it also illustrates the weakness in Leiss's organic approach, namely, that without something like Maslow's hierarchy, there is no way to distinguish the merits of different forms of satisfaction. The result may be a total inversion of Maslow's kind of hierarchy, an attempt to satisfy social and spiritual needs through material consumption. The way of consumption may then be promoted to fill the void caused by the loss of religious and moral certainties through secularization.[34] "What we see in our country today is a perfectly good economic process—the mechanisms for producing and consuming goods—made into a religion."[35] The way of consumption does not simply tell us what is good, it takes on the aura of goodness itself. It fills the vacuum created by the hesitancy of secularization with visions of security, status, and meaning attainable through accumulation and control. "Material goods have become substitutes for faith. It's not that people literally place their cars on the altar; rather, it is the function of these goods in a consumer society."[36] People do not place their cars on the altar because the cars themselves displace the altar. The consumer myth defines our perspective and priorities with a finality and authority that used to be reserved for religion.

If this recognition of consumer myth rings true, it should evoke deep resentment against this imposed orthodoxy. Once the mythic spell is broken, we begin to see that the promotion of consumption has moulded our aesthetic sensibility and our ethical standards as well as our religious vision. The shopping mall and the "golden mile" of fast-food franchises signal a new low in convenience architecture, and the glitz and gaudiness needed to attract the consumer's attention in ads of all forms must inevitably dull our aesthetic sensibilities. The constant promotion of consumption has to have a corresponding impact on our ethical outlook. "In fact, most advertising appeals directly to one or more of the seven deadly sins: pride, lust, envy, anger, covetousness, gluttony, and sloth."[37] How much is the violence and selfishness of contemporary life due to the constant promotion of hedonistic self-indulgence? That this finally amounts to an allegiance of religious proportions is indicative of how pervasive and impervious the consumer myth is.

The depth of devotion elicited by the ersatz religion of consumerism is missed unless we recognize that this characterization of it in religious terms is itself an acknowledgment of its massive hold over contemporary consciousness. As honest critics of consumerism, we must acknowledge its power and penetration not only in contemporary society but in ourselves, just as surely as do the most unwary adherents to its captivating faith.

> We are witnessing a violent verbal attack against the consumer society. Yet, on the other hand, the latter, and everything that goes with it, is the object of a religious exultation. Consumption, along with the technology that produces it and the advertising that expresses it, is no longer a materialistic fact. It has become the meaning of life, the chief sacred, the point of morality, the criterion of existence, the mystery before which one bows. Be not deceived, the rejection of consumer society is on the same level. The quarrel is really a religious one. The disputants never leave that world. To the contrary, they serve to reconfirm the religious fact.[38]

The consumer myth is not about materialism; it is about spiritual reality. It represents the most sustained attempt in the history of humanity to accord total spiritual significance to material consumption.

Notes

1. Paul F. Camenisch, "Business Ethics: On Getting to the Heart of the Matter," in Donald C. Jones, ed., *Business, Religion, and Ethics* (Cambridge, Mass.: Oelgeschlager, Gunn and Hain, 1982), p. 202.

2. Andrew M. Greeley, *No Bigger than Necessary* (New York: New American Library, 1977), p. 158.

3. Ibid., pp. 154ff.

4. Michael Schudson, *Advertising, The Uneasy Persuasion* (New York: Basic Books, 1984), p. 179.

5. William Leiss, *The Limits to Satisfaction, An Essay on the Problem of Needs and Commodities* (Kingston and Montreal: McGill-Queen's University Press, 1988), pp. 72ff.

6. Alvin Toffler, *Future Shock* (New York: Random House, A Bantam Book, 1971), p. 14.

7. Leiss, *The Limits to Satisfaction*, pp. 86ff.

8. Ralph Glasser, *The New High Priesthood, The Social, Ethical and Political Implications of a Marketing-Orientated Society* (London: Macmillan, 1967), pp. 113ff.

9. Ibid., p. 9.

10. Karl Polanyi, *The Great Transformation* (Boston: Beacon Press, reprint 1957).

11. John Francis Kavanaugh, *Following Christ in a Consumer Society* (Maryknoll, NY: Orbis Books, 1982), p. 35.

12. Bernard Eugene Meland, *The Secularization of Modern Cultures* (New York: Oxford University Press, 1966), p. 26.

13. Erich Fromm, *To Have or To Be?* (London: Jonathan Cape, 1976), p. 19.

14. Kavanaugh, *Following Christ in a Consumer Society*, p. 10.

15. Ibid., pp. 96ff.

16. Peter Singer, "The Place of Nonhumans in Environmental Issues," in K.E. Goodpaster and K.M. Sayre, eds., *Ethics and Problems in the Twenty-first Century* (Notre Dame: University of Notre Dame Press, 1979), pp. 191–98.

17. Lynn White, "The Historical Roots of our Ecological Crisis," *Science* 155 (1967): 1201–7.

18. Christopher D. Stone, "Should Trees Have Standing?—Toward Legal Rights for Natural Objects," in Tom L. Beauchamp and Norman E. Bowie, eds., *Ethical Theory and Business*, 2nd ed. (Englewood Cliffs, NJ: Prentice Hall, 1983), p. 425.

19. Abraham Maslow, "A Theory of Human Motivation," *Psychological Review* 50 (1943): 370–96; and *Toward a Psychology of Being* (Princeton: D. Van Nostrand, 1962).

20. Leiss, *The Limits to Satisfaction*, p. 58.

21. Ibid., p. 57.

22. John Kenneth Galbraith, *The Affluent Society* (Boston: Houghton Mifflin, 1968), p. xxvii.

23. Ibid., p. 131.

24. Ibid., p. 129.

25. Theodore Levitt, "Marketing Myopia," in E. Jerome McCarthy, John F. Grashof, and Andrew A. Brogowicz, eds., *Readings and Cases in Basic Marketing* (Illinois: Richard D. Irwin, 1984), p. 40.

26. Ibid., p. 42.

27. Ibid., p. 44.

28. Theodore Levitt, "Exploiting the Product Life Cycle," *Harvard Business Review* (Nov–Dec 1965): 81–94.

29. Theodore Levitt, *The Marketing Imagination* (New York: The Free Press, 1986), p. 36.

30. Ibid., p. 36 (emphasis in original).

31. Glasser, p. 12.

32. Ibid. p. 13.

33. Northrop Frye, *The Modern Century* (Toronto: Oxford University Press, 1967), pp. 27–8.

34. Glasser, *The New High Priesthood*, pp. 99f.

35. Fred W. Graham, "America's Other Religion," *Christian Century*, 17 Mar 1982: 306.

36. Jim Wallis, *The Call to Conversion* (San Francisco: Harper & Row, 1981), p. 49.

37. Ibid., p. xiii; see also E.F. Schumacher, *Good Work* (London: Abacus, 1980), p. 26.

38. Jacques Ellul, *The New Demons*, tr. C. Edward Hopkin (New York: Seabury Press, A Crossroad Book, 1975), p. 144.

5

A VALUES MYTH

In ordinary speech, we talk casually about "values." This casualness is a good indication that the notion of "values" operates as a mythic horizon that defines reality for us, without our being aware of it. Closer examination suggests that "values" represent an alternative to traditional ethical and religious perspectives. The prominence of the usage is indicated in the interviews reported and analyzed in *Habits of the Heart*, in which sociologist Robert Bellah and his colleagues found that when they spoke to people about what was significant in life and what was wrong with life as they experienced it in contemporary America, "almost everyone who talked with us spoke of 'values' in reply."[1] But the most significant finding, and a disturbing one, was not this confirmation of the widespread employment of "values" language, but the realization by the researchers that the more they probed for what lay behind this talk of values, the more they found themselves staring into an empty vortex. "'Values' turn out to be the incomprehensible, rationally indefensible thing that the individual chooses when he or she has thrown off the last vestige of external influence and reached pure, contentless freedom."[2] Thus, talk of values may be a way of fooling ourselves into thinking we are dealing with something substantial when there is really no substance at all except whatever we choose to inject.

The Emergence of "Values"

The prevalence and obviousness of references to "values" in the contemporary setting conceal the novelty of this language and perspective.

Prior to the modern period, it would never have occurred to people to talk about values. Because it is a modern Western phenomenon, identifying some of the most prominent elements that have contributed to this way of talking and thinking may help to clarify the meaning and implications of our references to values.

One of the basic sources of the modern notion of values, as of every other distinctive aspect of modern Western life, is the emergence of modern science, the accuracy and specialization of which put a particular premium on fact. As our understanding of reality came to be thought of more and more as a matter of the facts established by science, a term was needed to cover those wider areas that were not, or at least not yet, amenable to scientific determination. These areas—the arts, morality, and religion—became the domain of values. An intimation of the difference between fact and value is found in the distinction of the early modern Scottish philosopher David Hume between our interest in what is the case and our moral concern with what ought to be the case.

> In every system of morality, which I have hitherto met with, I have always remark'd, that the author proceeds for some time in the ordinary way of reasoning, and establishes the being of God, or makes observations concerning human affairs; when of a sudden I am surpris'd to find, that instead of the usual copulations of propositions, *is*, and *is not*, I meet with no proposition that is not connected with an *ought*, or an *ought not*. This change is imperceptible; but is, however, of the last consequence. For as this *ought* or *ought not*, expresses some new relation or affirmation, 'tis necessary that it should be observ'd and explain'd; and at the same time that a reason should be given, for what seems altogether inconceivable, how this new relation can be a deduction from others which are entirely different from it. But as authors do not commonly use this precaution, I shall presume to recommend it to the readers; and am persuaded, that this small attention wou'd subvert all the vulgar systems of morality, and let us see, that the distinction of vice and virtue is not founded merely on the relations of objects, nor is perceiv'd by reason.[3]

Although Hume does not speak of "value" or "values," his contrast between "is" and "ought" is directly parallel with what has come to be designated as a distinction between fact and value. In contrast to the factual realm, where we pursue empirical investigation and public debate over what "is" the case, there is this other realm of value, where we decide what ought to be the case, and this kind of value issue cannot be settled by knowing the "relations of objects" that are established through empirical investigation, or be "perceiv'd by reason" through applying the logical rules of inference. This schema set the agenda for some of the most influential philosophers of this century, through whom popular perception and expectations regarding what is true and real, and how we recognize this, have been established. The only secure source of knowledge is the empirical investigations of science. This is supported by the rules of logical inference, but these are totally formal and afford no knowledge in themselves. Apart from these factual and formal truths, there is no knowledge. This leaves large areas of life excluded from the domain of knowledge. Appreciation of beauty in the arts, ethical questions of what we should do (Hume's example of how "ought" differs from "is"), and statements about what is finally real and important that characterize philosophy and religion are all disqualified as claimants for the status of knowledge. Once strict standards for knowledge are established, such matters are seen to be too imprecise and debatable to meet them. They belong, rather, to the personal domain of values. Art is a matter of personal taste, morality is a reflection of personal preferences, and religion indicates an optional commitment and allegiance. In contrast to the public facts that science is progressively establishing, these areas all involve private values.

Science represents the wider context within which the notion of values has come to prominence. The notion itself, however, has more precise origins, emerging specifically from the field of commerce; "value" is an economic and commercial term. "The extension of the meaning and use of the term began in economics, or political economy, as it was then called."[4] It refers to the exchange ratio in the marketplace: the value of something is the measure of demand in relation to the available supply—that is, the price that purchasers are willing to pay in the current market.[5] It is the commercial usage that solidifies the sense of values as indicators of relative worth. The *Random House Dictionary*[6] describes the primary meaning of "value" as "relative worth, merit, or importance," and the second meaning it identifies leaves no doubt about the economic basis of this primary meaning, "monetary or material worth as in commerce or trade." That focus is also reflected in most of the other definitions proposed: "the worth of something in terms of the amount of things for which it can be exchanged or in terms of some medium of exchange," "equivalent worth of return in money, material, services, etc.," "estimated or assigned worth; valuation," "denomination as of a monetary issue, postage stamps, etc."; it is only subsequent to these economic variations that reference is made to the sense of designating importance or significance in some wider sense, to liking or wanting and affirmation of social ideals, an ethical application thought of as referring to "any object bof worth desirable as a means or as an end in itself" or an application to art and music.

While modern science provided the inspiration, and modern business the concept, for the values myth, the most prominent articulation of a values approach is to be found in the nineteenth-century philosopher and gadfly Friedrich Nietzsche, who called for the re-evaluation of all values in rebellion against the Judaeo-Christian legacy. Such a revolt, he felt, was necessary because that legacy itself really represented an inversion of the values appropriate to humanity. As Nietzsche saw it, Christianity imposed a distorted set of values on the whole of Europe.

> To turn upside down all valuations—*that* is what they had to do! To shatter the strong, to infect great hopes, to cast suspicion on the enjoyment of beauty, to break down everything autonomous, manly, victorious, dominating, all the instincts natural to the highest and best turned-out type of mankind, and bend it over into uncertainty, distress of conscience, and self-destruction—to reverse every bit of love for the earth and things earthly and control of the earth into hatred of things earthly and of the earth: *this* was the self-assumed task of the church.[7]

Christianity spiritualized life in depreciation of the natural order, and devalued humanity in what Nietzsche regarded as a slave morality that counselled submission and preoccupation with weakness and compassion. In direct opposition to this acquiescence to misery, he called for an assertion of strength: "We must seek *new philosophers*, spirits strong or original enough to give an impulse to opposing valuations, to trans-value and turn upside down the 'eternal values.'"[8] But this is not simply a matter of transforming or adjusting values. It entails the much more radical requirement of trans-valuation, of re-evaluation, that is implicit in this very notion of values itself. It is not a matter of a transition within a common framework. "The task itself is something else: it demands that he *create values*."[9] A new mandate is expected of the new philosophers. Their role is not to schematize and clarify; "*the real philosophers are commanders and legislators*":[10] "Their 'knowing' is creating. Their creating is legislative. Their will to truth is—*will to power*."[11] Such is the agenda of Nietzsche's superman, who not only will rise above the demeaning concessions of slave morality and assert his own will beyond good and evil, but will be constrained to act thus out of the realization that there is no higher reality to claim our allegiance or to constitute any possible source of guidance.

The Illusion of Values

The widespread appeal of the notion of values is no doubt due in significant measure to its comprehensive nature. "Values" can cover everything from the taste one displays in music or clothes to the stance one takes on life-and-death issues such as capital punishment or abortion. The term can also be employed on the individual level, as when we refer to a particular person's values, or to social groups or whole cultures, as in references to middle-class values or Western values. Within this wide range of reference, there are two senses in particular that can give the term very different meanings. On the one hand, "values" can refer to things that are valuable in themselves, out there, apart from whether or not any particular individual recognizes their value. These might include particular objects, such as forests and wildlife, as when we hear people say that wilderness values are threatened, or they might involve particular attributes or characteristics, as when people talk of family or traditional values. On the other hand, "values" can refer to one's own personal priorities, what one considers valuable, with the implication that value is in the eye of the beholder.[12] The potential gulf between these two senses is such that they can constitute directly contradictory meanings. Thus, in one of the most thorough treatments of the subject, Samuel L. Hart's *Treatise on Values*, we find what appear to be endorsements of both readings. At one point, Hart appears to be arguing for the objectivity of values, the fact that they exist out there, independently of our endorsement.

> Our preferences, our likings and dislikings refer to something beyond them. The value is not called into life in the act of gratification. Were values created in our acts of assent and dissent, our preferences would be arbitrary, which they are not.[13]

Yet, little more than thirty pages later, Hart seems to be insisting on exactly the opposite reading.

> Values do not descend upon us as a gift from heaven. They are not given in the universe as static, sublime entities, essences which we intuit. Rather, we create them; and as our own designs and discoveries, they mirror our frailty and strength, our shame and glory, our wants and satisfactions, likes and dislikes, griefs and joys.[14]

Values exist independently of us; and yet we create them. One solution to this dilemma is the standard academic expedient of declaring both meanings to be legitimate. Values are real, out there, apart from us, but their effect depends upon our appreciating them.

Such a combination may be behind many references to values. The primary sense of personal preference is seen to reflect our best access to what is really of value. That values as personal preferences can be expected to reflect what is valuable in any assured way, however, is not obvious in light of the discovery of the emptiness of references to values by Bellah and his colleagues. Even slight reflection on the prospects for a society where value is left to personal preference suggests that the values route faces formidable obstacles. Values as preferences are plausible so long as they remain on the individual level. The situation becomes more precarious when we move to the wider social context; then, personal preferences become a problem as soon as they represent real differences.

Today, one of the most difficult of such problem areas is the issue of abortion. On the personal level, everyone is entitled to his or her opinion on this issue. It is possible to be in favour of abortion, to be opposed to abortion, or to recognize a need for abortion in particular cases. If only this level of personal preference were involved, there would be no difficulty. Those who favoured abortion could have access to it; those opposed would avoid it; and those who approved under certain conditions could avail themselves of the option in those circumstances. When this neat accommodation of personal preferences is moved to the social level, this plurality of values runs into the reality that society as a whole either permits abortion or it does not. Personal preference can be no more than private whim, unless there has been a political decision that makes it possible. This is the first obstacle that values as personal preferences encounter. Because there are other persons in society, our own preferences have to face a political decision about which preferences can be met and which cannot. That decision may reflect the consensus of political democracy or the imposition of political expediency or dictatorship. By whatever means, some public posture will determine the scope for personal preferences, particularly in more important matters. It is not accidental that Nietzsche looked for an alliance of values and power. The values that would prevail would be those of the person with the power to assert them.

Whether or not abortion is available in a given society is a political, rather than a private, matter. A male-dominated society, in which abortion is not an immediate concern for those in power, might outlaw abortion out of lack of appreciation of the dilemma of unwanted pregnancy, or, more malevolently, as a means of maintaining restrictions on women. A society influenced by avid pro-choice proponents might make abortion virtually mandatory, in some situations, as a matter of social pressure. The scope for choice between these extremes depends on the nature of the authority in power; if the issue is a moral one, it will depend on the view of abortion itself. Here, the issue moves more explicitly from the subjective sense of values as personal preferences to the objective sense of value as what is of value. The abortion issue involves more than the question of access. To see the problem in those terms assumes an endorsement of abortion as morally right in itself.

This, of course, would not be conceded by opponents of abortion, for whom access to abortion is tantamount to access to murder. At this point, values as preferences run into not only the obstacles of political reality, but those of moral convictions about right and wrong. For opponents of abortion, it would be no solution to say that they do not have to avail themselves of access to abortion, if it is against their conscience. For them, abortion is not finally a matter of individual conscience, but of moral right and wrong in a wider sense. The conviction that abortion is wrong for everyone is held as deeply by opponents of abortion as the conviction of the primacy of individual choice is held by pro-choice advocates. As moral positions, these personal preferences run very deeply and are resistant to reconciliation. Pro-choice advocates are willing to leave abortion as a choice for individuals because they distinguish the termination of "preborn" life from the life of the "postborn." But they do draw the line somewhere. Murder is not an option for pro-choicers, any more than it is for anti-abortionists. Abortion can be left as a matter of choice because it is not regarded as murder. If values are not affirmed by sheer power, they will reflect some kind of social consensus that exceeds the level of personal preference.

Because personal choice is so circumscribed by wider circumstances, reliance on values may be not only unrealistic, but actually deceptive. Talk of values may reflect an impression that we are taking our own stands, when we are really reflecting a conformity that excludes precisely that possibility. Thus referring to values can be a highly effective way of avoiding the issue of value. One indication of this avoidance is to be found in the cliché that goes with the notion that values are personal preferences and that this allows for all kinds of different affirmations: "I don't want to impose my values on you." This really provides a convenient way of avoiding the issue of values altogether—or, at least, of appearing to do so. It does not have to address particular values, because these are held to be matters of personal preference. The catch, of course, is that this itself is a statement of values. It says that the most important things in life can and should finally be left to individuals. But this is precisely what we have just seen to be so problematic. Important matters of value can be left to individuals only if individuals live in virtual isolation; as soon as the connections of real life are taken into account, some kind of consensus on values becomes necessary. The stronger implication in this clichéd view of values, that they not only can but should be left to individuals, really amounts to an endorsement of whatever values prevail, perhaps simply those of the powerful. The notion that the values myth promotes, that we can deal with the important matters of life as essentially private preferences, obscures the real values that are operative precisely for those who think they are supporting the free endorsement of values by individuals. Questions about what is really valuable are obscured and avoided precisely through talk of values.

One of the clearest illustrations of this inherent dilemma in the values myth, from within the explicit promotion of the values approach itself, is to be found in the prominent movement in values education known as values clarification.[15] This movement reflects the basic values view that what is involved is the personal preferences of individuals. As a result, the fundamental method is for the teacher to remain completely neutral and encourage students to clarify their own values by inciting them to analyze the situation, determine the basic options, make a choice, and to stick with that choice. This might seem a sensible and practical approach to moral questions, and, no doubt, it is in the modern Western atmosphere that the values outlook has developed. However, if we pierce the obvious virtue that this managerial approach is likely to suggest to us, at least two significant limitations can be detected.

One source of reservation is that the identification of moral reflection with choosing carries the implication that the chooser has nothing to learn about value as such, but is in possession of mature and adequate values. A central conviction behind the values clarification method is that of the individuals in any group or perspective it can be said, "They have good reasons for the way they live, no matter how strange it may seem to outsiders."[16] All that is needed is values clarification, a procedure that will allow them to uncover the values they already possess. This optimistic view of humanity can claim an impressive precedent. If we put together Socrates' claim that the unexamined life is not worthy of living and his conviction that nobody would knowingly do what was wrong, so that matters of right and wrong are essentially matters of knowledge, we could regard the Socratic approach to wisdom, conveyed through Plato, as an early form of values clarification. This equation might do less than justice to Socrates, but values clarification bears some resemblance to his claim to be only a midwife, giving birth to knowledge that people really possess themselves. This whole approach finds a strong contrast in the attitude of Saint Paul, for example, for whom moral problems reach below knowledge to the will. "I can will what is right, but I cannot do it. For I do not do the good I want, but the evil I do not want is what I do" (Romans 7:18b–19). It is not enough to know what is right and what is wrong, for Paul, because he finds himself not doing what he knows to be right and actually doing what he knows to be wrong. For those who find this resonating with their own experience, values clarification is bound to reflect a very optimistic and superficial view of humanity.

The assumption that we have sound values and that all that is needed is methods to clarify and affirm them has another dimension in the implication that it does not really matter what values are affirmed. "Values clarification appears, at least by default, to hold the view that all values are equally valid."[17] The neutrality of the teacher and the identification of values with the choices of individual students carry the implication that there is no way of assessing or ranking values so that some are seen to be more important than others. If this approach were taken as fully adequate, one person's passion for raiding bird's nests and destroying unhatched eggs would be as good as another's dedication to preserving wetlands as a waterfowl habitat. The result is that values clarification is not only confined to uncovering the values that people already affirm, it can be seen to undermine values by according everything equal value. The notion of equal value may well carry a positive connotation, but a moment's reflection suggests that it is easily reversed. If everything is of equal value, this could amount to saying that nothing is of particular value.

The Depth of the Values Illusion

The bleak prospect of the affirmation of values turning out to be really a denial of value might seem so drastic as to be incredible. The other possibility, however, is that the emptiness of the values approach is not generally recognized because values provides its own content. The most obvious source of such content is the area that is the source of values language itself. This would mean that in constituting the source of the language of values, the commercial domain also defines the meaning of values to a considerable extent, for in its original commercial application, as a method for determining value, this approach is itself entirely without value—or at least, this is the claim that is often made on its behalf. The method, which consists essentially of cost-benefit analysis, does not in itself determine costs or benefits, but constitutes a neutral instrument for deciding what these are in a given situation for a business or for an individual buyer or seller. "This is the beauty of cost-benefit analysis: no matter how relevant or irrelevant, wise or stupid, informed or uninformed, responsible or silly, defensible or indefensible wants may be, the analyst is able to derive a policy from them—a policy which is legitimate because, in theory, it treats all of these preferences as equally valid and good."[18] Once this commercial background of the notion is considered, it should no longer be surprising that Bellah and his colleagues discovered that "the language of 'values' as commonly used is self-contradictory precisely because it is not a language of value."[19] What the origins of this language in the context of marketplace exchange ratios suggests, however, is that the contradiction is inherent in the notion itself, and is not simply a matter of a deterioration to which the language has become subject. For the values approach, nothing has any particular value, and at the same time everything is a candidate for potential value. It all depends on the whims of the market. It should not be surprising if this commercial consequence carries over to broader applications as the values method expands to become the values mythology.

Thus, the commercial sense of values comes to define what we take value to be. What determines value is willingness to pay. Value becomes more than just a personal preference by our willingness to put our money, or our lives, behind our choices. The dominance of the commercial presence today gives this a direct plausibility. If you value something, you should expect to pay for it. An unwillingness to pay exposes the fraudulence of any value claim. However, if we stop to think about what we really value, does this commercial standard hold, or is the situation not apt to be exactly opposite to what this would suggest?

> The things we cherish, admire, or respect are not always the things we are willing to pay for. Indeed, they may be cheapened by being associated with money. It is fair to say that the things we love are better measured by our *unwillingness* to pay for them. Consider, for example, love itself.[20]

The commercial notion of values provides a way of giving substance to personal preferences—the serious ones are the ones we back up with our commitment—by implying that everything is subject to a price calculus. Everything has a price. In that sense, everything is for sale; everything is a commodity.

Ivan Illich indicates the result of this wholesale adoption of the values approach in his suggestion that it would be obscene for him to say, "I value my wife."[21] The reason, Illich contends, is that as soon as "value" is mentioned, this immediately and automatically evokes the question, "How much?" Thus, for a man to say that he values his wife is equivalent to putting a price on her, because this sense of relative worth is what value means. It cannot allow for any sense of intrinsic worth.

Values language allows us to address the complexities and diversity of contemporary life. However, in precluding ascription of intrinsic worth, it renders the moral enterprise inherently arbitrary. An absolute distinction between right and wrong may be unrealistic in the circumstances of life, but values would seem to preclude even entertaining such ideals. The implications of this exclusion of considerations of intrinsic worth become more evident if we move beyond the moral realm into that of religion, an area that also evokes values language. People speak of values precisely to indicate that there is more to life than the technological-commercial preoccupations that so dominate the contemporary scene. Here again, though, when we consider that this values vision derives precisely from this technological-commercial background, we must begin to suspect that we are facing a peculiar irony, if not an outright contradiction, and one that might be particularly fatal to the reality of religion. George Grant was convinced of the latter reading of our situation. "What is comic about the present use of 'values' and the distinction of them from 'facts,'" Grant suggests, "is not that it is employed by modern men who know what is entailed in so doing; but that it is used also by 'religious' believers who are unaware that in its employment they are contradicting the very possibility of the reverence they believe they are espousing in its use."[22] When people appeal to the need for values in contrast to acquiescing in the technological and commercial preoccupations of contemporary life, they often intend it as a plea for recognition of the continuing relevance of religion in spite of the dominance of the secular outlook. What they fail to realize, according to Grant, is that in adopting the language of values as the vehicle for advocating this recognition, they are actually foreclosing what they want to promote. Far from affirming a reality that exceeds and precedes the technological and commercial preoccupations of the secular horizon, it functions as an instrument of that horizon. In affirming values, we are affirming a centre of life in ourselves, rather than in the comprehensive, transcendent reality that people of religious sensibility wish to affirm. Values language undercuts, rather than facilitates, affirmations of transcendent reality.

The supreme irony of undermining religious sensibility in the very act of seeking to promote it might be illustrated as clearly as anywhere by the great advocate of the values approach, Friedrich Nietzsche, in his depiction of the madman who announces the death of God. Arriving in the marketplace in the full light of morning with a lighted lantern in his hand, crying out "I seek God! I seek God!," the madman responds to the mockery of those standing around with the charge that they and he have killed God. But as he expounds on this to his astounded audience, their lack of comprehension provokes him to throw his lantern on the ground, breaking and extinguishing it, as he utters the lament "I come too early." The inability of the murderers of God to recognize what they have done is reflected in the churches which the madman castigates as "the tombs and sepulchres of God."[23] Nietzsche himself recognized that the values approach to life that he advocated was possible only after the death of God, for that approach involves the taking charge of life and the establishing of our own priorities. This is what values are. Only confusion confounded could allow us to think that we could use this language of total human autonomy to evoke and express a sense of ultimate human loyalty. If what we are about is affirming our own values, then we had better wake up and listen to the madman. He is surely right that such language could pass for articulations of religious faith only in the tombs and sepulchres of God.

In the wake of the impersonal and destructive visage that so dominates contemporary life, it is understandable that we should seek refuge in a domain of personal values in which possibilities for genuine humanity remain intact. When we recognize that that outlook and language itself emerge precisely from the vision that has spawned the impersonal and destructive tendencies, however, this suggests that the values myth really represents an illusory avenue of escape. As an apt vehicle for reflecting the complexity and confusion that characterize the present, it offers no way out of that complexity and confusion except through endorsement of the vision and priorities that have brought it on. Taking it as a means of voicing ethical concern in the face of massive injustice and destruction, we find ourselves reduced to expressing personal preferences that are deflections from the forces that actually shape life. Finding in it a vehicle for recovering some shades of religious sensibility in an increasingly monolithic secular culture, we find it functioning as a means of co-opting even religious sensibility in the surreptitious worship of ourselves as the positors of value. These endemic dangers make the obvious appeal of the values myth particularly chastening.

Notes

1. Robert N. Bellah, Richard Madsen, William M. Sullivan, Ann Swidler, and Steven M. Tipton, *Habits of the Heart, Individualism and Commitment in American Life* (New York: Harper and Row, 1985), p. 75.

2. Ibid., pp. 79–80.

3. David Hume, *A Treatise of Human Nature*, ed. L.A. Selby-Bigge, 2nd ed., P.H. Nidditch (Oxford: Clarendon Press, 1978), III.I.I., pp. 469–70.

4. William Frankena, "Value and Valuation," in Paul Edwards, ed., *The Encyclopedia of Philosophy*, vol. 8 (New York: Macmillan, 1967), p. 229.

5. Peter C. Danner, *An Ethics for the Affluent* (Washington, DC: University Press of America, 1980), p. 54.

6. *Random House Dictionary of the English Language* (New York: Random House, 1983).

7. Friedrich Nietzsche, *Beyond Good and Evil*, trans. Marianne Cowan (Chicago: Henry Regnery Co., 1955), pp. 70–1.

8. Ibid., p. 114.

9. Ibid., p. 134.

10. Ibid., p. 135.

11. Ibid.

12. Frankena, "Value and Valuation," p. 230.

13. Samuel L. Hart, *Treatise on Values* (New York: Philosophical Library, 1949), p. 36.

14. Ibid., p. 68.

15. Basic expositions of the values clarification approach are to be found in Louis Raths, M. Harmin, and Sidney Simon, *Values and Teaching* (Columbus, OH: Merrill, 1966, 1978), and Sidney Simon et al., *Values Clarification* (New York: Hart, 1972).

16. Clive Beck, *Learning to Live the Good Life, Values in Adulthood* (Toronto: OISE Press, 1993), p. 12.

17. Richard W. Kilby, *The Study of Human Values* (Lanham, MD: University Press of America, 1993), p. 162.

18. Mark Sagoff, "At the Shrine of Our Lady of Fatima, or Why Political Questions Are Not ALL Economic," in Donald Scherer and Thomas Attig, eds., *Ethics and the Environment* (Englewood Cliffs, NJ: Prentice-Hall, 1983), p. 231.

19. Bellah et al., *Habits of the Heart*, p. 80.

20. Mark Sagoff, *The Economy of the Earth* (Cambridge: Cambridge University Press, 1990), p. 68.

21. Ivan Illich, *Ideas*, CBC Radio, February 1989.

22. George Grant, *Time as History* (Toronto: The Hunter Rose Co., 1969), p. 45.

23. Friedrich Nietzsche, *The Gay Science* [125], in Walter Kaufmann, ed., *The Portable Nietzsche* (New York: The Viking Press, 1968), pp. 95–6.

6

AN ECOLOGY MYTH

T HE TWENTIETH century began in the optimistic buoyancy of the age of progress. The high expectations of this outlook were dashed by the destruction of two world wars and the intervening collapse of the stock market. However, by the middle of the century, things were back on track. The wars and the market collapse now seemed like unfortunate deflections from what once again appeared as an assured and inevitable improvement in the prospects for each succeeding generation. As we approach the end of the century, that outlook, in both early and mid-century forms, looks tragically romantic and naïve. The prospects for succeeding generations now appear to be diminishing rather than expanding. And this is true not only in economic terms, real and imme-diate though they are. There are indications that the quality of life, and perhaps even the very basis of life itself, is being placed in jeopardy by the very processes that were expected to produce the good life.

The Ecological Crisis

When the pursuit of the "good life" was launched with a vengeance in the middle of this century, the word "ecology" was virtually unknown by the general public. By the 1970s, it was beginning to appear in the press and on the bumper stickers of the partisans of nature causes. In the 1980s, it achieved a currency that made it seem like a long-standing staple of the general vocabulary. It would be difficult in the 1990s to find any reasonably intelligent adult or child who not only is not aware of the word, but who does not also sense an ominous foreboding attaching to it. There is no room for doubt that we have wreaked devastation and destruction on the natural order that sustains us. The only room for debate is over the seriousness and reversibility of this damage.

The ecological impact of humanity takes two primary forms—the depletion of nonrenewable resources and the creation of pollutants as by-products of the processes that we use to manufacture and consume the products made from these resources. These two dimensions are closely interconnected. The use of fossil fuels for industry, climate control, and transportation creates worrisome by-products at the same time as it depletes these resources themselves. What makes this two-sided process particularly significant is the way in which it has escalated. In this century, the world population has tripled, the economy is twenty times larger, fossil-fuel consumption has increased thirtyfold, and industrial production is fifty times greater than at the beginning of the century, and eighty per cent of this increase has been in the second half of the century.[1] The two dimensions of ecological impact, resource depletion and pollution creation, reflect these two ingredients—increasing population and dramatically increased demand.

Back in the 1960s, Paul Ehrlich was warning of the massive threat posed to the future by the rapidly escalating world population. He suggested that the dramatically shorter time spans it has taken for the world population to double indicate that within nine hundred years we will reach a state of standing room only.[2] No doubt, other factors, not the least of them human aggression, would take over before this situation was reached. However, the prospect of such incremental growth in demand on the earth's finite resources is a cause of considerable concern. But in the 1990s, Paul and Anne Ehrlich emphasize another dimension of this challenge. The impact of humanity on the environment is due not only to our numbers, but to the kinds of demands we make. We must distinguish, they suggest, between the situation in third world countries, where population demands are greatest, and the developed world, where population demands have stabilized but lifestyle expectations create far more extensive demands from each individual. The Ehrlichs offer a formula for environmental impact that incorporates this difference in demand: I = PAT (the environmental Impact in a given country is determined by Population multiplied by the level of Affluence and the state of Technology).[3] The dramatic increase in population growth in the third world is only one factor in environmental impact, and it must be balanced by the far more devastating demands made in the developed world. These two factors, population and consumer demand, act as multipliers on the basic ingredients of environmental impact, resource depletion, and pollution creation.

While both multiplier effects must be addressed, for us in the developed world, considerations of integrity would suggest that we focus on the level of demands that we make on the environment. Within this, a pattern of intensification is also evident. One readily identifiable aspect to begin with is the new chemicals that have been synthesized, and the potential they represent for repercussions that we cannot begin to anticipate. Among the most prominent chemical compounds that promised to provide miraculous solutions to serious human problems, but that turned out to be disastrous, are the chlorinated hydrocarbons of which DDT is the best-known variety. This insecticide helped control malaria, yellow fever, cholera, and encephalitis, but it also caused cancer.[4] This "side effect" was not recognized when the chemical was used so profusely in the early 1960s. Although its use has been restricted as its toxicity came to be acknowledged, it remains to be seen what the long-range effect of this "wonder chemical" will be. What we do know is that it is highly insoluble in water and incredibly mobile in air, but that it is soluble in fat, so that it becomes concentrated in living systems and gets passed along the food chain. Traces of it have been found in both the Arctic and the Antarctic.[5] The issue is not simply the long-term effect of DDT, but the possibility, some even say the inevitability, of that experience being repeated with an even more deadly concoction, which will not be recognized for what it is until it is too late.[6]

In purely quantitative terms, production of chemical compounds increased ten thousand times between 1940 and 1980, going from ten million pounds to one hundred billion pounds over the period.[7] Much of this involved plastic compounds, which might be relatively harmless except for their indisposable disposability, but with the total number of different chemical compounds ranging somewhere between forty and seventy thousand, the benignity assumption is severely strained. What makes the situation particularly worrisome is not these huge numbers, but the fact that these compounds can magnify the toxicity of the chemicals being combined in a scale of synergistic effects that is terrifying.[8] "The result to be assessed is not that of a few thousand deaths or obvious cases of genetic mutation (already observed in newborn infants with every fiftieth new basic pesticidal chemical or every ten-thousandth new commercial formulation marketed), but that in the long run we shall all be dead of synergistic poisoning."[9] This frightening prospect suggests that we are well on the way to becoming the victims of our own ingenuity. If we are to avoid this destiny, it may well be only through a collective recognition that we are not nearly as smart as we thought we were.

An obvious instance of this chastening insight is the recent realization that our chemical tampering has probably contributed significantly to creating holes in the ozone layer that protects the earth from dangerous elements in the sun's rays. The suspected culprit is chlorofluorocarbons (CFCs), a chemical compound that proved to be a very useful substance in fire extinguishers, as a refrigerator coolant, in aerosol sprays, and for producing rigid foam insulation. It was neither toxic nor flammable. Unfortunately, it seems that CFCs float up from the earth's surface into the upper atmosphere, the stratosphere, in six to eight years, and remain there for up to one hundred years, during which time each chlorine atom that is released as CFCs break down is capable of destroying tens of thousands of ozone molecules.[10] Exposure to ultraviolet rays that are not filtered out because of the depletion of this protective layer poses risks of dramatic increase in skin cancers and eye problems such as cataracts.

The essential thrust of ecological awareness is not so much a matter of recognizing specific threats implicit in technological innovations, however, as systemic ones. The issue is not simply that innovations may have unforeseen "side effects," but that all innovation has inevitable repercussions. Ecology may be defined as the study of connections. It entails the awareness that there are no isolated innovations. Every tampering with the givenness of the natural world has ramifications that we cannot anticipate. The development of CFCs is only one part of a complex chemical mix that defies clear analysis. One of the more common natural chemical compounds, for example, is carbon dioxide, the gas that we all breathe out and that plants, in turn, take in to assist in the process of photosynthesis. Although carbon dioxide represents only one thirtieth of one per cent of the atmosphere, in combination with water vapour and trace gasses such as methane and CFCs it contributes to the other major atmospheric change that has become a cause for concern, global warming. These gasses let more light through, but they trap heat in, thus producing a greenhouse effect. Through the burning of fossil fuels and the cutting of trees that absorb carbon dioxide and produce oxygen in return, the content of carbon dioxide in the atmosphere has increased by about twenty-five per cent since the beginning of the industrial revolution. There is not much doubt that this will result in long-term global warming. Global circulation models used for long-term weather forecasting suggest that a doubling of these greenhouse gasses would result in an increase in the average surface temperature on the earth of between three and 5.5 degrees Celsius. This might not sound like very much, but it corresponds to the difference between the average temperature of the earth at the peak of the last ice age, about eighteen thousand years ago, and the present temperature, a difference of some five degrees Celsius. To this must be added the much more compressed time period in which this could happen, perhaps ten to one hundred times faster than the eighteen thousand years for the last transition.[11] The prospect of melting polar ice caps and rising sea levels not only evokes speculation about what this could mean for us as inhabitants of this planet, but might also invite clearer recognition of the difficulty of predicting where our ingenious innovations may lead.

What is at stake, from the interconnected perspective of ecology, is not the consumption of particular nonrenewable resources or the pollution of particular waterways or even of the air, but the threat of fundamental disruption in basic life cycles themselves. "The kind of breakdown which most alarms biologists at present is not a simple physical alteration in the air or water, but a breakdown of these biological chains of cause and effect."[12] What is ultimately at stake begins to emerge only when we consider directly the arrangement in nature between us animal species and the world of vegetation. Our lives are sustained by the reciprocal arrangement whereby we breathe in oxygen and breathe out carbon dioxide, while plants, especially trees because of their size, provide a significant portion of the oxygen we need, by absorbing the carbon dioxide we breathe out. We are threatening this arrangement from both sides. We are increasing the carbon-dioxide side of the equation through the burning of fossil fuels. This also serves to deplete the oxygen side through the acid rain that is produced from the same processes, damaging and killing trees that absorb carbon dioxide and produce oxygen, aggravating the effect of the loss of forests through commercial exploitation, and adding to the impact of our increasing pollution of the oceans, which provide some seventy per cent of the oxygen we require. We may be in the final stages of destroying the fundamental necessity of life, air, through disruption of the natural balance between oxygen and carbon dioxide.

The prospects for more deliberately ingested items, water and food, are not very different. We may well be doing to water something very similar to what we are doing to the air. Besides direct pollution of waterways through industrial and domestic effluent, our pollution of the land through casual use of chemicals, and perhaps particularly through the massive chemical component of modern agriculture, threatens water supplies as these chemicals leach into the ground and find their way into the water table or are propelled through run-off directly into lakes and rivers. At the same time, the food chain is infiltrated not only by the preservatives and additives introduced in the final stages of processing, but also at the earliest stages as blossoms and trees and plants are sprayed with insecticides and herbicides. This brings us back to the chilling prospect of creations of chemical engineering such as DDT. The systemic nature of life recognized by ecology renders the isolationist approach of technological manipulation and commercial capitalization extremely precarious. We simply cannot anticipate the systemic impact of procedures and products designed to address particular situations. Life might be made easier or even healthier in immediate terms, but that very development might be destroying the fundamental bases of life on a much wider scale.

Proposals for Solutions

The simplest solution to the ecology crisis is to deny that there is a crisis at all. Those who take the warnings of ecologists seriously are seen to be doomsayers, obsessed with finding potential disaster in every new development. Advocates of such a denial point to predictions of environmental devastation that have not materialized. One of the earliest of such dramatic forecasts was the initial report of the Club of Rome, *The Limits to Growth*,[13] published in 1972. At that time, the complex communications systems on which modern civilization depends seemed to be in jeopardy because of the prospect that the supplies of copper required for these lines would soon be exhausted. That fear appears amusing in retrospect, in light of the development of fibre-optic cables, which are made essentially from sand.[14] Another telling instance is the bet made between Paul Ehrlich and a prominent economist. In 1980, Ehrlich bet that the price of five important minerals would increase over the following decade because these resources would be used up; the economist bet that prices would drop because new deposits would be discovered and substitutes would be developed. In 1990, the economist won the bet, and he would have won even if allowance had not been made for inflation.[15] The ecologist's dire expectations simply did not materialize.

The confidence that concern over the environment is exaggerated rests on two main factors. One is a fundamental confidence in modern technology. Even if a particular resource is depleted, technological innovation can be expected to come up with alternative ways of performing the function for which that resource was required, and this will probably result in more efficient performance, as in the displacement of copper by fibre-optic cables. This confidence is supported by a parallel confidence in the economic mechanism of the market system. The supply of essential minerals will not be exhausted, in fact, because the market will not permit this. As supplies dwindle, the price of that resource will increase. Thus, any particular resource will become prohibitively expensive as it becomes more and more scarce. Not only will this serve to protect what remains of the resource, it will provide the economic incentive for the technological innovation that will devise a substitute.[16] Therefore, technology and the market, far from being sources of environmental crisis, are really primary vehicles for the solution of whatever environmental problems do exist.

That the symbiosis of technology and market can dispense with concerns about the symbiosis of depletion of resources and creation of pollution is a consoling prospect. Whether the consolation can extend to the dimensions we have seen to be involved in 'the ecology crisis, however, is not so obvious. The market can be expected to preserve only what is too expensive to consume at any given time. This may involve not only a very short-term view of the value of certain natural resources, but may even encourage the depletion of irreplaceable elements of nature. Oil reserves may never be exhausted, although, in retrospect, they will appear to have been increasingly underpriced the more abundant the reserves were thought to be; elephants, on the other hand, may be hunted to extinction as their tusks become increasingly valuable.[17] Thus, the market mechanism can promote the destruction of elements of nature, and may be expected to preserve only such reserves as become too prohibitively expensive to exploit.

The other side of the environmental sword, the creation of pollution, is even more precariously suspended. Technological innovations may be developed to deal with emissions and effluent, but the economic incentive for this will emerges only as the quality of air and water deteriorates. That such developments will happen soon enough is far from assured. In fact, it is virtually certain that they will not for some, if not all, of us. Technological innovations always come with an immediate price tag, not to mention the hidden costs that sometimes appear only much later. The most vulnerable would once again be excluded from this kind of solution. That this has happened and that the range of the excluded is being extended is obvious. Through market mechanisms, we have created a world where only those who can afford it can eat. We are rapidly approaching a situation where only those who can afford it will be able to breathe. Without entering into the debate about the relationship between first-world affluence and third-world poverty, the food banks and soup kitchens of our so-called developed world are ample testimony to the market's exclusion of the poor from even this basic necessity. A similar situation is developing with regard to water, as public supplies require more and more chemical treatment and those who can afford it resort to bottled water. It does not take much imagination to envisage filtration systems for buildings and cars and portable breathing apparatuses that will allow those who can afford these devices to breathe. Those who cannot afford these will have to take their chances with the poisoned air that causes disease and hastens death.

The social selectivity of market and technological solutions to environmental challenges will be reason enough for some people to dismiss this direction, which appears to be a narrow, vested-interest avoidance of the real crisis. For others, the difficulty is still more fundamental: not only does it favour certain people and disadvantage others, but it is fundamentally flawed in its focus on people. It represents, at best, an instrumental approach to ecology. Only those elements of nature that are viewed as resources for us will be candidates for concern, or else specious arguments will have to be developed to attribute some economic significance to species we might want to preserve. The pioneer ecologist Aldo Leopold points out that something like this was done with songbirds at the beginning of the century, when it was argued that we would be eaten alive by insects if the birds were not around to control them.[18] The value of the songbirds themselves could not be recognized. This outlook is interested in nature for the sake of humanity; its perspective is exclusively anthropocentric.

The anthropocentric approach to ecology can itself involve different levels. For example, it is possible to distinguish between "resource conservation and development," which attempts to ensure that particular dimensions of the natural order produce the maximum sustainable yield, and "resource preservation," which involves attempts to preserve areas and species for their future potential for research, recreation, or aesthetic enjoyment.[19] Where "resource conservation and development" is intent on making the most of a particular resource, "resource preservation" seeks to maintain a resource for the long term. Beyond this difference in their range of vision, however, both of these approaches reflect the view of nature as a collection of resources for human exploitation. The contrast with these anthropocentric visions is an approach to ecology that takes the natural order seriously in its own right. Leopold's land ethic moves in that direction, but the strongest version of this alternative is Arne Naess's deep ecology.

Naess refers to concerns with resource depletion and pollution as shallow ecology because these are really expressions of concern for ourselves; it is our survival and affluence that are primary. In contrast, deep ecology reflects the perspective of the biosphere as a whole. This means affirming *"the equal right to live and blossom"* for all life forms and recognizing that *"its restriction to humans is an anthropocentrism with immoral effects upon the life partnership with other forms of life."*[20] In this advocacy of a biocentric, as opposed to an anthropocentric, perspective, Naess does not intend to promote a total levelling in which all life is seen to have the same value. He recognizes that life feeds on life. A biocentric perspective does not mean a romanticizing of nature as completely inviolable. Death is the common lot of all life, and death of some life forms may be hastened by the needs of other life forms. The difference is that this necessity is not engaged in thoughtlessly or wantonly from the biocentric perspective, as it is apt to be from the anthropocentric perspective.

The difference between shallow and deep ecology suggests that the source of, and any significant solution to, the ecology crisis has a lot to do with basic perspectives. Whether or not we think there is a crisis, and what we regard as a crisis, will be determined by the extent to which our outlook is anthropocentric or biocentric. Not only our ability to recognize a crisis, but also a crucial part of the background that accounts for there being one, may involve a particular attitude toward the natural order. In a very influential article, "The Historical Roots of Our Ecological Crisis," published in 1967, Lynn White, Jr., contended that the ecology crisis derived ultimately from the Judaeo-Christian creation mandate to take dominion over the earth and subdue it.[21] This sense of human authority over the rest of creation is seen to underlie the abuses that have resulted in the current crisis. Wendell Berry finds the Christian source of ecological devastation to be even more basic. Apart from the sense of a divine mandate to control other species, the theological emphasis on the transcendence of God is seen to render the earth mundane and vulnerable. "If God was not in the world, then obviously the world was a thing of inferior importance, or of no importance at all."[22] The basic direction of Christianity in finding ultimate significance beyond the world, involved a devaluation of the world that left it exposed to environmental exploitation. When the environmental crisis is seen to arise out of this background, it can really be addressed only by a change in basic perspective. Attempts to address particular resource or pollution problems appear piecemeal and preliminary at best. The seriousness of the situation will only be realized when we see that our most basic visions of life are what is at stake.

Ecology will be taken seriously, in this visionary view, only when nature is taken seriously in its own right. This common direction takes several prominent forms. One version is the Gaia hypothesis advanced by James E. Lovelock. The name of the ancient Greek earth goddess is used to refer to "a complex entity involving the Earth's biosphere, atmosphere, oceans, and soil; the totality constituting a feedback or cybernetic system which seeks an optimal physical and chemical environment for life on this planet."[23] For Lovelock, Gaia is a biological concept. References to Gaia in personal terms are not to be taken literally; they are not intended to imply suprahuman consciousness.[24] Gaia refers to the whole biosphere as an interactive system, but the only consciousness that is recognized is human consciousness. On the other hand, this does not imply any dominating role for humans. This

is a fundamental difference between Gaia and the anthropocentric outlook that underlies the ecology crisis. "The Gaia hypothesis implies
that the stable state of our planet includes man as a part of, or partner
in, a very democratic entity."[25] As the only known form of consciousness, humans may have a unique role to play, but that role depends on
a sensitivity to and integration with the total biosphere that has yet to
be realized.[26] Although Lovelock is speaking from the viewpoint of the
life sciences, as he acknowledges himself, the Gaia hypothesis is more
like religion than science.[27] It represents a fundamental vision rather
than a theory that might be subject to scientific confirmation. What is
at stake is of mythic proportions.

The appeal to Mother Earth, in contradistinction to the reliance
on Father God that is seen to have provided the metaphysical ground-
ing for the human domination that figures so prominently in the ecology crisis, has received enthusiastic endorsement from some feminists,
who generally have less reservation about attributing consciousness
and personality to the Earth Mother. Archaeological evidence is interpreted as confirming an original stage of matriarchy in which the
Goddess was the comprehensive divinity, before it was diluted in poly-
theism and eliminated by patriarchy.[28] In this early, natural stage of
human life, the feminine qualities of nurture and care prevailed, so that
human beings lived in perfect harmony with nature.[29] This outlook is
closer to Lovelock's Gaia hypothesis than it is to conventional Christianity, for example, because the Goddess is understood essentially in
immanent terms in contrast to the transcendence of the Christian God.
The domineering divinity who sanctions human domination over nature is seen as a deviation from the immanent deity, the Earth Mother,
who permeates the natural order and induces care for all living things.
With this vision, ecofeminism offers its alternative as a basis for ecological salvation.

The tendency to replace what is seen as a mechanical, domineering Christian-based outlook with an organic, holistic perspective lends
particular appeal to Eastern religious traditions as a source of alternative vision that may address the ecology crisis. While we in the West,
following the Judaeo-Christian monotheistic direction of identifying
the divine in terms of exalted isolation, have understood holiness in
terms of separateness, religions in the Far East have seen life in more
integrated terms. "All beings and things, animate or inanimate, were
thought to be permeated with divine power or spirit."[30] Hindu and
Buddhist traditions, for example, see life as an intricate interconnected
web in which all life forms have their place, with human distinctiveness consisting not in domination of lesser forms but in the contemplation that is not concerned about particularity at all. In the West, this

tradition has had its widest appeal through Zen Buddhism, which is really a Chinese development in the Buddhist tradition that reached the West by way of Japan. A more direct contribution of Chinese religion to current ecological visions is represented in Taoism, which sees all life as a flow of pervasive rhythms. This sense of a natural flow to life to which we can become better attuned, or of a comprehensive meaning that may be appreciated through contemplation, is seen by some as an essential change in vision that can lead to the kind of organic, holistic perspective that is essential if the real roots of the ecology crisis are to be recognized and addressed.

The Mythic Dimensions of Ecology

Deep ecology is distinguished from shallow ecology by its recognition of the importance of the mythic dimension. It sees the challenge posed by the environmental situation as not simply a matter of particular problems but something of crisis proportions because it sees it in mythic dimensions. As we have seen, Lovelock acknowledges that he has stepped from science into religion in advocating his Gaia perspective. In contrast, the science of ecology tends to remain on the shallow side in retaining the piecemeal, specialized approach that has characterized modern science and has helped to contribute to the unravelling of the ecological web of life. Some ecologists suggest that one of the main obstacles to appreciating the crisis is that the science of ecology gives the impression of addressing the situation through things like wildlife management and impact studies, but through these approaches it is really reinforcing the technocratic, managerial mentality that is behind the crisis.[31] The ecological challenge begins to be appreciated, for deep ecologists, only when it is seen in mythic proportions.

Although deep ecologists see the issue as one of mythic proportions, their proposals also suggest that they do not really seem to appreciate the depth and formative influence of myth. This is indicated by the standard suggestion that the solution is to be found through a change in mythic perspectives. That we can be expected to change from managerial specialization to holistic ecologism, or from modern Western secularism to ancient Eastern mysticism, anticipates conversions that match the expectations of the most ardent evangelical missions. Of course, this is expected without benefit of the divine agency relied upon by evangelicals, which makes the feat even more amazing. Advocates of deep ecology seem to assume that myths are basically at our disposal, to be chosen and changed as circumstances demand. This not only contradicts what we have seen about the depth and elusiveness of living myth; it is also at variance with the emphasis of deep ecologists themselves on the importance of fundamental visions and perspectives.

The mythic conversions sought by deep ecologists not only betray a lack of recognition of the depth and tenacity of mythic commitments, they are indicative of a mythic commitment on the part of deep ecologists themselves. The view that myths can be exchanged generally in such direct ways implies that myths are fundamentally at our disposal. We preside over our myths. As we have noted, this contradicts the formative and elusive qualities that are characteristic of living myth. This expectation is understandable and natural, however, from the modern managerial perspective. Myths should be at our disposal, if we are really in charge. The irony, of course, is that deep ecology would then share the same basic mythology as shallow ecology. Indeed, it would amount to an intensification of this in the extension of our managerial ability from the nonhuman environment to encompass human perspectives. Thus, rather than representing our incorporation in the web of life, what is really being advocated is that we assert our human distinctiveness and superiority over other life forms and adopt the correct mythology.

What is being advocated as the correct mythology is a naturalistic holism or a cosmic spiritualism, but, if the present analysis is credible, what is really being offered is a sophisticated version of the modern, technological managerial outlook. This means that the operative mythology is really that of modern anthropocentrism, and so what is being offered is not so much a cure as an intensification of the disease.

This strange prospect raises the wider consideration of whether this mythic perspective may not be the effective source of the ecology crisis. Perhaps what underlies the ecology crisis is not the basic orientation of the Judaeo-Christian tradition, as White contends, but the exact opposite, the abandonment of that tradition. The ecology crisis occurred not when Christianity was at the height of its influence, but after its advocacy of certain directions as divine revelations had been rejected and replaced by secular humanism. Secularization may be seen as an extension of the Christian assurance of the superiority of humanity and its mandate to exercise dominion over the rest of creation, but that extension has also involved the abandonment of the notion of creation, especially insofar as this involves any answerability to a Creator. James Barr has no doubt that this is what underlies the ecology crisis.

> I would say that the great modern exploitation of nature has taken place under the reign of a liberal humanism in which man no longer conceives of himself as being under a creator, and in which therefore his place of dominance in the universe and his right to dispose

of nature for his own ends is, unlike the situation in the Bible, unlimited.[32]

It is not the divine mandate to dominate the earth that accounts for the ecology crisis, then, but the abandonment of that mandate, which came with restrictions and responsibilities.

Those who want to retain Lynn White's thesis that the Christian background is what really underlies the ecology crisis may do so by insisting that the Christian mandate to take dominion over the earth and the modern secular anthropocentric assumption that the earth lies at our disposal are more closely linked than Barr's dissociation would allow. Indeed, they might contend that talk of a divine mandate to take dominion over the earth is really just a way of reinforcing our own human superiority, so that there never were any serious restrictions and responsibilities attached to it. These, too, were of our own devising, and so were further diversions to camouflage the naked human aggression that has finally come clean in modern secular humanism. This reading may be a plausible one, but if so, it would be from the viewpoint of modern secular humanism. It assumes that this outlook is the only legitimate one, so that any reference to the divine can only be illusory. Such a reading would clearly be unacceptable to followers of the Christian tradition. Consequently, for them, the restrictions and responsibilities would be as real as the sense that they constitute divine mandates. This is not to say that Christians have been particularly faithful in following these restrictions and responsibilities. In every age, Christians have hardly been immune to committing abuses that would rival those that might be attributable to modern secular humanism. But to see such abuses as evidence that Christian belief in divine creation is simply a ruse for human assertion is a reductionistic reading that depends on endorsing the modern secular perspective.

Indeed, Christian mythology involves more than a sense of responsibility beyond ourselves that is lacking in secular humanism; to the answerability to our Creator, it adds the conviction that we have a tendency to fail miserably in that answerability. Between the creation mandate to take dominion over the earth and subdue it and us, there lies the Fall. The recipients of the mandate were ejected from their earthly paradise because of their disobedience to their Creator. That the ecology crisis is to be attributed to this mythic outlook, which, in addition to recognizing transcendent answerability, includes such a sombre self-assessment, may not seem so obvious when there is an alternative mythology that glories in unlimited human potential.

In its advocacy of myth management, deep ecology could be seen as an intensification of the crisis promoted by the ambitions of secular humanism, rather than as a source of resolution. This extends to the

Eastern religions option as well as to the Gaia alternative insofar as these, too, appear as management strategies. No doubt there are Westerners who learn to see reality through Far Eastern traditions. The poet Gary Snyder, winner of the Pulitzer Prize in 1975 for his book *Turtle Island*,[33] who combines insights of Zen Buddhism, Native American traditions, and deep ecology, may well be a case in point. There is merit in the assessment that "his knowledge of Zen Buddhism is not that of a dilettante, but insofar as this is possible for an occidental, of an adept."[34] That many Westerners can be expected to be more than dilettantes when it comes to Far Eastern religious traditions, however, is not so clear. If the ecology crisis is due particularly to modern secular anthropocentrism, it would be ironic that people who have arrived at this state through the abandonment of their own religion should be counselled to find salvation by embracing other religious traditions. Far Eastern traditions suggest an organic perspective in contrast to the hierarchical orientation of the Middle East traditions, but this appeal is compromised if the source of ecological abuse is not acknowledgment of divine hierarchy, but the assertion of human hierarchy without that wider divine restraint, and if this Eastern option is thus subordinated to the modern secular mandate.

The obvious appeal of what appears to be an organic direction in Far Eastern religions is thus subject to two particular reservations. One concerns the accessibility of these traditions to us, or, from the other side, our ability to appreciate these traditions. If the ecology crisis has resulted from our abandonment of our own religious tradition in the West, why should we think that we can readily appreciate other religious traditions? The appeal of these traditions in modern secular culture may be a further means of avoiding serious spiritual confrontation. Toying with the exotic not only provides a diversion from the ordinary, it may also represent an escape from the claims of our own reality. Serious spiritual interest may be expected to manifest itself in exploration of one's own spiritual heritage, problematic though this may be, before looking to alien traditions.

That the appeal to Far Eastern religions may represent a further avoidance of spiritual seriousness, rather than a return to spiritual depths, tends to be further confirmed by the other source of reservation. From its base in the modern secular West, this appeal may be suspected of attempting to use these traditions for its own purposes, rather than respecting their integrity. Here, again, we encounter the manipulative mentality that is more congenial with the source of environmental devastation than with prospects for its reversal. The current point of interest, however, is in the lack of spiritual sensitivity implicit in such an approach. These ancient and venerable traditions are mined as resources for dealing with the ecology crisis. In this way, these traditions are clearly subordinated to the perceived demands of ecology. Ecology is the basic religion, in the interests of which Buddhism or Taoism are secondary and auxiliary. As one ecospiritualist puts it, "I do not advocate Taoist religious beliefs any more than I advocate that we believe in the existence of Pan or the bear god, nor do I advocate that we adopt Taoist metaphysics. Still, there are ideas and attitudes in Taoism from which we can well profit."[35] Does an attempt to profit from ancient religious traditions, on which we look with condescension, represent a promising source of solution to a mentality that has been intent on profiting from the natural order, which we have assumed to be at our disposal? The appeal to Eastern traditions thus seems to offer promise of ecological salvation by an intensification of the approach that has produced the crisis in the first place. Even ancient religious traditions have become resources for our avaricious appetite.

If deep ecology thus constitutes an intensification of the approach that has caused the ecology crisis because it really fails to appreciate the depth and elusiveness of myth, how does the present analysis escape this hazard? If myth is so foundational and resistant to identification, how is it that we can detect that even deep ecology reflects the modern managerial myth of secular anthropocentrism? It can only be because we occupy some other mythic base. A prime candidate for this is a sense of depth and integrity in classical religious traditions that is apt to remain foreign to modern secular sensibility. Whether this or the deep ecology direction, or indeed the shallow ecology one, is true is for individuals to decide for themselves in light of what speaks to them. In the most optimistic reading, the ecology situation raises frightening prospects. It would be irresponsible to deflect attention from the real problems it poses with considerations of deep ecology, much less of the mythic considerations we have pursued here, unless these latter directions are true. If it is the case that even deep ecology represents an intensification of the very mentality that underlies the crisis in the first place, then the seriousness of the situation will not be faced until this mythic dimension is recognized. Nothing short of full spiritual conversion will be adequate. This still leaves us with what may be the most basic irony of all, however; truly sincere spirituality would seem to issue its own insights and disciplines that would resist utilitarian employment for ecological or any other purposes. In posing issues of life and death in a particularly dramatic way, the ecology crisis may be posing the issue of our fundamental mythic allegiance today more forcefully than does any other area. Whether that allegiance is ultimately an ecological one is another matter.

Notes

1. Jim MacNeil, "Strategies for Sustainable Economic Development," in *Managing Planet Earth: Readings from Scientific American Magazine* (New York: W.H. Freeman, 1990), p. 109.

2. Paul R. Ehrlich, *The Population Bomb* (New York: Ballantine Books, 1968), p. 18.

3. Paul Ehrlich and Anne Ehrlich, *The Population Explosion* (New York: Simon and Schuster, 1990).

4. Donald M. Thompson, *The Economics of Environmental Protection* (Cambridge, MA: Winthrop Publishers, 1973), p. 128.

5. Ibid.

6. Ralph O. Brinkhurst and Donald O. Chant, *This Good, Good Earth: Our Fight for Survival* (Toronto: Macmillan, 1971), p. 31.

7. Gerard Piel, *Only One World: Ours to Make and to Keep* (New York: W.H. Freeman & Co., 1992), p. 92.

8. Thompson, *The Economics of Environmental Protection*, p. 127.

9. Ibid.

10. Cynthia Pollock Shea, "Protecting the Ozone Layer," in *State of the World 1989: A Worldwatch Institute Report on Progress toward a Sustainable Society* (New York: W.W. Norton, 1989), pp. 85ff.

11. Stephen H. Schneider, "The Changing Climate," in *Managing Planet Earth: Reading from Scientific American Magazine* (New-York: W.H. Freeman, 1990), pp. 25ff.

12. Gordon Rattray Taylor, *The Doomsday Book* (London: Thames and Hudson 1970), p. 19.

13. Donella H. Meadows, Dennis L. Meadows, Jørgen Randers, William W. Behrens III, *The Limits to Growth: A Report for the Club of Rome's Project on the Predicament of Mankind* (New York: Universe Books, 1972).

14. Martin W. Lewis, *Green Delusions, An Environmentalist Critique of Radical Environmentalism* (Durham and London: Duke University Press, 1992), p. 184.

15. Ibid., p. 185.

16. On the virtues of technology and the market as sources of solution to environmental challenges, see Wilfred Beckerman, "The Case for Economic Growth," in Thomas Donaldson and Patricia H. Werhane, eds., *Ethical Issues in Business* (Englewood Cliffs, NJ: Prentice-Hall, 1983), and Charles Maurice and Charles W. Smithson, *The Doomsday Myth* (Stanford: Hoover Institution Press, 1984).

17. Frances Cairncross, *Costing the Earth: The Challenge for Government, the Opportunities for Business* (Boston: Harvard Business School Press, 1992), p. 9.

18. Aldo Leopold, *A Sand County Almanac* (New York: Oxford University Press, 1949), p. 210.

19. Alan Drengson, "Protecting the Environment, Protecting Ourselves: Reflections on the Philosophical Dimension," in Raymond Bradley and Stephen Duguid, eds., *Environmental Ethics*, vol. 2 (Burnaby, BC: Institute for the Humanities, Simon Fraser University, 1989), pp. 44–5.

20. Arne Naess, *Ecology, Community and Lifestyle*, trans. and rev. by David Rothenberg (Cambridge: Cambridge University Press, 1989), p. 28.

21. Lynn White, Jr., "The Historical Roots of Our Ecological Crisis," *Science.* 155 (1967): 1203–7.

22. Wendell Berry, "A Secular Pilgrimage," *The Hudson Review.* 23 (Autumn 1970), 403.

23. James E. Lovelock, *GAIA: A New Look at Life on Earth* (Oxford: Oxford University Press, 1979), p. 11.

24. Ibid., p. ix.

25. Ibid., p. 145.

26. Ibid., p. 148.

27. Ibid., p. vii.

28. See Merlin Stone, *When God Was a Woman* (New York: Dial Press, 1976), and Elizabeth Gould Davis, *The First Sex* (Baltimore: Penguin Books, 1971).

29. See Riane Eisler, *The Chalice and the Blade* (San Francisco: Harper and Row, 1987).

30. Roderick Nash, *The Rights of Nature: A History of Environmental Ethics* (Madison: University of Wisconsin Press, 1989), p. 113.

31. John Livingston, "The Ecological Imperative," in Bradley and Duguid, *Environmental Studies*, vol. 2, p. 130.

32. James Barr, "Man and Nature: The Ecological Controversy and the Old Testament," in David Spring and Eileen Spring, eds., *Ecology and Religion in History* (New York: Harper and Row, 1974), p. 73.

33. Gary Snyder, *Turtle Island* (New York: New Directions, 1974).

34. Thomas Parkinson, "The Poetry of Gary Snyder," *Southern Review.* 4 (1968): 616.

35. Lawrence E. Johnson, *A Morally Deep World, An Essay on Moral Significance and Environmental Ethics* (Cambridge: Cambridge University Press, 1991), p. 269.

7

A SEX MYTH

In what must be at least the fourth decade of the sexual revolution, we might expect that the legacy of hang-ups and misconceptions about sexuality would have been largely dissipated. The massive clandestine market for sexual materials and services, the pervasive exploitation of sex in mainstream commercial activity, and the apparent escalation of allegations of sexual abuse, however, suggest that the revolution has by no means resulted in the development of general sexual maturity. Sex is still very much a furtive activity; insecurities and lingering confusions leave us susceptible to "sexploitation"; and the frighteningly frequent victimization of the vulnerable belies any hope that some significant level of sexual mutuality has been achieved. When to this is added the potentially lethal results of sex in the age of AIDS, apparent failures of the sexual revolution are a cause for concern. Where previous generations faced the connection of sex with life, the present generation has solutions to that difficulty available, only to be confronted by the far more sinister connection between sex and death. Serious though this situation obviously is, when the topic of sex is raised in terms of the question of basic visions that are at stake in myth, a specific dimension of the sexual revolution appears even more prominent than issues of sexual practice and their potential dangers: the redefinition of sex instigated by feminism.

Few recent developments can compare with the emergence of feminism for prominence and influence in any field. In the area of sexuality, feminism has been particularly formative. This might seem too trite to deserve mentioning; after all, is feminism not a movement based on issues of sex? The curious thing, however, is that the central thrust of feminism has been to minimize, rather than emphasize, sex; many feminists would say that feminism is not about sex, it is about gender. The point of this distinction is that sex is a basic biological reality—we are born male or female. Leaving aside the question of sexual orientation, which means avoiding the difficult questions raised by homosexuality in either gay or lesbian forms, we may say that sex is determined by birth. How the sexes are perceived, however, is determined by culture. It is this issue of gender, what it means to be male or female, that is the central concern of feminism. This is also clearly the dimension of sex that is most obviously of mythic proportions.

Feminist Protests

Even allowing for the claim that feminism is concerned with gender, rather than with sex as such, it is still not clear how important gender is for feminism. Different visions are apparent from the earliest stages of the movement. While it is always a precarious matter to date major movements, there is not much room for argument that feminism as we know it received a formative impetus from Betty Friedan's *The Feminine Mystique*, published in 1963. Friedan's protest was primarily against the identification of women with the role of wife and mother. "The new mystique makes the house wife-mothers, who never had a chance to be anything else, the model, for all women; it presupposes that history has reached a final and glorious end in the here and now, as far as women are concerned."[1] Not only did this outlook, which was largely taken for granted when Friedan wrote, not represent a pinnacle that women had reached, but it was a reflection of an arrangement that had emerged only in the modern period. The industrial revolution created the division between public and private domains, where men went out into the industrial world and earned incomes that supported the family, over which women presided. Prior to this, family and work had been much more organic; both women and men supported the family. With the division between public and private realms, male and female roles diverged so totally that women were identified with the home, while the wider world belonged to men. "The separate sphere ideology succeeded in driving bourgeois women into lives of enforced domesticity, sexual repression, economic dependency, and unpaid 'good works.'"[2]

This pattern had become particularly noticeable in light of its disruption during the Second World War, when women worked in factories, making the machines and armaments that supplied the troops. When the war ended, women returned to what had become their conventional roles in industrial society, but memories of the diversity and opportunity of the war years lingered, and this is what surfaces in Friedan's protest. In fact, there are indications that women did not return to domestic roles as fully as is generally supposed: "Two years after the war, working women had recouped their numerical setbacks in the job market, and by 1952 more women were employed than at the height of the war economy's output."[3] In any event, at its origins, the present wave of feminism represents a revolt against the confinement of women to, and their identification with, the home sphere.

In what would generally be seen to be the most prominent articulation of feminist protest after Friedan's *The Feminine Mystique*, Germaine Greer's *The Female Eunuch*, Friedan's position is both endorsed and challenged. While Greer applauds Friedan's launching of the feminist wave, and notes that her organization, NOW (the National Organization of Women), has achieved the most influence politically, she is critical of the apparent limitation of Friedan's agenda to achieving recognition and acceptance in the world of men. "She represents the cream of American middle-class womanhood, and what she wants for them is equality of opportunity within the status quo, free admission to the world of the ulcer and the coronary."[4] This is tantamount to contending that women should really have the opportunity to be men. The feminine mystique that Friedan opposed was the equation of women with femininity. The problem, as she saw it, was that femininity had been so isolated and romanticized as intuitive, life-giving, and nurturing that women became identified with these qualities and confined to the roles they permitted,[5] roles that were underpaid or not paid at all in the male-structured economy.

The irony of the difference between Greer and Friedan is that they both identify Freud as a prime source of the misunderstanding of women, suggesting that, in terms of vision, the problem stems from the influence of Freud's assumption that women are incomplete men. The classic concept in this vision is Freud's characterization of women as victims of penis envy. The obvious sexual difference between girls and boys is that girls lack a penis. This lack shapes their identity, according to Freud, so that they go through life regretting the fact that they are not men. While there might have been some basis for this in the middle-class women patients Freud saw in Vienna amid the repressions of the Victorian era, Friedan suggests, it is unfortunate that this account "was seized upon in this country in the 1940's as the literal explanation of all that was wrong with American women."[6] The misfortune, though, Greer would suggest, has been confined to exclusion from male opportunities, for Friedan. Greer herself contends for opportunity for women to be themselves.

The title and focus of Greer's book, *The Female Eunuch*, is a direct reference to Freud's characterization of women as victims of penis envy. "In traditional psychological theory, which is after all only another way of describing and rationalizing the status quo, the desexualization of women is illustrated in the Freudian theory of the female sex as lacking a sexual organ."[7] There is nothing wrong, then, with Friedan's diagnosis. It is her prescription for remedying the situation that is deficient. The answer is not to provide opportunity for women in a men's world, but to recognize the legitimacy of women in their own right. Women are not deficient men who should have more scope. Rather, the legitimacy of women as human beings, and sexual beings, has to be recognized.

In spite of Greer's dissatisfaction with Friedan's direction, there may well be more similarity in their protests than this divergence would suggest. Both oppose the identification of women with the home, the private as opposed to the public sphere, and their corresponding exclusion from the public domain. Not only is this so, but Friedan seems to come very close to Greer's concern with the way women are perceived as being the heart of the problem. "I think that this has been the unknown heart of woman's problem in America for a long time, this lack of a private image."[8] It is not simply a case of making room for women in the world of men, but of women coming to appreciate themselves, so that they may find their own way as fully human persons. Where Greer sees Friedan's direction falling short is in allowing the scope for women to develop, without having to conform to priorities and expectations deriving from male dominance. This difference in aim continues to render feminist protest ambiguous.

The dilemma has been posed more recently by Naomi Wolf in *The Beauty Myth*. As she sees it, the beauty myth has taken the place of the feminine mystique: "As women released themselves from the feminine mystique of domesticity, the beauty myth took over its lost ground, expanding as it waned to carry on its work of social control."[9] When women could no longer be confined to domestic life through the identification of that life as a woman's true vocation, new restrictions emerged in terms of expectations regarding beauty. Where women were spared the rigours of public life in business and politics because they were too pure for that, now they are enticed to replace such preoccupation with purity with a preoccupation with beauty.[10] In one sense, the beauty myth has been around since about 1830, when the feminine mystique really got under way.[11] However, it has really come into its own as the feminine mystique has been eroded by the onslaughts of feminism. In fact, Wolf suggests that "the ideology of beauty is the last one remaining of the old feminine ideologies that still has the power to control those women whom second wave feminism would have otherwise made relatively uncontrollable."[12] Women who cannot be shamed into domesticity may still be vulnerable to concern with measuring up to the standards of the beauty myth.

The insidious thing about the beauty myth is that it is not really about beauty at all, but about power.[13] It creates an image of beauty, which in the present version is extremely artificial and unhealthy in its preoccupation with thinness, and portrays this as the natural destiny of women. Women must qualify on the beauty scale before they can hope to qualify for positions in the public world, which remains the masculine domain. What is even more insidious is that it is women who keep the beauty myth functioning by imposing its expectations on one another: "The remarkable truth is that though the marketplace promotes the myth, it would be powerless if women didn't enforce it against one another."[14] To recognize this and to defy it in practice, however, are two different things. This is indicative of its depth and influence. The catch is that any woman who would challenge the beauty myth is apt to be immediately subjected to its scrutiny. How does she measure up against the current image of beauty? will almost certainly be one of the first questions that arises about her challenge to the myth. Many people must have had that reaction to photos of Naomi Wolf herself on the back cover of one edition of *The Beauty Myth* or on the front cover of her more recent *Fire with Fire*. Those photos clearly display someone who could feel comfortable with current images of beauty, and who also clearly takes some pains to meet this standard and some pleasure in doing so. This suggests a continuing endorsement of the beauty myth at the same time as it is challenged, sending even more ambiguous signals about whether the point is to be more feminine or more like men.

Wolf identifies the movement launched by Friedan as the second wave, following the first wave represented by the women's suffrage movement from the nineteenth century that achieved the vote for women in the United States in 1920 through the introduction of the Nineteenth Amendment to the Constitution, and in Canada in 1917 (although it was not achieved in Quebec until 1940). However, once the vote was achieved, the feminist cause faltered. "In the 1930s and 40s, the sort of woman who fought for woman's rights was still concerned with human rights and freedom—for negroes, for oppressed workers, for victims of Franco's Spain and Hitler's Germany. But no one was much concerned with rights for women: they had all been won."[15]

Thus, when Friedan and others took up the cause in the 1960s, they were launching the second wave of feminism. Wolf calls today for a third wave, or rather announces its arrival. According to her, the year 1991 saw the beginning of the "genderquake" [16] in the confirmation hearings for Supreme Court justice Clarence Thomas. Although the challenge of sexual harassment launched by Anita Hill did not prevent his confirmation, it did raise awareness about sexual harassment and opened new prospects for recognition of the liabilities that exist for women under male power structures.

It is not clear what this post-genderquake third wave is expected to accomplish. In negative terms, the hope is that it will eliminate the harassment and disadvantages to which women are subjected because they are women. What this is expected to produce in positive terms, however, is not so clear. "To look however we want to look—and to be heard as we deserve to be heard—we will need no less than a feminist third wave." [17] This call for choice for women begs the fundamental question as to the point of that choice. Is it to allow women to become more like men, or to allow women to be more distinctively women? Greer's difference with Friedan continues to haunt feminism.

Feminist Proposals

Ambiguity in feminism about the importance of gender—about the way women and men should be characterized, whether the aim is to promote sameness or difference—reflects a more basic ambiguity about the importance of sex itself. The reservations Germaine Greer expresses over Betty Friedan's version of feminism are indicative of a fundamental rift that runs through feminist diagnoses and prescriptions. Greer's reading that Friedan's concern is to achieve admission to the male-structured world represents one fundamental version of feminism, according to which feminism is basically about human rights for women. Greer's concern for women to pursue their own integrity as women is indicative of another basic direction that understands feminism as the promotion of the distinctively female.

The irony of this situation is that far from avoiding sex in the interests of gender, prominent feminists can be found opposing sex. *Women Against Sex* (WAS) is a national organization in the United States that opposes freedom of sexual expression. Its members oppose pornography on principle, contending that it cannot be defended as a matter of rights for those in favour of it because it is inherently exploitative of women. WAS reflects a split in the feminist movement, the other side of which is represented by the *Feminist Anti-Censorship Task*

Force (FACT), which opposes censorship in the name of freedom for all. Members of FACT are not necessarily in favour of pornography; indeed, they might find it abhorrent. However, they find it necessary to support the right of those who want access to pornography in the interests of human rights as such. If women expect to have their rights respected, they have to be ready to acknowledge the rights of others, even those they might not approve of. Of course, supporters of FACT might also favour pornography, and want it available to, and appropriate for, women.

This division over pornography illustrates that what is at stake in the feminist movement is not simply gender, but sex. That women should have the same rights as men may seem obvious as an issue of human rights, but if this is how feminism is perceived, it can be taken as affirmation not only of equality but of sameness—of the view that when it comes right down to it, women are not really different from men. For feminists who insist that women have their own distinctive concerns and needs, the feminist cause is not one of human rights but of assertion of the interests of women. This is what underlies the WAS position, and for feminists of this view the FACT position represents the abandonment of feminism. Catharine MacKinnon speaks for supporters of WAS in their reaction to the emergence of FACT: "At this point, for me, the women's movement I had known came to an end."[18] The cause of women has been abandoned to the priorities of modern liberalism, the mistaken view that rights of the individual must take priority over substantive issues like the abuses to which women are subject. For supporters of FACT, it is WAS that endangers feminism by claiming special rights for themselves at the same time as they seek to restrict the rights of others.

This divergence within feminism is depicted vividly by Naomi Wolf in her distinction between power feminism, which she advocates, and victim feminism, which she deplores. Power feminism is decidedly pro-feminist, but it allows women to decide for themselves what they want, rather than offering doctrinaire prescriptions. Thus, it shares the liberal outlook of the FACT position, rather than presuming to speak for women as a whole, as WAS attempts to do. Wolf expands on the basic direction of promoting freedom for women to choose for themselves in terms of five basic tenets that might be taken to characterize power feminism.

1. Women matter as much as men do.

2. Women have the right to determine their lives.

3. Women's experiences matter.

4. Women have the right to tell the truth about their experiences.

5. Women deserve more of whatever it is they are not getting enough of because they are women: respect, self-respect, education, safety, health, representation, money.[19]

Power feminism is concerned with the empowerment of women. It demands for women, and encourages women to demand for themselves, the opportunities and attention they deserve.

Power feminism shares with victim feminism a concern for women, but they differ fundamentally over their diagnosis of the liabilities women suffer and the prognosis for improvement of their situation. Power feminism identifies the liabilities in order to challenge and overcome them; victim feminism tends to dwell on the liabilities. It sees women as victims of male power structures; rather than seeking to penetrate those structures, as power feminism does, it emphasizes the superiority of women to them:

> "Victim" feminism is a composite. It evolved out of the aversion to power of the radical left, the identification of women and nature popularized with the "cultural feminism" that came of age in the 1970s, old habits of ladylike behavior that were cloaked in the guise of radicalism, and dollops of the work of such writers as Adrienne Rich, with her belief that language is male; Carol Gilligan, with her view of women's different moral reasoning; and Andrea Dworkin and Catharine MacKinnon . . . with their vision of overweening male oppression and female lack of choice.[20]

Thus, where power feminism challenges men at their own game, victim feminism reflects a preoccupation with differences between women and men. Wolf has no patience with this preoccupation because it dwells on problems and siphons off energy from the more practical and promising prospects for increasing power for women.

In fact, Wolf herself represents the two sides of feminism. In *The Beauty Myth*, she can be seen to be championing the cause of victim feminism. Women are seen as victims of expectations of "beauty," as previously they were victims of domestic confinement. In *Fire with Fire*, she challenges women to take control of their own lives, to adopt the agenda of "power feminism," in contrast to the unprofitable preoccupation with obstacles that characterizes victim feminism. The shift is pointed out by Christina Hoff Sommers in *Who Stole Feminism?*, in which the earlier Wolf is aligned with Susan Faludi, author of *Backlash*, as an example of promoters of what Sommers calls "gender feminism."[21] The point of this designation is that women are singled out as victims of a male system. Yet while gender is important in this regard, in another sense Faludi is as opposed to emphasizing the distinctiveness of the feminine, and, conversely, just as insistent on the rights of women as human beings as Sommers is. From that point of view, Faludi and the later Wolf would belong to the equity feminist camp just as surely as Sommers.

One possible resolution to these confusing categories is to make yet a further distinction. Wolf and Faludi would seem to approve of what Sommers calls equity feminism. The complication is that Faludi and at least the earlier Wolf also give some scope to what Sommers derides as gender feminism. The quarrel Sommers has with this is close to the position of the later Wolf, that it diverts attention from positive possibilities for furthering the cause of achieving equity by wallowing in victimization. Sommers concludes her book with confidence that all feminists will one day be equity feminists. The apparent shift in Wolf's position would seem to confirm this. Whether those represented by Faludi will follow suit remains to be seen. Even if this should prove to be the case, however, victim feminism does not represent the only form of gender feminism. In fact, the real contrast with equity feminism might be the positive form of gender feminism that insists on a distinctiveness of women that would not be satisfied with goals of equality.

Sommers seems to regard the negative strain of victim feminism as the only alternative to the equity version she endorses. She opposes gender feminism because it challenges women to see men as the enemy and to oppose virtually every aspect of the present situation as a reflection of male dominance and female imprisonment. Some see this as the inevitable result of the WAS position. The irony is that this view, focused on the distinctive concerns of women and intent on protecting them, ends up being opposed to sex, because there really is no healthy female sexuality. Taken to the extreme, these women are against sex because all sex is seen to be patriarchal.[22] Thus, sex is opposed in the name of gender. An extreme expression of this view sees all women as prostitutes and slaves; marriage is merely generalized prostitution in a patriarchal society. Women have to break free from this male-defined way of seeing life.

> As long as we're concentrating on the men, doing everything with our pimps in mind, we're never going to break free. Our pimps are the men around us. They're the legislators, professors, ministers— none of you still *has* ministers or priests, I trust? Our pimps are our fathers, our husbands, our sons. To be everything in relation to them is slavery.[23]

In one sense, this call to arms sounds like Wolf's promotion of power feminism. It is fundamentally different, however, in that its castigation of men places it decidedly in the victim feminism camp. Wolf wants space for women in the world dominated by men. This version of victim feminism calls for total rejection of that world, on the assumption that that is the only world there is. The apparent compromise with patriarchy, which the later Wolf and Sommers would be seen to promote from this perspective, is not the only alternative to such victim feminism, however.

There is also a positive version of gender feminism, which emphasizes the distinctiveness of women's experience of life as a positive alternative to the directions seen by men. Through interviews with women about their approach to moral issues, Carol Gilligan discovered that the vision of moral maturity of her mentor in moral psychology at Harvard, Lawrence Kohlberg, not only did not have a corner on moral understanding, but, in fact, was assuming a view of morality that was very different from that reflected by the women. On Kohlberg's scale, women generally did not manage to reach more than half-way to moral maturity. They seemed to lack the ability to stand back to gain the impartial perspective necessary for appreciating moral principles. What Gilligan discovered was that seeing this as indicative of moral immaturity was not the only possible reading. The responses of the women she interviewed suggested another explanation: that women see morality in very different terms. Further research in this area "suggests a new mapping of the moral domain."[24] This mapping results in a morality of care emerging as characteristic of women, in contrast to the morality of justice assumed by the male point of view, and taken to be definitive of morality as such.

> Justice and care as two ideals of human relationship provide the coordinates for a new theory of human development. Two ways of thinking about moral reasoning and moral emotions when taken together can account for observed similarities and differences between males and females.[25]

Our understanding of morality has been shaped by men, who tend to stand back and attempt to arrive at impersonal moral principles that will assure the most just balancing among the interests of the individuals involved in a moral dilemma. Women do not seem to be particularly adept at this, not, Gilligan suggests, because they are morally inferior, but because they see morality differently. They are not inclined to try to work out impersonal principles; their inclination is to enter into the situation, identifying with the people experiencing the moral dilemma and seeking to resolve the difficulty through this direct form of caring.

The proposal that women have a unique perspective on morality has drawn criticism from feminists, who contend that Gilligan is playing into the hands of advocates of the conventional differentiation between men and women, whereby men are seen to be rational and women emotional. Men see morality as a matter of rational principles of justice; women see morality in terms of emotional caring. Gilligan replies that it is her critics who are assuming that the standard male view of morality is the only possible one. She illustrates the point in terms of the issue of male and female approaches to violence.

> My critics are concerned about stereotypes that portray women as lacking in anger and aggression; but they do not consider the lower incidence of violence in women's fantasies and behavior to be a sex difference worth exploring. Thus my critics essentially accept the psychology I call into question—the psychology that has equated male with human in defining human nature and thus has construed evidence of sex differences as a sign of female deficiency.[26]

To deny distinctiveness in female experience may be more reflective of the acceptance of male definition than to claim uniqueness for female experience. From this perspective, what Sommers calls "equity feminism" and Wolf "power feminism" appears not so much the only positive alternative to victim feminism, but a capitulation to male visions and structures.

The basic differences among feminists as to the analysis of the problem and proposals for solutions may ultimately revolve around this difference between equity feminists and gender feminists in the positive sense. Thus, the proposals of feminists remain ambiguous because of uncertainty over whether the point is for women to have more scope to become more like men or more scope to develop their distinctive identities as women. Wolf's proposal to leave it to women to choose what they want might sound like a neutral solution, but this is only because it reflects the modern liberal outlook that has come to be taken for granted. The proposal, then, is really for women to become more like men. The alternative would be to seek to transform our fundamental structures and ways of living in terms more peculiar to the outlook and experience of women, as Gilligan suggests. Either way, fundamental mythic visions are at stake.

Feminist Programs

The conventional feminist claim to be dealing with the cultural issue of gender, rather than the biological issue of sex, does not correspond to the realities of the feminist debate. Feminism faces a basic division over the importance of sex, of whether the difference between male and female is to be denied or emphasized. The result of this is that not only does sex occupy a prominent place on the feminist agenda, but it is elevated to mythic proportions as a fundamental perspective on reality. What is involved in approaching reality from the vantage point of sex? Is it sensible to think that sex could constitute the clue to the meaning of life? Feminism represents the implicit claim that it is. For committed feminists, nothing takes priority over gender. This scope of the sex myth is most evident in how feminism deals with the divine.

An initial concern of feminism in terms of divinity is with masculine language. Identification of God as Father or Lord, and the corresponding pronouns, he and him, are seen to be indicative of patriarchy. A pioneer of feminist theology, Mary Daly, contended that if God is male, then male is God.[27] If God is thought of in male terms, then male supremacy is reinforced in society. The response that this should demand varies among feminists. Some find feminist possibilities in the traditional language, so that the doctrine of the Trinity, for example, may be seen to allow for a balancing of the masculine connotations of Father and Son by understanding God as Spirit as feminine. When this is combined with the proposal of some theologians that Spirit should be thought of as the comprehensive reality of God, in contrast to the attribution of this role to Father in the traditional reading, it could involve a significant recognition of feminine dimensions of divinity. Others propose new terms in an effort to balance male language with female designations; for example, God may be identified as Mother as well as Father. Sallie McFague suggests a revised trinity of Mother, Lover, and Friend.[28] For many feminists, however, such responses amount only to tinkering with patriarchy. They insist on replacing God with the Goddess, or even dispense with the whole notion of divinity.

The displacement of God with the Goddess has even given birth to a new term for the reflection that this involves; theology becomes thealogy.[29] The reflection that thealogy involves reveals a variety of meanings in affirmation of the Goddess. For some, it is a feminine version of God, meant to counter the male connotations of traditional representations of the divine. For others, however, any sense of a reality out there represents the lingering legacy of patriarchy.[30] "It is the political legacy of White Christianity that seeks to ally Goddess thealogies with God the Mother or the Great Mother, Earth Mother, or other such designations."[31] Radical feminist references to the Goddess are not pointing to an immanent substitute for the patriarchal God, but to a new way of relating among women themselves, a way of mutuality, which stands in sharp contrast to the hierarchical, patriarchal God.[32]

The most distinctive theological stances in feminism once again reveal the basic division that runs through the whole movement. Advocacy of the Goddess, in opposition to the patriarchal God, represents a theological insistence on the distinctiveness of the feminine; rejection of any wider reference for the Goddess in insistence on the social reality of mutuality can be seen to parallel the direction of secularization in patriarchal culture, however much the social shape of mutuality itself may be seen to contrast with the hierarchical shape of patriarchal society. The theological expression of these two basic directions in feminism highlights this unresolved schism at the heart of the feminist movement and also illustrates what is at stake in elevating sex to the level of myth.

That the focus on social mutuality represents a version of the central direction of modern Western secularization is illustrated directly in Mary Daly's early quarrel with the patriarchal nature of Christianity. The complaint that male imagery and language support male dominance in society turns into references to deity for social purposes. When Daly says that if God is male, then male is God, it can carry two quite different meanings: it can involve recognition of the social significance of theology or extend to a theologizing of society. As recognition of the social significance of theology, it challenges us to recognize the social basis and implications of all our views of deity. How we think of God will reflect our situation in life and the directions we take for granted; referring to the divine in male terms means social advantage for males. To make this relation absolute and equate views of divinity with social arrangements, however, is tantamount to subordinating divinity to society, so that views of deity are nothing more than reflections of social arrangements, in this case, a means of assuring male superiority.

This inversion may even be a central ingredient of the feminist program, insofar as that program centres on promoting equality in contrast to the hierarchical stance identified with patriarchy. "We understand then that that paradigm—that power-over paradigm, that sadomasochism paradigm which is patriarchy—extends to everything, that it is the model for all social institutions, for all economic structures, for international politics."[33] In social relations, this means men over women, whites over blacks, big nations over small ones, humans over other life forms. Feminism seeks to expose and oppose this hierarchical stance in the interests of equality and mutuality. This direction carries a certain intuitive appeal in the wake of modern democratic sentiments, but how feasible radical egalitarianism would be in practice is another matter. People differ in abilities and ambition, and social stability and progress would seem to demand an inevitable element of direction from the top. More significant for our present purposes are the theological implications of radical egalitarianism.

Hierarchy is equated with patriarchy, so that any element of vertical social arrangement is seen to be a reflection of male perspective and priorities. This critique also extends, as in the inversion of society and God by Daly, to any understanding of the divine. Not only on the social level, but with deity as well, hierarchy is out. But what kind of deity is limited to our level? Are we really dealing with divinity at all, if hierarchy is ruled out? To pose the issue in more directly feminist terms, is hierarchy exclusively a male characteristic, or is it an indispensable quality of the divine? When it engages in an absolute onslaught on hierarchy, denouncing hierarchy as such, and not only social hierarchy, feminism can be seen to involve an intrinsically atheistic bias. The result is striking even to feminist theologians.

> What strikes me about much modern theology—and this is not least true of feminist theology—is how profoundly secular it is. It is as though theology has lost its moorings. In the case of feminist theology, what seems to have replaced talk of God is largely talk of women's experience. It is not even women's experience of God; it is simply women's experience.[34]

Whatever the prospects for a significantly different social form of life characterized by genuine mutuality, on the theological level, this approach to feminism stands directly in line with modern secular rejection of any serious consideration of the divine.

In the other basic theological direction of feminism, where the transcendent God is replaced by the immanent Goddess, some sense of hierarchy is retained insofar as the divine is seen as distinctive from us. The substitution of the Goddess, then, remains explicitly theological, rather than abandoning theology entirely for a secular social agenda. However, advocates of the more radical pursuit of this direction end up with positions that do not seem so different from the direct abandonment of the divine. The need for the Goddess arises, according to Carol Christ, because women cannot see themselves represented in the male God of the Bible.

> For me the biblical God was "beyond sexuality" as theological tradition asserted, but he retained a certain aura of masculine presence and authority. It wasn't until I said Goddess that I realized how significant that remaining aura of masculinity was in my image of God. Not until I said Goddess did I realize that I had never felt fully included in the fullness of my being as a woman in masculine or neutralized imagery for divinity.[35]

Although the official line is that God is beyond sexuality, masculine designations have predominated, with the result that the God who is above sexuality evokes male associations.

Christ's depiction of the sense of exclusion sounds a note that must be heard, just as does Daly's insistence on the social significance of theogical imagery. However, just as Daly's concern can flip to the opposite extreme, resulting in a theologizing of the social, so Christ's lament for female exclusion can reflect an absolutization of the female. She complains, for example, that in the singing of the Gloria, a girl "must begin to recognize that the power and glory are not to be hers."[36] The implication is that the power and the glory are restricted to boys and men. The point of the Gloria, however, is to ascribe power and glory to God.

As with the hierarchical displacement of equity feminism, the theological expression of gender feminism, when pursued to its extremes, results in complete displacement of the divine. Christ is quite frank in her admission that the fundamental consideration is not the Goddess, but the experience and aspirations of contemporary women. "Ancient traditions are tapped selectively and eclectically, but they are not considered authoritative for modern consciousness."[37] The Goddess represents a symbolic expression for the empowerment of women. "The night when I expressed my anger at God and heard a still, small voice saying 'in God is a woman like yourself' was the beginning of my remembering, which was also a re–membering, enabling me to claim my female being and my female body in a new way."[38] The hurt and anger of feminists such as Daly and Christ raises serious questions for traditional theological imagery. That the resulting displacement of the divine is the answer, however, represents a massive mythic shift.

The implication of the concern with substituting the Goddess for God in order to have a symbol of divinity relevant to women, is that the divine is a direct reflection of ourselves. Women can identify only with a female divinity, and a male deity is appropriate only for men. But this can be true only if sex is more basic than divinity. Where traditional Western religion identified God in male terms, giving rise to the charges of patriarchy, this form was quite different from the intent of these traditions. What distinguished the God of Israel was that "He" was above identification in terms of sex, in contrast to the gods and goddesses of the fertility religions, who were identified by and with sex. This was understood to distinguish God not only from the gods and goddesses, but from us. The God of Israel was holy—that is, separate. Feminism has made us aware of how far this intent was compromised through masculine designation of this supposedly suprasexual divinity.

The theological import of feminism is really to sharpen the modern question as to whether there can be any sense of divinity that is not a human projection. The answer of feminism, in either form, would seem to be "No!"

Not only does ardent feminism reach beyond its own professed focus on issues of gender to involve direct confrontation over the significance of sex, but this confrontation is made possible only because of a more pervasive unspoken agreement that sex is the all-important issue. So important is it that these two sides of feminism end up according sex definitive status, so that even the divine must be defined in terms of sex in order to have any credibility at all. Those who see sex as largely insignificant tend to follow the direction of male-shaped secular culture in abandoning the divine for direct concentration on the social agenda; those who emphasize the importance of sex seek to replace God with the Goddess. Insofar as the divine does come into the picture, it is almost bound to be as barrier to, or means for promoting, aspects of gender. Serious feminism thus illustrates the considerations that are involved when priority is given to the sex myth.

Notes

1. Betty Friedan, *The Feminine Mystique* (New York: Dell, 1963), p. 37.

2. Naomi Wolf, *Fire with Fire: The New Female Power and How to Use It* (Toronto: Vintage Books, 1994), p. 167.

3. Susan Faludi, *Backlash: The Undeclared War Against American Women* (New York: Crown Publishers, 1991), p. 53.

4. Germaine Greer, *The Female Eunuch* (New York: McGraw-Hill, 1971), p. 294.

5. Friedan, *The Feminine Mystique*, p. 37.

6. Ibid., p. 96.

7. Greer, *The Female Eunuch*, p. 61.

8. Friedan, *The Feminine Mystique*, p. 68.

9. Naomi Wolf, *The Beauty Myth* (Toronto: Vintage Books, 1991), p. 10.

10. Ibid., p. 91.

11. Ibid., pp. 11 and 15.

12. Ibid., p. 10.

13. Ibid., p. 13.

14. Ibid., p. 282.

15. Friedan, *The Feminine Mystique*, p. 93.

16. Wolf, *Fire with Fire*, p. xxv.

17. Wolf, *The Beauty Myth*, p. 274; cf. pp. 280ff.

18. Catharine A. MacKinnon, "Liberalism and the Death of Feminism," in Dorchen Leidholdt and Janice G. Raymond, *The Sexual Liberals and the Attack on Feminism* (New York: Pergamon Press, 1990), p. 9.

19. Wolf, *Fire with Fire*, p. 138.

20. Ibid., p. 143.

21. Christina Hoff Sommers. *Who Stole Feminism? How Women Have Betrayed Women* (New York: Simon and Schuster, 1994), pp. 228, 244–5.

22. Wendy Stock, "Toward a Feminist Praxis of Sexuality," in Leidholdt and Raymond, *The Sexual Liberals and the Attack on Feminism*, p. 148.

23. Sonia Johnson, "Taking Our Eyes Off the Guys," in Leidholdt and Raymond, *The Sexual Liberals and the Attack on Feminism*, p. 59.

24. Carol Gilligan, "Preface," in Carol Gilligan, Janie Victoria Ward, and Jill McLean Taylor, with Betty Bardige, eds., *Mapping the Moral Domain* (Cambridge, MA: Center for the Study of Gender Education and Human Development, Harvard University Graduate School of Education, 1988), p. ii.

25. Ibid., p. iv.

26. Carol Gilligan, "Reply," *Signs.* 11 (1986): 331.

27. Mary Daly, *Beyond God the Father* (Boston: Beacon Press, 1973), p. 13.

28. Sallie McFague, *Models of God: Theology for an Ecological, Nuclear Age* (Philadelphia: Fortress Press, 1987).

29. Carol P. Christ, "Why Women Need the Goddess," in Carol P. Christ and Judith Plaskow, eds., *Womanspirit Rising* (New York: Harper and Row, 1979), p. 287, n. 12.

30. Ibid., p. 278.

31. Susan Brooks Thistlewaite, *Sex, Race, and God: Christian Feminism in Black and White* (New York: Crossroad, 1989), p. 123.

32. See Christ, "Why Women Need the Goddess," pp. 284ff., and Thistlewaite, *Sex, Race, and God*, p. 111.

33. Johnson, "Taking Our Eyes Off the Guys," p. 56.

34. Daphne Hampson, *Theology and Feminism* (Oxford: Basil Blackwell, 1990), p. 170.

35. Carol P. Christ, *Laughter of Aphrodite, Reflections on a Journey to the Goddess* (San Francisco: HarperSanFrancisco, 1987), p. 67.

36. Ibid., p. 95.

37. Ibid., p. 120.

38. Ibid., p. 100.

8

A SOCIETY MYTH

W ITH EVERY myth we have considered, we have ended up in the realm of religion. Science, sport, sex, and consumption may fill roles for us that formerly would have involved religion. How this has happened, and in particular how we can be doing something like this without generally realizing it, is explained to some extent by the fact that the transcendent horizon of religion has been replaced by the kinds of myths we have considered. However, in itself, this would leave us with a collection of rather loose-fitting interests and perspectives that could provide at best a series of preoccupations and diversions, something like the eclectic images suggested by Roland Barthes. This would mean that we have left religion behind, no longer sensing any need for its unifying focus. More careful consideration of our present outlook would probably find that among these contemporary myths that give life shape and meaning, some are more fundamental than others, and, indeed, one in particular will tend to assume the unifying role that used to be performed by religion. Although this source of unification might be different for some, for most of us, and for our culture at large, that role is apt to be performed by the society myth. The basic comprehensive reality we refer to in our discussions, the horizon of meaning that we take for granted, as our ancestors took the reality of God for granted, is society.

In one sense, "society" is simply ourselves, collectively, and so it is just an easy way of talking about our immediate situation in more general terms. At the same time, however, "society" stands over against each of us, and perhaps also over against all of us collectively, if not in some mystical fashion, at least in the form of institutional structures to which we are subject, however much they may be of our own devising. This comprehensive range of reference gives the notion of "society" a prominence that makes it a leading candidate to be one of the major metaphysical realities of present-day academia in particular and of Western, and increasingly world, culture in general. It is the horizon of meaning that we take for granted as the bounds of reality as we know it. "Society" can thus be seen as the God-substitute of secular culture.

Consider how "society" is used in such an absolute sense in a recent best-seller, *The Beauty Myth*, by Naomi Wolf. She says things such as, "Under the myth, women's bodies are not our own but society's"[1] and "Society really doesn't care about women's appearance per se, what generally matters is that women remain willing to let others tell them what they can and cannot do."[2] What is this reality that controls women? This could be simply a way of referring to all of us collectively; it could refer to the institutional structures and expectations that shape our lives, but it seems to mean more than this. It carries the connotation of the ultimate horizon of meaning. Society is the context of life itself. The emergence and extent of that connotation is most evident among those who concentrate on society as a subject itself: sociologists.

Society Explains Religion

If society represents the secular substitute for God, this means that it has come to occupy roles formerly filled by religion. How society has filled the vacuum created by the demotion of religion is an involved process, but it is possible to identify some distinctive highlights. We have already seen how the acknowledged founder of sociology, Auguste Comte, consigned religion to the distant past and welcomed the opportunities afforded for a mature human society. Yet his attempt to replace the vagaries of mythology and the speculations of metaphysical religion with a positive religion of science was too contrived to catch on, and so it withered away far more decisively than the religion he sought to replace. Karl Marx's tirades against the class exploitations of religion and call for an egalitarian society in which religion would no longer be needed were more influential. Yet Marx was more significant as a prophet and inspirer of social vision than as a theoretician of the social itself. The social displacement of religion has been presented most influentially by Émile Durkheim.

While Marx dismissed religion as a symptom of an ill-structured society, real and significant in but confined to those circumstances, and so dispensable when they were corrected, Durkheim regarded it in more positive terms. While Marx begins from the premise that religions themselves are fundamentally false, Durkheim assumes that "all are true in their own fashion."[3] In this vein, he focuses on the most elementary forms of religion in the confidence that what can be discovered there will be relevant for more developed forms because there is a common thread running through all religion. The form that he identifies as most distinctive is totemism. The alternatives of animism and naturism are rejected because animism is too nebulous, with spirits abounding all over the place, and naturism too mundane, being confined to the scope of nature itself. Totemism illumines that middle area where there is something that elicits the respect and reverence that characterizes religion. That something cannot derive from ourselves or from the natural order but represents something beyond. That other domain is symbolized by the totem, which elicits this kind of respect from the clan that embraces it. Further, the object of respect expands beyond the totem when the clan becomes incorporated into wider levels of association, and gods, or even one supreme God, become the object of devotion. The significance of this recognition, Durkheim contends, is that it indicates how the process that produces such reverence is itself essentially social.

The claim is not, of course, that people actually believe in society rather than in the totem or in God. The point is rather that the practice of religion actually involves the emergence of these beliefs because of the effect of social experience. The definition of the source of loyalty and devotion develops out of the dynamics of group associations. Ritual, and not belief, is the basic religious reality. But the reality behind religious ritual is society: "Religion ceases to be an inexplicable hallucination and takes a foothold in reality. In fact, we can say that the believer is not deceived when he believes in the existence of a moral power upon which he depends and from which he receives all that is best in him: this power exists, it is society."[4] Durkheim is advancing what has come to be known as a functionalist account of religion. It is explained in terms of its function, which is essentially to promote the cohesion of society. Religion provides the common allegiance that makes social life possible, which is why it is significant, true, and finally indispensable. That significance, truth, and indispensability, however, are simply functional—or are they?

As Durkheim sees it, we are caught between eras: "The old gods are growing old or already dead, and others are not yet born."[5] He is confident that a new effervescence will provide a guide for humanity, but the form it will take remains to be seen; that it will be quite different from traditional religious versions seems to be taken for granted. Durkheim sees no significant difference between "an assembly of Christians celebrating the principal dates of the life of Christ, or of Jews remembering the exodus from Egypt or the promulgation of the decalogue, and a reunion of citizens commemorating the promulgation of a new moral or legal system or some great event in the national life."[6] That Durkheim can equate civil ceremonies with religious rituals indicates that he is moving beyond a functional treatment of religion toward an endorsement of the subject matter of religion itself. His treatment of the ritual practices of religion as forms of social bonding involves a substantive assumption that the reality of religion is social. In the end, the restriction to a functional focus on ritual is not sustainable. Ideas and beliefs emerge as the inevitable core of the position being advanced.[7] Not just functionally, but metaphysically, "God is a symbol of society."[8] Thus, society is more basic than God. It is society, rather than God, that constitutes the horizon of reality. "Durkheim gives a wholly sociological analysis of not only the origin and function but also the content of religion."[9] The social function of religion exhausts its reality. The collective impact of social experience is what underlies religious phenomena, and that is all that underlies them.

Thus, the results of the Durkheimian analysis are no more reassuring for religion than are those of Comte or Marx. In fact, as Talcott Parsons has suggested, the results are doubly disturbing precisely because Durkheim seemed to be defending religion against those who would write it off: "Perhaps no proposition could awaken more instantaneous indignation in religious circles than this. The man who has started out to vindicate the permanence of religion against those who would dissolve it into illusion emerges with an even more objectionably 'materialistic' view than those he criticizes."[10] The disappointment of believers who might have looked to Durkheim for vindication of the enduring significance of religion is particularly poignant because in the end the position being advocated, far from assuming the truth of all religions, "in their own fashion," as initially suggested, really requires that every religion be false in its own terms, except Durkheim's own sociological religion. This was put to Durkheim himself directly by Gustave Belot when the former attempted to defend his position at a meeting of the *Union des Libres Penseurs et des Libres Croyants pour la Culture Morale* in 1914. "Durkheim, Belot insisted, was (despite his claim to the contrary) maintaining that all religions were false, in so far as they did not accept his own theory."[11]

What is more, this conviction that religion is false except as a social adhesive is Durkheim's assumption, and not simply the conclusion at which he arrives.[12] Indeed, he openly states his conclusion at the beginning of the book: "The general conclusion of the book which the reader has before him is that religion is something eminently social."[13] The vigour with which he develops this thesis suggests that this indication of the conclusion is far more than a concession to the reader. It is the cardinal assumption, which the whole book is dedicated to bolstering. It represents what W.E.H. Stanner has called Durkheim's "sociocentric fixation," a fixation that Stanner regards as "all-consuming."[14] In retrospect, perhaps the most distinctive element in Durkheim's position is not that he has inverted society and religion, but that he is so explicit about this, which makes him one of the most influential pioneers in this transition. In looking at what he says, we see what we are likely to take for granted today. We assume the reality and significance of society. We might not be too sure what to make of religion and the transcendent reverence it connotes. What we will be inclined to assume is that whatever it is, religion is a social phenomenon.

Society Defines Reality

The genuine myth is the perspective that is so taken for granted that it is never isolated for explicit attention. Not many candidates remain for this status amid the penetrating searchlights of contemporary self-consciousness. "Society" can lay claim to it more credibly than most, not only because of the ease with which the social horizon is taken for granted today, but, more intrinsically, because it seems to provide the thread that holds the diversity of perspectives on life together. The wide variety of positions and proposals at least share the formal base of coming from a particular social configuration: they reflect the outlook of a society in terms either of a whole culture or of some specific segment of more restricted interests or ambitions.

Once the importance of locatedness is recognized, it becomes impossible to retreat behind social consciousness to retrieve a more immediate grasp on reality. This grasp is mediated through the peculiarities of our social inheritance, especially through its linguistic possibilities. So fundamental does this recognition become that language and society can come to be seen not only as the media through which reality is mediated but as the defining parameters of reality as such. This process is illustrated by Durkheim himself: "Since the universe does not exist except in so far as it is thought of, and since it is not completely thought of except by society, it takes a place in this latter; it becomes a part of society's interior life, while this is the totality, outside of which nothing exists."[15] The suggestion that the universe exists within society is bound to be perplexing, if not ludicrous, to everyday common sense that has been sheltered from the explicit complications of modern self-consciousness. Even with some sense of those complications, however, the starkness of the stance is striking. It is one thing to be told that our view of the universe is shaped by the culture in which we live; it is something else to be told that outside of that cultural context nothing exists. We have to wonder whether the means have not become transformed into an end; the language, images, and concepts of a particular society are taken as the subject matter they are intended to articulate.

The inversion is indicated by Durkheim's location of the universe within society, but it is articulated more fully in Peter L. Berger and Thomas Luckmann's *The Social Construction of Reality*, in which they illustrate this prominence of society as horizon of meaning in three short sentences. *"Society is a human product. Society is an objective reality. Man is a social product."*[16] Society is what emerges from our collective interaction; it, in turn, shapes us. This dialectical process is reality. The import of Berger and Luckmann's summation is indicated in their depiction of the sociologist as standing between the philosopher and the "man in the street." The latter functions with a naïve immediacy that is largely untroubled by questions of the nature of reality and how we know it. What is generally accepted is taken to be an accurate reflection of the way things are. On the other hand, such questions are the preoccupation of the philosopher, who is concerned to attempt to know what is real and to clarify how we know it. In this understanding of philosophy, Berger and Luckmann might be overlooking how much philosophy has come under the same spell that has spawned the social sciences. Be that as it may, in this perhaps more traditional view of philosophy, sociology falls between the naïve immediacy of the "man in the street" and the reflective ambitions of the philosopher. It looks at different approaches to life in terms of the social circumstances at stake in those approaches.

Berger and Luckmann present the differences most graphically in terms of the presence or absence of quotation marks in the speech of these three principals. The "man in the street" does not notice the quotation marks that surround his own speech; he simply assumes that he is talking about reality. The philosopher is aware of the quotation marks and attempts to remove them, so that we will have reliable access to reality. The sociologist is stuck with the quotation marks.[17] Social scientists are neither condoning the generally accepted view of reality in any time or place, nor seeking to get behind it to see if it is really accurate; their role is to investigate the social circumstances in which various views are articulated. While the "man in the street" naïvely thinks that he is talking about reality directly, and the philosopher seeks to gain critical access to reality, social scientists do not profess to have any such access. The most they can do is to consider how different people "construct reality." This is the official line. If we notice what social scientists actually do, however, this modesty certainly seems to be misplaced. Remember, they have assured us that "Society is an objective reality," and they have defined and restricted this reference through the further dialectical assurances that "Society is a human product" and "Man is a social product." In their original form, not only do these statements lack quotation marks; they are presented with the emphasis of italics. This is the way things are. This is the reality that both the "man in the street" and the philosopher exemplify, even though they might not appreciate it themselves. "Society is an objective reality."

We have seen that Berger and Luckmann insist on asserting that "Society is an objective reality." Far from a hypothetical, working principle, this clearly seems to represent an uncompromising articulation of the way things are. It seems clear that amid the complexity of contemporary experience, and the self-consciousness that this complexity elicits, there remains an indispensable intention to know, deal with, and give articulation to a vision of reality itself. However provisional our perspectives may be, they are serious only because they are characterized by what Michael Polanyi has called "universal intent."[18] In the present context, this means that we must pursue this self-consciousness to ask whether the society myth can really carry the weight it has come to be routinely assigned. Granted the very different understandings of the universe involved in a Hindu outlook, for example, and in a modern Western secular perspective, what is at stake in these is this common reality that we in the West call a universe. There may be a "world of difference" between our sense of universe and a Far Eastern sense of the illusory nature of this present realm of attachments, and it is also quite clear that we can gain some sense of this difference only through our own conceptual frameworks, but it is the nature of reality that we are concerned with and not these formulations in themselves.

Although we are social beings, and achieve any of the understanding we do through the vehicles of particular categories and concepts formed in particular linguistic communities, our self-conscious awareness of our locatedness causes a short-circuit when that context itself becomes the horizon of meaning and reality. In our social self-consciousness, we seem to be in danger of turning the windows through which former ages looked out on life into mirrors in which we see only reflections of ourselves. To claim that the universe exists within society, as Durkheim does, is a dangerous half-truth. The truth is more adequately portrayed in Charles Hartshorne's contention that while reality is inherently social, as Whitehead held, there is a wider reality than society as such. "That we are social through and through is a Whiteheadian idea. The final society, however, is the cosmos."[19] As both Hartshorne and Whitehead recognized, this appreciation of the cosmos as the wider and inevitable context of our lives opens out finally into theological questions evoked by the cosmos and by the fact of life itself. To regard society itself as the ultimate horizon equates humanity with ultimate reality.

Society Is Reality

The extent of the inversion, whereby society has come to bear connotations of the Absolute, is indicated by the way in which even sociologists sympathetic to the distinctiveness of religion and its transcendent reference end up subsuming religion under the category of society. In recent years, some prominent sociologists and anthropologists have displayed an interest in, and sympathy for, religion that stands in stark contrast to the all but totally secular horizon that characterized sociology in its formative phase. These social scientists want to recognize the significance and legitimacy of religion in its own right. "What is true of Geertz is also true of Berger, Turner, Bellah, Douglas and other contemporary sociologists of religion: religion primarily originates and functions to fulfil the individual's innate need for meaning."[20] Where classical sociologists such as Comte, Marx, and Durkheim, in their different ways, allowed religion to be absorbed entirely by the social horizon, these contemporary anthropologists and sociologists see social forces shaping religion through particular social and cultural influences, but the reality itself is taken to involve a realm of meaning that transcends the social horizon.

In spite of his interest in the social construction of reality, Peter Berger insists on the independent integrity of religion.

> It seems to me that the essence of religion has been the confrontation with an *other*, believed to exist as a reality in the universe external to and vastly different from man—something that is indeed "out there," as Robinson puts it. The fundamental religious proposition, therefore, is that man is not alone in reality. Whether this is or is not part of the socially objectivated world view of a particular society is as irrelevant to its possible validity as, for instance, the absence from the world view of Zulu society of any notion of quantum theory is irrelevant to the validity of the quantum theory. The theological enterprise reduces itself to absurdity if it engages itself with the fundamental proposition of religion on any terms other than those of its validity.[21]

At the same time, however, as a sociologist, Berger is committed to the view that we have no access to that *other* apart from the categories and perspectives provided by the society to which we belong. From that point of view, claims about a reality other than ourselves must be particularly suspect as the sociological sin of "reification," which "can be described as an extreme step in the process of objectification, whereby the objectivated world loses its comprehensibility as a human enterprise and becomes fixated as non-human, non-humanizable, inert facticity."[22] The theological object that Berger insists constitutes the essence of religion would seem to be a prime candidate for dismissal as an extravagance of sociological reification. As Berger himself notes, when speaking from the perspective of a sociologist who sees affirmations as human projections: "Symbolic universes which proclaim that *all* reality is humanly meaningful and call upon the *entire* cosmos to signify the validity of human existence, constitute the farthest reaches of this projection."[23] It is not surprising that Gregory Baum should complain that Berger moves from a functionalist understanding of concepts in terms of social processes to an affirmation of particular concepts as true and reflective of reality, without any indication of how he distinguishes one from the other.[24] If our grasp of reality is mediated through concepts and language that have developed in a particular society to the point where those vehicles actually construct reality for us, how can we ever have any confidence that those constructs are really significantly referential? Berger's stance as a sociologist undermines the theological affirmation he also wants to make.[25] The social self-consciousness that underlies this dilemma can easily result in the functional significance of the social dimension acquiring such importance that it takes on ontological status itself, so that society becomes the assumed reality, regardless of what one might want to affirm on a more personal level.

The dilemma faced by Berger is intensified for Robert Bellah. Like Berger, Bellah departs from the anti-religious bias of traditional sociology by insisting on taking religion seriously in its own right. "I believe those of us who study religion must have a kind of double vision—at the same time that we try to study religious systems as objects we need also to apprehend them as religious subjects ourselves."[26] His chief method for developing this direction has been through his repudiation of what he calls "symbolic reductionism," the various attempts to explain religion in other terms, in favour of "symbolic realism," which involves taking religious symbols seriously in their own right. "Symbolic realism simply holds that religious symbols are not primarily social or psychological projection systems (though they always contain some projective elements) but the ways in which persons and societies express their sense of the fundamental nature of reality, of the totality of experience."[27] His answer to Berger's dilemma is to affirm the neutral, scientific inquiry that sociology presumably involves, but to reserve the right to inject personal insights that emerge in the course of this endeavour.

> I do not wish to deny to any scholar the "neutral zone" within which he can carry out his studies. There is no obligation that I would place higher than defense of that zone. But if a conception of religion which has in part grown out of the scientific study of religion has profound implications for the integration of my life, the life of my students and the validity of my culture then I intend to say so.[28]

Thus, he directly confronts Berger's dilemma of recognizing that religion has its own focus and subject matter, although it is also a human phenomenon subject to study by the human sciences. His solution is to allow for recognition of that focus and subject matter in the very pursuit of scientific analysis. Whether this reconciliation is as straightforward as Bellah makes it sound, however, is another matter.

The central difficulty in such alignment of religious faith and social science has to do with the neutrality that is attributed to social science. The "neutral zone" that Bellah regards as the highest priority can be taken to be constituted by the distance between the investigator and the subject. The social scientist can claim a certain impartiality because of lack of vested interest in the subject under consideration. Thus, Robert A. Segal suggests that social science deals with the origin, function, and meaning of religion and not with its object.[29] This means that the social sciences attempt to identify the mechanics of belief and even to clarify the meaning of beliefs for believers, but they do not, and cannot, pronounce on the truth of belief or of religion.[30] However, there is an interesting ambiguity in Segal's treatment for elsewhere, he contends that the focus is even narrower. "More frequently, contemporary social scientists avoid the issue of origin altogether and focus directly on function, which they assume, has even less bearing on truth."[31] There is no contradiction in Segal's proposals. The omission of consideration of origin simply represents a further restriction of the sociological horizon. Yet it does raise the interesting question of how social scientists could deal with the origin of religion and not be involved in the issue of truth. The implication of the suggestion that dropping consideration of origin results in the social scientist being even less involved with truth is that involvement with truth is a relative matter. By focusing exclusively on function, social scientists have reduced this involvement to a minimum. Whether this could ever approach zero involvement, so as to constitute neutrality, however, is another matter, especially as Segal also asserts that although a social scientific explanation cannot refute or preclude a theological explanation, it can render such explanation superfluous.[32] If this is not a truth claim, it is difficult to know what would be. One hardly expects to find truth in a dimension dismissed as superfluous; conversely, such dismissal is possible only on the basis of firm confidence that what constitutes truth is clearly known. In this case, the social horizon has acquired an epistemological and metaphysical status that displaces theological considerations.

The perspective implied in Segal's treatment of the relation between the social sciences and religion corresponds closely to what we saw in Durkheim. Society becomes the ultimate subject. But what we must now consider is the possibility that this tendency is also present even among those social scientists who display religious sensibility. For if the engagement of social science with the truth of the area it is dealing with, in this case religion, never reaches zero, how can Bellah equate the pursuit of social science with a "neutral zone"? More significantly, why does he assume that social science occupies a neutral zone, but that religion does not? Is this not tantamount to identifying with Durkheim in his contention that social dynamics are the basic reality, in defiance of the collective religious experience of humanity? The horizon that is taken for granted is humanistic and secular; religion represents an additional dimension that is controversial and problematic. "In fact, by definition Bellah views religion as an anthropological and societal universal."[33] It is humanity and society that are taken for granted; religion has to make its case in their terms. Obviously this is directly contrary to Berger's recognition that "the theological enterprise reduces itself to absurdity if it engages itself with the fundamental proposition of religion on any terms other than those of its validity."[34] Bellah's flirtation with this absurdity threatens to eliminate the gap between his "symbolic realism" and the "symbolic reductionism" he wishes to avoid insofar as the preferred realism of religious symbols is undermined. Since the social symbols are the primary ones, religious affirmations come in as personal qualifications of this assured anthropological base. "Bellah thus paradoxically ends up seemingly 'reducing' religion to social science."[35] That this can happen with the social scientists who are most sympathetic to the distinctive significance of religion is indicative of the thoroughness with which the social has displaced the theological in modern secular culture.

In retrospect, social consciousness appears to be the inevitable successor to the self-consciousness that launched the modern West. Having become aware of our own responsibility for making sense of life, it was only natural that we should proceed from there to become aware of the diversity and precariousness that results from this situation. That we see things as we do is a reflection of the particular society that has shaped our perspective. And further, the way we see things has implications that give advantages to some and disadvantages to others. However, when the recognition involved in the inevitability of the social that constitutes social consciousness moves beyond conditioning our view of reality to the point where it comes to be taken as definitive of reality itself, we have become totally immersed in the society myth.

Once we become aware that we are attributing this status to society, we have three options. We can repudiate it as error and reclaim the direct metaphysical and theological vision that prevailed prior to modern secularity and its expression in social consciousness. We can recognize that society is not God and that it is ridiculous to acquiesce in the society myth in this total and comprehensive sense. If it seems naïve and impractical, if not impossible, to effect such a direct reversal, another option is to accept the inevitability of the social horizon and try to ignore its pretentiousness. Of course, society is not God, but it is the widest horizon that we can get hold of. The third basic possibility is to seek to develop a more subtle understanding of the social, so that its inevitability does not amount to tyranny. This could involve challenging the confinement of society to a secular range, as is involved in the conventional assumption that sees society as totally a human phenomenon or, at least, regards humanity in closed and final terms. To see society as involving more than humanity, or to see humanity as open to a wider dimension of mystery, would involve recognition of the religious dimension of society. Our associations with one another, and the institutional arrangements under which we live, would be seen to open out into a wider mystery, rather than being seen as management targets of social engineering. The success of such attempted penetration of the secular captivity of "society" would depend on maintaining both the insights of social consciousness and the distinctive integrity of the theological dimension. This would mean acknowledging that our only access to the theological depth of reality is through our own particular social location, while at the same time resisting the equation of theological reality with the social as such. This means that the classical displacement of theology by social science must be challenged. "Sociology was offered as an alternative to theological knowledge, and its positive and empirical orientation was set against both metaphysical speculation and the arbitrary 'truths' of Christian revelation."[36] That society can be taken for granted as the neutral horizon of meaning is abundant testimony to the extent to which theology has been sociologized. Once we are aware of this, we must not only question whether society can bear this theological weight, but, if we decide that it cannot, we shall be obliged to pursue a more subtle integration of genuine theological scope with the sociological factors that have been brought to light through social self-consciousness.

What is at stake is illustrated in the emergence of liberation theologies, which seek to present Christian faith in terms of the needs of particular segments of society—the poor in Latin America, blacks in the United States, women, particularly in North America and Europe. One of the most ardent advocates of the feminist version of liberation theology, Mary Daly, proposed early on that if God is male, then male is God.[37] That is, if God is designated in male terms, it has the effect of endorsing and enforcing male dominance in society. This recognition of the reciprocal relation between our understanding of God and the way our society is structured can represent recognition of the social significance of theology or amount to attributing theological significance to society. The difference between these directions is the difference between the application of social consciousness to theology and replacing the object of theology by society in a full endorsement of the society myth. Recognition of the social significance of theology calls for social consciousness in theology. Once we have become aware of the ways in which social arrangements and the social context of theologians impinge on the theological visions they articulate, the social significance of those visions must thereafter be taken into account. Social consciousness leads us to recognize how identifying God almost exclusively in male terms serves to legitimize male superiority in society, and, in retrospect, can be seen to reflect the patriarchal structure of the society in which that vision developed. To take the reference to God to be exhausted by this social significance, however, is possible only by according society itself theological significance. This might be legitimate, even from a theological point of view, if the understanding of society is broad enough to encompass the depth and mystery that has evoked reference to God. In this way, "society" could constitute a way of affirming the divine mystery in ways that are too easily compromised by the confining object connotations of the word "God." To carry this theological level of meaning, however, the understanding of society would have to be divested of the formative secular range of reference with which it has been stamped in its modern usage, particularly through its treatment by the social sciences. Such divestiture represents a formidable agenda for those who would employ social language with theological integrity. It amounts to challenging the cumulative weight of a century and a half of the equation of society with a secular horizon. On the other hand, such a translation may be one of the few ways in which theological sensibility might be tapped in the present. Few frames of reference reach the theological proportions of "society," in the contemporary flourishing of the society myth.

Notes

1. Naomi Wolf, *The Beauty Myth* (Toronto: Vintage Books, 1991), p. 187.

2. Ibid., p. 99.

3. Émile Durkheim, *The Elementary Forms of Religious Life* (New York: Collier Books, 1961), p. 15.

4. Ibid., p. 257.

5. Ibid., p. 475.

6. Ibid. This is perhaps why Jeffrey K. Hadden suggests that Robert Bellah's concept of civil religion might be the clue that eluded Durkheim. Jeffrey K. Hadden, "Editor's Introduction," "The Sociology of Religion of Robert M. Bellah," Review Symposium, *Journal for the Scientific Study of Religion.* 14 (1975): 386.

7. Susan Budd, *Sociologists and Religion* (London: Collier-Macmillan, 1973), p. 42.

8. Randall Collins, *Sociological Insight, An Introduction to Non-Obvious Sociology* (Oxford: Oxford University Press, 1982), p. 35.

9. Robert A. Segal, *Religion and the Social Sciences* (Atlanta: Scholars Press, 1989), p. 114.

10. Talcott Parsons, *The Structure of Social Action* (Glencoe, IL: The Free Press, 1949), p. 417.

11. Steven Lukes, *Émile Durkheim, His Life and Work* (Stanford, CA: Stanford University Press, 1985), p. 518.

12. "In fact, *petitio principii* is, in a sense, a feature of the book as a whole, for Durkheim begins it with his conclusion, building it into his very definition of religion and then seeking to prove it by finding examples." Ibid., p. 481.

13. Durkheim, *The Elementary Forms*, p. 22.

14. Lukes, *Émile Durkheim*, p. 481.

15. Durkheim, *The Elementary Forms*, p. 490.

16. Peter L. Berger and Thomas Luckmann, *The Social Construction of Reality, A Treatise in the Sociology of Knowledge* (Garden City, NY: Doubleday Anchor Books, 1967), p. 61.

17. Ibid., p. 2.

18. Michael Polanyi, *Personal Knowledge, Towards a Post Critical Philosophy* (London: Routledge and Kegan Paul, 1958), pp. 214ff., 301ff., 309, 396.

19. Charles Hartshorne, *Creativity in American Philosophy* (Albany: SUNY Press, 1984), p. 135.

20. Segal, *Religion and the Social Sciences*, p. 123.

21. Peter L. Berger, *Facing Up to Modernity, Excursions in Society, Politics, and Religion* (New York: Basic Books, 1977), p. 181.

22. Berger and Luckmann, *The Social Construction of Reality*, p. 89.

23. Ibid., p. 104.

24. Gregory Baum, "Peter Berger's Unfinished Symphony," in Gregory Baum, ed., *Sociology and Human Destiny* (New York: Seabury Press, 1980), p. 125.

25. As Susan Budd points out, Berger subsumes the sociology of religion under the sociology of knowledge. See Budd, *Sociologists and Religion*, p. 4.

26. Robert N. Bellah, "Christianity and Symbolic Realism," *Journal for the Scientific Study of Religion*. 9 (1970): 95.

27. Robert N. Bellah, "Response to Comments on 'Christianity and Symbolic Realism,'" *Journal for the Scientific Study of Religion*. 9 (1970): 113; see also Robert N. Bellah, *Beyond Belief* (New York: Harper & Row, 1970), pp. 251ff.

28. Bellah, "Response to Comments on 'Christianity and Symbolic Realism,'" p. 115.

29. Segal, *Religion and the Social Sciences*, p. 39.

30. Ibid.

31. Ibid., p. 90.

32. Ibid., p. 78.

33. John A. Coleman, "The Renewed Covenant: Robert N. Bellah's Vision of Religion and Society," in Baum, *Sociology and Human Destiny*, p. 92.

34. See above, n. 21.

35. Dick Anthony and Thomas Robbins, "From Symbolic Realism to Structuralism," "Review Symposium: Robert Bellah," *Journal for the Scientific Study of Religion*. 14 (1975): 404.

36. Bryan Wilson, "The Return of the Sacred," *Journal for the Scientific Study of Religion*. 18 (1979): 269.

37. Mary Daly, *Beyond God the Father* (Boston: Beacon Press, 1973), p. 13.

9

A RELIGION MYTH

Recognition of the presence of living myth indicates that we have not left myth behind nearly as decisively as the prevailing view assumes. The journalistic sense of myth as falsehood that reflects naïveté of the past or of other people does not begin to recognize the pervasive presence of mythic commitments that give shape and direction to our own lives. What we have seen is that not only do we live by myth, but these mythic commitments become most evident when they take on religious proportions. Every living myth we have considered ends up reaching into religious proportions, and this is the point at which the myth itself becomes most visible. This suggests a close connection between myth and religion. It might even be taken to imply that we should equate religion with living myth as such. In order to do this, however, we must have a sense of what religion in itself involves. Is there a religion myth in its own right? Because it can become evident in every other myth, a religion would be a unique form of living myth in comparison with the ones we have considered.

Living Myths as Religion

That every living myth we have considered reaches out to religious proportions suggests that religion is something that permeates the whole of life. What is involved in seeing living myths as instances of, or at least approximations to, religion has been addressed most directly by a German-American theologian whose influence is still felt from the mid-point of this century, Paul Tillich. Tillich challenged the reading of modernity as straightforward secularization. Such a reading is inappropriate, he contended, because religion represents an indispensable and inevitable dimension of human life. Each of us is, by nature, a religious being, Tillich contends, *homo religiosus*. From his own perspective, that identification carries strong existentialist connotations. In contrast to animals, which presumably approach life as a matter of immediate needs, human beings are characterized by more long-range needs, including in particular a fundamental need for meaning. In spite of the intense messages of modern consumer culture, human beings cannot finally be satisfied by eating, drinking, and merriment, enjoyable though these are. We also have an inescapable curiosity about life itself, not just the processes that science investigates, but the point of it all. This distinctive feature of human beings represents the inescapable religious preoccupation intrinsic to humanity as such.

The most striking illustration of Tillich's insistence on the indispensability of religion is his transposition of faith into "ultimate concern."[1] Where devotees of conventional religion might be inclined to assume a monopoly on faith and advocates of a secular perspective are apt to think that they have left faith behind, Tillich proposes a new vocabulary that poses the issue of faith as one arising out of our common humanity, regardless of what orientation we explicitly approve. Whether conventional believer or convinced secularist, as human beings we are characterized by a search for meaning that indicates our situation as one of concern. If we pursue this, Tillich contends, we will find that there is some central and foundational concern that supports the others; this ultimate concern discloses our real faith. What we are really concerned about fundamentally, what we could not abandon without risking personal disintegration, is the faith that provides coherence and depth in our lives. In this sense, we are all religious beings, whether we make the effort to identify our religious vision or not.

Tillich's treatment can be taken as vindication of the importance and inescapability of myth and religion in the basic, comprehensive sense of living myth. If people do not see themselves as subscribers to any of the conventional religions, this does not mean that they have left religion behind. It means, rather, that something else is filling this definitional and directive function, which some people do find in conventional religion. It may be assumed by any of the myths we have considered, or, more realistically, by some combination of these and others that we have not identified. The science myth defines reality today in ways formerly established by religion, and this is true even for those who continue to find significance in religious traditions. To varying degrees, the sports myth performs religious functions for some, ranging from occasional release from the routine demands of life and renewal somewhat similar to what the believer experiences from religion, to a total orientation that represents a surrogate sacred calendar. Issues of sex can become so important to some people, such as ardent feminists, that sex can represent a defining horizon that prevents recognizing any other horizon, even the divine, as more comprehensive or fundamental. The values approach entails a vision of ourselves as determiners of value that similarly excludes serious acknowledgment of any reality greater, of more value, than ourselves. Society affords a horizon of meaning for the person who does not find overt religious reference meaningful. There is no shortage of religion substitutes in contemporary life. Identifying these as myths, and thinking of them in terms of Tillich's notion of ultimate concern, provides ways of recognizing that rejection of conventional religion does not by any means entail dispensing with basic perspectives and loyalties.

Living myths imply that religion, as well as myth, is more relevant to contemporary life than is generally assumed. How these myths involve religion, however, is another matter. Science, sport, sex, and ecology can be seen to take on religious significance, but they are not themselves religions. They may be more adequately understood as substitutes for religion. To assess the adequacy of this substitution, or indeed even to identify these living myths as religion substitutes, we have to have some sense of what constitutes religion itself. Can we identify a distinctive religion myth in its own right? A basic difficulty with Tillich's approach is that it does not help us to answer that question. Although he sees intimations of religion all over the place, Tillich does not permit comparison between these religion substitutes and the real thing because he does not identify the real thing in any direct way. Critics of Tillich suggest that he does not deal with religion in its own right precisely because he takes such a broad approach. As Jacques Ellul puts it, Tillich's definition of religion is too all-inclusive; it does not recognize the specifics that constitute the religious itself.[2] For Tillich, religion is a depth that might be available in any serious concern; what religion involves in itself, beyond this dimension of depth, resists identification.

The ironic situation in which the comprehensive approach to religion cannot really deal with religion itself suggests that this approach involves a basic contradiction. It is as though in finding religion everywhere, "religion" is given such a broad connotation that it has no identifiable meaning of its own. The real difficulty with this is not the apparent logical contradiction, but the implications for the reality of religion itself. Religion is seen as a depth that may be encountered in many ways, but that multiplicity tends to displace any distinctive characterization of the depth. Thus, the characterization of religion as depth tends to result in what is really a depiction in terms of breadth. The result is that religion can be identified with any area of life, or, at least, any area of life can be seen to open out into religion, but what religion itself involves defies identification, except in the most abstract terms.

The difficulty of identifying religion in its own terms reflects back on the religion that is supposedly encountered in these other areas. If we cannot say what religion is in itself, how do we know that we are encountering religion through these other avenues? What we are encountering may be not religion, but secular alternatives to religion. We have seen, for example, that sports, may come to fill the roles that were previously filled by religion. In this case, sport becomes a religion in itself. But can sport really be regarded as a religion? Although it has often had religious overtones, to see it as a religion in itself is to see religion in secular terms. Then what we are involved with is not religion so much as a religion substitute, a surrogate religion. This would suggest that far from affording access to religion in a secular culture, such substitutes represent false or pseudo-religion. Living myths, then, may be not so much indications of the persistent presence of religion in secular culture as of a continuing hunger for religion and a tendency to seek to meet this hunger through secular substitutes. Then, Tillich is not rescuing religion from secularity, but demonstrating its captivity. To see this, however, would depend on a sense of what is distinctive about religion, but this is precisely what would be precluded by the secular horizon.

Religion as Living Myth

What religion itself would involve, in distinction from these living myths that can serve as secular substitutes for religion, poses a difficult question because something distinctive seems to be indicated that would not be available from these substitutes. One approach to what is involved is offered by Martin Buber's insistence that genuine religious sensibility involves a "turning."

For Buber, the inductivist approach, implied in Tillich's discovery of religion all over the place, assumes a basic continuity that does not do justice to the distinctiveness of religious sensibility. Failure to recognize that distinctiveness, Buber contends, involves failure to reckon with the risk of idolatry. "This conception presupposes that man's relation to the finite goods he has 'idolized' is of the same nature as his relation to God, and differs only in its object."[3] Obviously, God is different from finite objects, but we expect to be able to deal with God as though we were dealing with a finite object. Finite objects, such as scientific theories, sports, sex, values, and society, are seen to be at our disposal, and we extend this presumption to God, the only difference being, of course, that God is much larger. In order to be open to God at all, Buber contends, our basic attitude has to change. "He who is dominated by the idol that he wishes to win, to hold, and to keep—possessed by a desire for possession—has no way to God but that of turning, which is a change not only of goal but also of the nature of his movement."[4] We cannot expect to possess God the way we seek to possess objects or particular areas of life involved in our living myths. Knowledge of God is personal, not possessive. It involves a relation in which we find ourselves claimed and challenged by the eternal Thou. The nature of the movement, as well as the goal, are different from the way we seek to capture and possess life through our living myths.

The problem, though, is not that we cannot possess God in the way we seek to possess finite objects and concerns. Buber is not making the obvious point that God is different from finite objects and concerns; nor is he only saying that we cannot approach God in the possessive way that we approach these finite matters. Buber's main point is not that God demands a different attitude and approach than do finite things, but that our approach to finite things has to change. The "turning" is not from the world to God, but a change in our basic attitude toward both the world and God, our fundamental approach to life as such.

> Life cannot be divided between a real relation with God and an unreal relation of *I* and *It* with the world—you cannot both truly pray to God and profit by the world. He who knows the world as something by which he is to profit knows God also in the same way.[5]

To know God is not a matter of an approach different from how we know the world; it is of a piece with how we know the world. The problem is not that we become so wrapped up in the world that we forget God, but that we approach the world possessively, and assume that God is to be approached in the same way. What has to change is the whole approach to the world as well as to God. That is the "turning" that is required, according to Buber, rather than the natural progression that is implied in Tillich's increments of concern.

The "turning" is necessary because of the distinctiveness of religion, because of the transcendent claim that it involves, in contrast to the possessive approach to life that is so natural to us. What makes this "turning" particularly urgent and elusive is that this possessiveness can characterize religion too. In fact, it has come to characterize religion especially through the impact of secularization. For secularity marginalizes religion not only by dismissing it, but also by tolerating it in its own separate compartment. Insofar as secularity involves the dismissal of religion, this leaves religion free to find its own way, even though that is destined to be on the margins of life as structured in secular terms. When religion is assigned to its own separate compartment, however, this changes the nature of religion itself.

There is reason to think that this is really what has happened to religion through the impact of modern secularity. Rather than being dismissed, it has been fundamentally distorted, and it is tolerated by secular interests in this distorted form. What is involved is portrayed in the work of the world religions scholar Wilfred Cantwell Smith. Smith has shown how what we think of as religion is something that has emerged only in recent times; it has developed particularly in the Western world.[6] Where many religious traditions see practice as the most important dimension, Christianity has given prominence to the intellectual dimension. If we were asked how to identify Christians, we probably would not point to the way they live or even to how they worship. Our first inclination would probably be to focus on what they believe. Christians are people who believe in God and who believe that God is known through the man Jesus, whom they call the Christ. We distinguish other religious traditions in terms of the different things their followers believe. For many of the major traditions, however, believing is not especially important in itself; a basic direction in life, devoutness, and treatment of others and the world they live in are the central considerations. The tendency in Christianity to give such importance to the intellectual element has resulted in a natural progression whereby we have come to assume in the West that what is at stake is the total package that is identified particularly by a set of beliefs.

Smith sees this development resulting in isolation of the notion of religion in the modern era.[7] While the intellectual orientation of Christianity is of long standing, the term "religion" has taken on a specific importance and connotation in the modern period. Insofar as the word was used at all before the modern era, it referred to personal involvements, rather than to something out there in which a person might or might not participate. It was used in conjunction with a profession of faith and referred to things such as worship rites or a vision of God endorsed by the user of the term. Smith notes how "Christian religion," as a living context, became transformed into "the Christian religion" as an external entity. He traces the transformation of the range of application of the label "Christian" from an attestation of personal orientation to an expression of an ideal, then to an abstraction, and ultimately to an institution.[8] The term "Christian" used to be essentially a personal confession of faith and an expression of the confidence that one lived "in Christ." That sense gave way to the expression of an ideal for which to strive; one sought to emulate the way of Christ. It ends up being a name for what we have come to think of as a religion, a movement to which one might subscribe. Now one might ask, What is so surprising about this? It simply seems to be pointing out the obvious: people used to believe in Christianity, but now people are more likely not to. But that is the point—people did not believe in Christianity or in any other religion. People of religious sensibility believe in Christ or in the way of the Buddha. To think we have to believe in Christianity or in Buddhism is a secular notion. Religion as a compartment that bears these different labels—Christianity, Buddhism, Islam, Hinduism—is very different from the practice of religion by people for whom these traditions are a way of life.

Secularization makes identification of a religion myth very difficult. It tends to dismiss religion completely, so that we are left treating all sorts of areas of life in what amounts to religious terms. Insofar as it tolerates religion, it is as a separate compartment that reduces religion to the parameters of the secular. Religion is identified with historical phenomena like Christianity or Buddhism, rather than with the transcendent meaning that these traditions stand for. A serious religion myth would have to reflect this sense of transcendent claim, which is precluded by a secular outlook. This is the distinctiveness that will distinguish a religion myth from any other instance of living myth. It is the distinctiveness of this claim that Buber insists must be affirmed, in contrast to Tillich's more direct association of religion with what we have been calling living myths.

As a living myth, a religion myth would be distinctive in recognizing its implications in transcendence. This recognition implies another characteristic that would be peculiar to a religion myth. In recognizing its implication in transcendence, it should also recognize its inadequacy to that claim. The self-critical stance that is implied here is illustrated forcefully by the scholar who has few rivals as most prominent theologian of the twentieth century, the German Protestant Karl Barth. Barth devoted a long section of his massive *Church Dogmatics* to promoting the abolition of religion.[9] Why would a theologian call for the abolition of religion? One possible answer is that he is rejecting the compartment that has come to be identified as religion through the influence of secularization. Insofar as "religion" refers to the area that is expected to be meaningful in itself, it must be rejected by those who take religion seriously. But Barth's rejection of religion is more basic than that. He is challenging not just the artificial compart-ment that religion has become through the process of secularization, but religion as such. He is able to do this because he is assuming and endorsing what we would consider to be religion in a wider sense. From within a religious perspective, he is challenging religion in the name of religion.

The contrast that Barth makes is between religion and faith. "Faith" is his Christian term for what religion is involved with when seen from the inside. Faith refers to living from beyond ourselves; it is living by the grace of God, rather than out of our own independence. It is living as recipients of life, rather than possessively, to put it in terms that would reflect Buber's perspective. But such a transcendent claim does not come in such vague terms. For Barth, it takes the concrete form of the assurance and claim of the Christian gospel. Genuine reli-gion takes such specific forms. It is knowing the gift and claim of God in Christ; it is pursuing, and ultimately achieving, the way of enlight-enment shown by the Buddha. There is a world of difference between this concreteness of sincere religious sensibility and the possessiveness that would identify religious faith with a particular historical religion, much less with an essentially secular activity such as sport or shop-ping. The sense of transcendent meaning and direction precludes pre-cisely the possessiveness that Buber sees as the antithesis of religion. It is particularly ironic that religion itself should take on this character-istic, and at times become the most possessive of postures. This is why religion must be rejected in the name of religion. A vital religion myth reflects a sense of direction received from beyond ourselves, individu-ally and collectively, and a humility about our own grasp and execution of that direction. There is nothing more pathetic than religion that takes itself seriously. By its very nature, religion is concerned with a re-ality that is beyond its grasp. It is real and significant only insofar as it plays that role. This is what requires a religion myth to be qualitatively different from every other living myth.

We can speak of religion as a living myth so long as we take this distinctiveness into account. It is not one more myth alongside the oth-ers because it reflects this explicit sense of transcendent claim. This is how it is able to expose the pretentions to transcendent claim, to total visions, in other living myths. It is also what requires it to be critical of its own grasp and articulation of the glimpse of transcendence it reflects. Religion at its best, as Buber insists, is not about possession but relation. A religion myth will thus be aware of its mythic nature, as no other myth is likely to be.

Religion and Myth

A religion myth is more difficult to identify and define than any of the living myths we have considered because it is distinctive in being involved with transcendence. The other side of this, however, is that because of this involvement with transcendence, religion has a peculiar affinity with myth. Because of its transcendent focus, religion requires the indirect expression that myth affords. The result of this elusiveness of a living religion myth in its own right and the appropriateness of myth as the expression for religion is that religion might be thought of mythic self-consciousness. It is the place where our involvement in myth is recognized and taken seriously.

One expression of this alliance of religion and myth is that it is the transcendent perspective of religion that allows us to develop the concept of living myth and to seek to identify some of the more prominent of our own living myths. Identification of living myths reflects a religious perspective. It operates from the assumption that we live by fundamental visions and priorities. That assumption is of religious proportions. It reflects the sense that we operate out of some vision of totality. That religious sense is what allows for the identification of the visions and priorities that we have considered as living myths. Consideration of these myths, in turn, confirms the religious assumption. It seems clear that we do live by such visions and priorities, and that, in a secular culture, these can even appear to assume religious proportions themselves. Thus while religion allows us to identify living myths, living myths indicate a continuing functional religion, even in a secular culture. Religion then involves mythic self-consciousness in this basic form. It represents the most direct recognition that we live by myth, and affords the perspective from which our particular mythic involvements may best be identified.

Once we become aware that we are involved with myth in the positive sense of visions and perspectives that give life shape and direction for us, the religious scope of this invites us to consider the myths that play these roles for us, and to notice the ways in which they perform religious functions, as we have been doing. The place where the aspiration to total vision became most apparent was in the science myth. Contrary to the official version, which sees science as a humble, inductive accumulation of facts, extending the secure base of established knowledge piece by piece, we saw how science really reflects a fundamental vision of the nature of reality that is as total in its own way as any religious vision. It is not just that some scientists aspire to a theory of everything as their ultimate goal, but that science itself reflects a sense of what reality is like as a basic working vision. This includes a sense of reality as fundamentally consistent, even in the wake of the complications detected at the quantum level, and that it is and should be expected to be amenable to human comprehension. Appreciation of living myth, made possible from the perspective of religion, allows us to recognize that some such total vision is inevitable. We cannot finally live by piecemeal visions; we live by myth, by assumptions about what life is like deep down. If we do not identify and confront these directly, as religion attempts to do, they are no less present and influential for us. Religion shows that we live by total mythic visions of religious proportions. Thus far, Tillich is surely right.

As well as indicating the inevitability of a vision of totality, however little identified and owned, through its identification of how we live by myth, religion discloses how we ourselves are at stake in these visions. How we think of ourselves, how we see our possibilities and prospects in life, follows from the mythic vision that defines reality for us. Through its deliberate raising of this dimension of total vision and fundamental commitments, religion exposes this mythic horizon in our lives. We saw how, in aspiring to a theory of everything and assuming that reality should lend itself to such explanation, science also has reflexive implications that involve visions of ourselves and our place in the scheme of things. The quest for a theory of everything has a direct corollary in the expectation that we will be masters of the universe. Other myths have corresponding reflexive implications. They are far from being theoretical perspectives, such as we might associate with science; we live by them, and our lives are shaped by them.

When we have been led to confront the direct religious involvement in totality, this allows us to see that we are grasping for assurances that have totality proportions in all sorts of ways, through the visions and priorities that we have identified as living myth. At this point, religion may serve the further purpose of challenging the religious pretentions of these total visions. For someone like Buber, the vantage point of religious sensibility suggests that the reliance on living myths to perform religious functions is ignorant of what he identifies as the idolatry factor. Secular culture is particularly conducive to overlooking the idolatry factor, to assuming that we can live fully and adequately in terms of the kinds of living myths we have considered. However, as we have also seen, this temptation is by no means peculiar to our secular era. As Barth's treatment implies, it is the perennial temptation of religion itself. This is where myth is able to return the favour, and to perform a service for religion.

Because religion not only reveals the limitations of living myths that have a tendency to assume religious proportions, but also, at its best, is aware of its own limitations, myth can provide the appropriate medium for expressing this self-conscious form of religious sensibility. Myth, as we are using the term, refers not to falsehoods to be rejected or to the naïveté of others to be avoided, but to the partially glimpsed visions and priorities by which we live. Is this not precisely what religion involves? To take religion as the possession of absolute truth is to overlook the idolatry factor from within religion itself. Such an approach also tends to reflect that view of truth as possession and accuracy that identifies myth with falsehood. To take the "living myth" approach and apply it to religion is no guarantee of avoiding idolatry, but it does represent an approach that incorporates an idolatry check as a possessive approach may not. Living myth is congenial to the mystery of knowing and not knowing, of seeing through a glass darkly, that has always characterized religion at its most profound. The dismissal of myth goes with the possessive, positivistic approach to truth for which it is a matter of all or nothing, either we know or we do not know. This is precisely the outlook that has rendered religion peripheral and incredible in secular culture. Living myth reflects the mentality that is open to religious vision, recognizing that we live by intimations of the eternal rather than by doctrinal or institutional possessions.

An illustration of how religion might function as myth is provided by a successor of Karl Barth, the German theologian and Second World War martyr Dietrich Bonhoeffer. Drawing on Barth's contrast between the possessiveness of religion and the openness of genuine faith to transcendent claim, Bonhoeffer proposed directions for religious sensibility in the wake of secularization. In the latter stages of the Second World War, from his prison cell in Nazi Germany, Bonhoeffer was led to conclude, "We are proceeding towards a time of no religion at all: men as they are now simply cannot be religious any more."[10] As with Barth, this does not mean the dismissal of religion as such, as would be expected from a secular point of view. What Bonhoeffer offers is not a secular dismissal of religion, but a religious appraisal of secularization. The transcendent claim of religion is affirmed (for Bonhoeffer, as for Barth, this meant the claim and promise of the Christian gospel); what is to be abandoned is not what would be slated for abandonment by the priorities of secularity, but the use of this transcendent claim for "religious" purposes.

Bonhoeffer has specific things in mind when he calls for the abolition of religion. "What do I mean by 'interpret in a religious sense'?" he asks rhetorically about the religion he seeks to abandon. "In my view, that means to speak on the one hand metaphysically and on the other individualistically."[11] To speak metaphysically is to use religion as though it were science, to use God as a hypothesis to explain what we cannot yet account for. It is to assert a firm grasp on transcendence, which diminishes the awesomeness of transcendent reality and exaggerates our grasp of it. Bonhoeffer referred to this assertion of knowledge of God as the "God of the gaps," fitting God into gaps in our knowledge or looking to God in emergencies, when we come to the end of our own resources. This is one of the religious ways in which we attempt to use God that must be abandoned in the wake of secularization. Religion can infringe on the science myth, just as, in its aspirations toward a theory of everything, science can assume religious proportions. Rather than attempting to compete with science, by providing explanations for the emergence of life, for example, religion should leave such explanations to science. The religious affirmation is that life is God's gift; the vehicles by which the gift has been and is conveyed are for science to discover, insofar as they can be discovered.

The other characteristic of religion that Bonhoeffer identifies involves using religion in our own self-interest. The most obvious form of this is to think of religion as the way of assuring that we will get to heaven. As Bonhoeffer saw it, modern people are not particularly concerned with saving their souls in this sense. This individualistic form of religion invites the suspicion that religion has come to represent the opposite of what it professes. It is supposed to deliver us from ourselves, but it so often comes across as an appeal to our worst instincts, elevating them to spiritual proportions. This "security blanket" manoeuvre is another of the religious ways in which we attempt to use God, and in so doing we discredit religion, rather than promote it.

What Bonhoeffer is challenging, then, is metaphysical and individualistic abuses of religion. In explanations about the workings of the universe and in coping with actual living, there is no going back on the maturity to which secular insight calls us. In challenging these abuses of religion, however, Bonhoeffer assumes an underlying positive form of religion. He advocates a "religionless Christianity" that permeates what we think of as the secular world, a Christianity that is thought of not in religious terms, but as a way of living that is not distorted by the hypothetical or hypocritical abuses that so readily characterize religion. From his Nazi prison cell, Bonhoeffer sketched his expectation in these terms:

> During the last year or so I have come to appreciate the "worldliness" of Christianity as never before. The Christian is not a *homo religiosus*, but a man pure and simple, just as Jesus was a man, compared with John the Baptist anyhow. I don't mean the shallow this-worldliness of the enlightened, of the busy, the comfortable or the lascivious. It is something much more profound than that, something in which the knowledge of death and resurrection is ever present.[12]

Christianity is not about religion; it is about fully human living. It is mythic living that draws on a vision that defies our articulation and manipulations. Our attempts to express such transcendent claims are as feeble as our attempts to live by them. Yet express them in words and actions we must; thus the appropriateness of living myth.

We all live by myths. The more seriously we give ourselves to any particular myth, the more it is inclined to assume religious proportions. This becomes recognizable from the vantage point of religion, where the final and total meaning of life is at stake. That vantage point also reveals the inherent limitations of these living myths in that they cannot themselves perform the function of religion because they are essentially finite. Although these living myths are particularly characterized by this limitation as expressions of the secular horizon in which they emerge, such limitation is also shared by religion itself as a human activity. Religion avoids this inherent limitation only insofar as it reflects the genuine participation in transcendence that is available only through faith. The appropriate vehicle for expressing this precarious state of religion is precisely living myth. Thus, a living religion myth shares with other living myths the precariousness and tentativeness of the human condition; it is a distinctive living myth in that it addresses the mythic issue of totality directly and self-consciously, and in so doing provides perspective on the other myths by which we live.

Notes

1. Paul Tillich, *Dynamics of Faith* (New York: Harper Torchbooks, 1957), pp. 1ff.

2. Jacques Ellul, *The New Demons* (New York: Seabury Press, 1975), p. 125, n. 3.

3. Martin Buber, *I and Thou*, trans. Ronald Gregor Smith (New York: Charles Scribner's Sons, 1958), p. 105.

4. Ibid.

5. Ibid., p. 107.

6. Wilfred Cantwell Smith, *The Meaning and End of Religion* (Toronto: New American Library of Canada, Mentor Books, 1964), p. 22.

7. Ibid., pp. 42ff., 46, 70ff., 73.

8. Ibid., p. 73.

9. Karl Barth, *Church Dogmatics*, I/2 *The Doctrine of the Word of God*, ed. G.W. Bromiley and T.F. Torrance (New York: Charles Scribner's Sons, 1956), sec. 17, "The Revelation of God as the Abolition of Religion," pp. 280–361.

10. Dietrich Bonhoeffer, *Letters and Papers from Prison* (London: SCM Press, 1953), p. 91.

11. Ibid., p. 94.

12. Ibid., p. 124.

MEANINGFUL MYTH

T HE LIVING myth approach that we have been considering is a fairly novel one, in contrast with the conventional dismissal of myth in the journalistic sense and the academic interest in scholarly myth. However, this usage is not entirely idiosyncratic. There are indications of an increasing recognition of our self-conscious involvement in myth in the sense of basic perspectives and priorities that shape life for us. But this living sense of myth must make its way against the domination of the journalistic and scholarly senses. Just how formidable these associations are is indicated by the way in which even an international authority on myth such as Joseph Campbell misses the sense of living myth, although he wants to display the relevance of scholarly myth for us today.

The Brokenness of Myth

Audacious though it must seem, it can certainly be argued that for all his interest in myth, Campbell really does not take myth seriously. In *Myths to Live By*,[1] he proposes that as relics from past cultures, myths remain significant because they reflect psychological dimensions of the humanity we share with people who did take those myths seriously. For Campbell himself, direct implication in myth is a thing of the past. One of the clearest indications of this is his treatment of horizons. "There were familiar horizons within which people lived and thought and mythologized. There are now no more horizons."[2] What makes this characterization of our present situation particularly significant is that it is precisely this notion of horizons that has been used by others to identify myth. Thus, Langdon Gilkey combats the journalistic tendency to equate myth with falsehood by contending that "this term specifies the form of language with which any community objectifies for reflection the ultimate historical horizon in which it lives."[3] And Raimundo Panikkar suggests, "We could call myth that invisible common horizon that allows communication."[4] If there are no more horizons, this would seem to be tantamount to contending that there is no more myth, in the sense that myth itself can have no significance for sophisticated contemporaries.

For Campbell, myths are "facts of the mind;"[5] "images of myth are reflections of the spiritual potentialities of every one of us."[6] This is why there are no more horizons, because we are all "centres of mind at large—each in his own way at one with all, and with no horizons."[7] There are no horizons because we contain all horizons within ourselves. "Each of us—whoever and whatever he may be—is then the centre, and within him, whether he knows it or not, is that Mind at Large, the laws of which are the laws not only of all minds but of all space as well."[8] The significance of this assumption of our own centrality, which eliminates all need for horizons, is suggested particularly in Campbell's treatment of Thomas Merton's depiction of the workings of symbols. He quotes approvingly Merton's account of "symbol" in terms of the circumference and centre of a circle: "A true symbol takes us to the centre of the circle, not to another point on the circumference."[9] In his interpretation of this depiction, however, Campbell seems to contradict Merton's fundamental understanding of how symbols work. "Whereas theologians, reading their references counterclockwise, so to say, point to references in the past (in Merton's words: 'to another point on the circumference') and Utopians offer revelations only promissory of some desired future, mythologies, having sprung from the psyche, point back to the psyche ('the self'): and anyone seriously turning within will, in fact, rediscover their reference in himself."[10] Although Campbell thinks he is reflecting Merton's position, their visions would seem to be virtual contraries; where Merton seems to imply that we are located on the circumference, seeking access to the centre, from Campbell's psychological vantage point, through the symbols and myths originating from the human psyche, we already occupy the centre. So while Merton seeks to catch a glimpse of the centre through circumferential horizons, Campbell plays with circumferential images in the knowledge that they are really reflections of the centre that he occupies directly without the need for horizons.

As images of our psyche, reflections of our central location at the heart of reality, the significance of myth is tied to this function of identifying our own inner potentialities. The implication is that myths do not really have any significant external reference. Our view that people who believed these myths did not realize that they were dealing with psychological projections seems to require that once the psychological dimension of myths is recognized, it follows that they are essentially, if not exclusively, psychological. This, in turn, carries the further implication that what we are dealing with may not be far from the popular journalistic view of myth as naïvetés of the past. At most, it might be construed as the scholarly approach that recognizes myth as significant for other people. What is completely lacking, insofar as these myths themselves are concerned, is what we have been considering to be living myth, myth significant for ourselves. This may account for the difference between Campbell and Merton. Campbell's scholarly treatment of myth does not involve the personal religious sensitivity that animates Merton.

Because of the personal nature of living myth, it is difficult to pursue this area without getting involved in such *ad hominem* considerations. Without presuming to gauge Campbell's religious sensitivity, it is clear that he does not see his own fundamental stance as in any significant sense mythical; he does not regard the psychological approach to life and the anthropocentric perspective implicit in it as mythical. His perspective is true, and accurate, and absolute. He sees things as they are, in contrast to the naïveté of people who took their myths seriously. But this sense of having direct access to reality is precisely what myth involves. "Our prejudices (prejudgments), our presuppositions, our unreflective convictions, these all have a mythic character."[11] In identifying myth with reflections of psychic impulses, Campbell does not recognize the mythic nature of his own basic perspective.

Campbell's identification of myth with "ancient legends," as the blurb on the book jacket puts it, and his dissociation of his own position from mythic associations are obviously not unconnected. That myths belong to the past and that a contemporary perspective would not involve myth are two sides of the same outlook. Myths are "prescientific." This exempts scientific perspectives from the domain of the mythical, even when those perspectives take on cosmic and absolute proportions. Science represents fact, truth, the way things are; previous perspectives on life are at best crude approximations and anticipations. This is precisely the understanding that underlies the popular journalistic sense of myth as exposed falsehood.[12] It is characteristic of the science myth that it exempts itself from the mythic domain to which it assigns other perspectives. The irony is that it is the elevation of science to mythic proportions that entitles it to claim this exemption. "Those who define myth as illusion overlook the mythic dimensions of the believed-in reality of their own location."[13]

Campbell's position is not so simple as to permit a direct identification with the popular media equation of myth with falsehood. Myths are significant as clues to our own psychic procedures and potentialities. But that indirect significance that myth retains is distinctly subordinate to the anthropocentric perspective that sees myths as products of our own psychic activity, which is not in any sense seen in mythic terms itself. Thus, the significance that is accorded to myth is decidedly secondary to the point at which the equation with falsehood is not entirely inappropriate. This can be seen most readily if we consider a contrary perspective on myth, such as that implicit in the suggestion that "we have no right to regard ourselves as fully the creators of myth, but rather as its discoverers."[14] This does not necessarily deny the recognition of the humanness of our myths. What it challenges is the assumption that the subject of myths is humanity. Although myths are human creations, we are not "fully the creators of myth." They reflect something of reality other than ourselves. That is where Campbell's treatment becomes particularly ambiguous. His own subscription to the modern scientific myth in the form of a humanistic psychological perspective undermines the seriousness that he accords to traditional myths.

By identifying myths with the past and seeking to make use of them for contemporary purposes, Campbell comes dangerously close to adopting the popular journalistic understanding of myth as naïvetés of the past and overlooking the mythic nature of his own location. However, we must consider the possibility that in advocating a contemporary approach to ancient myths, Campbell is really practising myth in its purest state. This could mean that our reading of Campbell's treatment of myth misses the point completely. Perhaps his appreciation of myth is so profound that someone who has not lived with myth in the range and depth that Campbell has simply cannot appreciate the obviousness with which he takes myth. The casualness of his references to the mythic lore of widely disparate peoples bespeaks a respect for myth that is not easily matched. What is more, that respect includes a sense of the continuing relevance of those myths for us today. Serious confrontation with myths of other times and places, as well as those of our own inheritance, can provide clues for our own orientation in life. Thus, maybe the failure to appreciate myth is reflected in the critique of Campbell more than in Campbell himself. Perhaps he represents a vibrant alignment of classical mythic themes with the prevailing and effective mythology of the present.

The case for this positive reading of Campbell's treatment of myth is enhanced through a consideration of the comprehensive range of myth implied in the four functions he identifies as requisite to a vital mythology.[15] The "mystical function" is "to waken and maintain in the individual a sense of awe and gratitude in relation to the mystery dimension of the universe"—hardly a restrictive notion of the scope of myth! The second function of a significant mythology is to provide a credible contemporary picture of the universe—again, a function that implies a vital continuing place for myth. A third role involves the validation of moral norms for the society of the day. And finally, the individual will be sustained and guided personally by a living mythology. Thus, Campbell not only demonstrates a profound respect for myth through his intimate acquaintance with the mythologies of diverse times and places, but also expects myth to perform a significant role in the present. It is through myth that we come to grips with reality at large, with the universe, with our social context, and with ourselves. Whatever we may make of these characterizations of the functions of myth, to see them as a denigration of myth is likely to be very far down the list of possible reactions.

Yet in spite of the comprehensiveness and contemporaneity implied in this portrayal of myth, if we consider Campbell's own treatment of myth in light of these criteria, shades of the reservations that have been identified re-emerge. The "mystical function" of an operative mythology, "to waken and maintain in the individual a sense of awe and gratitude in relation to the mystery dimension of the universe," is fulfilled as the individual "recognizes that he participates in it, since the mystery of being is the mystery of his own deep being as well."[16] As a result, the need to consider the universe is eliminated inasmuch as we contain its mystery within ourselves, and, for Campbell, that containment seems to be virtually complete. He explicitly rejects religions of otherness; the religions of the Middle East, which see the mystery of the universe epitomized in God, are dismissed in favour of more immediate approaches. Thus, he reverses the course of Christian doctrinal history by dismissing every version of Christian faith that would find particular significance in the historical reality of Christ, and will consider only a kind of mystical significance that he recognizes would amount to "the very essence of Christian gnosticism."[17] This sense of a direct gnosis that gives us access to the mysteries of life is seen to be exemplified most adequately, though, in the religious traditions of the Far East. Apart from the presumably rare enlightened gnostic, Western religion involves second-hand conformity to a metaphysical fiction called God. "In the great East, on the other hand, the accent is on experience: on one's own experience, furthermore, not a faith in someone else's."[18] To pursue this would lead us to the question of how far the appeal to religious traditions of the Far East is really modified through the influence of modern anthropocentrism, but what is of immediate relevance here is the fact that Campbell rejects any form of God myth, and, irrespective of the legitimacy of his reading of Buddhist tradition in particular, permits only a mythology of immanence and immediacy as an articulation of the mystery of the universe.

The contradiction between Campbell's designation of the first function of myth as that of awakening and maintaining awe and gratitude in relation to the mystery dimension of the universe, and his confinement of this possibility in his own practice to what he considers non-Western forms, and perhaps ultimately even to anthropocentric ones, is exceeded in his treatment of the second function. For in spite of his contention that myth provides a contemporary picture of the universe, he makes no reference at all to myth in his repeated articulations of his own picture of the universe. The anthropocentric vision of the universe, which is the basis on which he dismisses religious visions that affirm significant otherness, is regarded as scientific fact; myth is psychological projection from this anthropocentric base. Thus, we find reconfirmed the impression that for all his concern with myth, Campbell ultimately exempts himself from its influence.

From the point of view of the reality of myth, of course, this is perfectly consistent. When Campbell quite unself-consciously promotes his anthropocentric vision of life, he is practising myth. Thus, he bears witness to the tenacity and abiding relevance of myth precisely by affirming his own view of the universe so insistently, and in not at all naming this as mythic. However, that he never acknowledges that this stance is mythic stands at odds with his own recognition that it is myth that gives us our basic picture of the universe, carries the implication that he really consigns myth to the past, and does not seriously consider the perspectival, living form of myth that is most characteristic of our era. Another way to state the difficulty would be to suggest that he has not come to grips with the brokenness of myth. To identify something as myth is to be dealing with broken myth. The "ancient legends" that represent the main focus of Campbell's treatment of myths are broken myths for him. However, in spite of the comprehensive functions of myth that he designates, his lack of express acknowledgment of his implication in myth in terms of his own visions and priorities suggests that he continues to live by myth himself, without a sense of brokenness where his own myth is concerned.

Living with Broken Myth

In contending that there are no more horizons, Campbell is, in fact, affirming a horizon. To propose that horizons have been eliminated and to assume that we are seeing life whole and direct is, of course, precisely what myth involves. Myth is direct appreciation of the way things are. The difference in this proposal is that it recognizes the brokenness of myth for other people, those who accept other horizons. The exemption of its own vision not only surreptitiously constitutes its own horizon or myth in spite of itself, it is in fact a version of the journalistic view of myth. It is surely supremely ironic that it is precisely this outlook, which sees itself as the exposer and disposer of myth, that so clearly exemplifies the most characteristic features of myth in its sense of the immediacy and absoluteness of its own vision. The irony is heightened when this inversion is exemplified by one of the most ardent champions of myth. Perhaps what Campbell should have said, to promote an appreciation of myth, is not that there are no more horizons, but that we have become aware of having horizons. To do that consistently, though, he would have had to acknowledge the mythic nature of his own position. The fact that someone as immersed in myth as Campbell does not do this suggests that such acknowledgment may be more difficult than we have been inclined to realize.

That it even makes sense to talk about acknowledging our own horizons is by no means obvious. Horizons constitute our field of vision, and by that very token they resist becoming the object of our vision. It might be that "only the other is able to recognize and criticize my myths, my silent presuppositions."[19] We can identify Campbell as an exponent of the psychological form of the modern anthropocentric myth because we occupy some other mythic perspective. What that vantage point is will be more readily identifiable to those who do not share it. If this is all that can be said, however, this recognition of the unavoidability of myth acquires a fundamentally negative connotation as we engage in exposing each other's most cherished convictions. The most promising alternative to this all-or-nothing situation would be a position in which we are able to move in and out of our mythic involvements, so that we really live by broken myth.

The comprehensive and absorbing nature of myth militates against any easy identification, much less verification. Myth encompasses us, and is changed by attempts to encompass it. "The interpreter who sets out to understand the myth must first consent to being interpreted by the myth (at least provisionally) or the meaning of myth has been lost altogether."[20] This distinctive character gives myth an independent integrity that Hans-Georg Gadamer takes to be constitutive of the only good definition of myth: "That myth neither requires nor includes any possible verification outside of itself."[21] To take myth seriously will necessitate according it a respect that recognizes its transcendent quality. To want to identify and assess the myths by which we live is itself a reflection of the mythic stance of modern post-enlightenment rationalistic ambitions to catalogue and control reality precisely and definitively.

Having acknowledged the foundational and formative role of myth, however, it is also true that we are heirs to this enlightenment myth. This is precisely what has led to the rise of this category of myth to the prominence it has acquired in recent years. To speak and think of myth is already to be dealing with broken myth. Our dilemma resides in the tension between the self-consciousness of broken myth and the immediacy and totality of living myth. Thus, the issue for us is whether we can live by broken myth. Where Campbell appears to be divided between the exposure of myths of others and total immersion in his own, the reality of broken myth poses the question of whether we can move in and out of our own myths.

One aspect of the dilemma is identified by Raimundo Panikkar: "One cannot be a witness and an exegete at the same time."[22] We are not inhabiting a myth when we are looking at it. But perhaps a more significant question is whether we can be a witness and an exegete of the same myth. To say that we cannot is to divorce myth and rationality completely. To allow for some commerce between the two dispositions suggests that we can move in and out of myths without complete compromise of the mythic quality. Of course, this kind of dialectic is not without its dangers. There is an obvious compromise position, which Panikkar identifies as a shift in focus from belief in the reality to which the myth testifies to a focus on the myth in itself. "When we cease to believe the *myth*, when it no longer 'goes without saying;' we try to believe *in* it by means of our interpretation."[23] This is what we considered the rationalized stage of myth, which succeeds the compelling myths that grasp us in their immediacy and the supplemental myths that run so deeply that we do not even identify them. Something of this rationalized stage is involved in the very recognition of myth. That designation signals the loss of the immediacy where that vision "goes without saying," and that means that some other myth has become operative. That this new myth must remain completely concealed, however, and the old myth be rendered completely dysfunctional assumes that myth can only be naïvely affirmed or totally broken. Panikkar himself suggests a more realistic possibility in his distinction between the stance of a witness and that of a confessor. "A witness does not bear witness to himself; whereas a confessor confesses his belief."[24] In our era of broken myth, it would seem that we are all some combination of witness and confessor. The depth and tenacity of myth make us witnesses to perspectives that resist our detection because they mould our vision, while the self-consciousness implicit in the very identification of myth impels us not only to seek to detect the myths by which we live but to attempt to justify those myths that we do confess.

Just how deliberately we can live with broken myth will itself reflect our own mythic stance and our own sense of its brokenness. At one end, there can be a quite explicit attempt to identify, assess, and co-ordinate our mythic horizons, and basic criteria can be proposed for this. One set of criteria[25] include: 1) internal consistency, 2) cohesion among all the myths one accepts, 3) comprehensiveness, so that the more inclusive the myth the more adequate it will be, and 4) pragmatic success in sustaining a person through providing a positive sense of meaning in life. In an era of broken myth, when our own cherished myths lose their obviousness, when different and even antithetical myths attain the status of obviousness, and when there is a growing sense of legitimacy in other myths that was not recognized before, criteria such as these become significant. How significant they become will depend on the degree of brokenness of our own myths, on the one hand, and the resistance of myth itself to treatments of brokenness, on the other. These criteria reflect a scale of manageability from deliberate considerations of consistency, cohesion, and comprehensiveness to a more immediate sense of adequacy that would be endemic to a fully functioning living myth. Ultimately, the deliberate considerations of consistency, cohesion, and comprehensiveness will be sustained by a sense of dealing with bedrock truth that simply cannot be avoided or evaded. The result would be confessional criteria of the kind that Schubert Ogden proposes: "The criteria for assessing the truth of myths may be formulated as follows: mythical assertions are true insofar as they so explicate our unforfeitable assumptions that life is worthwhile that the understanding of faith they represent cannot be falsified by the essential conditions of life itself."[26] We are constrained to identify and testify to the fundamental convictions that sustain us, even as we recognize that the sustenance resists identification and that the identifications have a way of becoming the objects, rather than the vehicles, of the testimony. As the exponent of the more deliberate criteria just noted, Robert Ayers, acknowledges, "the very presuppositions of our truth-criteria are themselves mythical."[27] From within orientations too wide and deep for strict demarcation, we are bound to confess, as best we can, the realities that evoke our witness.

Notes

1. Joseph Campbell, *Myths to Live By* (New York: Bantam Books, 1972).
2. Ibid., p. 263.

3. Langdon Gilkey, *Reaping the Whirlwind* (New York: The Seabury Press, 1976), p. 151.

4. Raimundo Panikkar, *Myth, Faith and Hermeneutics* (New York: Paulist Press, 1979), p. 248.

5. Campbell, *Myths to Live By*, p. 10.

6. Joseph Campbell, *The Power of Myth* (New York: Doubleday, 1988), pp. 217ff.

7. Campbell, *Myths to Live By*, p. 275.

8. Ibid., p. 274.

9. Thomas Merton, "Symbolism: Communication or Communion?" *New Directions* 20 (1968): 11–12, quoted in Campbell, *Myths to Live By*, p. 265.

10. Campbell, *Myths to Live By*, p. 266.

11. Panikkar, *Myth, Faith and Hermeneutics*, p. 345.

12. Robert H. Ayers, "Religious Discourse and Myth," in Robert H. Ayers and William T. Blackstone, eds., *Religious Language and Knowledge* (Athens: University of Georgia Press, 1972), p. 91.

13. Charles S. McCoy, *When Gods Change* (Nashville: Abingdon, 1980), p. 91.

14. Leszek Kolakowski, *The Presence of Myth* (Chicago: University of Chicago Press, 1989), p. 32.

15. Campbell, *Myths to Live By*, pp. 221ff.

16. Ibid., p. 221.

17. Ibid., p. 57.

18. Ibid., p. 96.

19. Panikkar, *Myth, Faith and Hermeneutics*, p. 346.

20. Theodore W. Jennings, Jr., *Introduction to Theology, An Invitation to Reflection upon the Christian Mythos* (Philadelphia: Fortress Press, 1976), p. 52.

21. Hans-Georg Gadamer, "Religious and Political Speaking," in Alan M. Olson, ed., *Myth, Symbol and Reality* (Notre Dame: University of Notre Dame Press, 1980), p. 92.

22. Panikkar, *Myth, Faith and Hermeneutics*, p. 237.

23. Ibid., p. 132.

24. Ibid., p. 237.

25. Ayers, "Religious Discourse," p. 94.

26. Schubert Ogden, *The Reality of God and Other Essays* (San Francisco: Harper & Row, 1977), p. 116.

27. Ayers, "Religious Discourse," p. 86.

BIBLIOGRAPHY

THE NATURE AND SIGNIFICANCE OF MYTH

AYERS, Robert H., and William T. BLACKSTON, eds. *Religious Language and Knowledge.* Athens: University of Georgia Press, 1972.

BARTHES, Roland. *Mythologies.* Trans. Annette Lavers. London: Jonathan Cape, 1972.

CAMPBELL, Joseph. *Myths to Live By.* New York: Bantam Books, 1972.

————. *The Power of Myth.* New York: Doubleday, 1988.

COX, Harvey. *The Secular City.* New York: Macmillan, 1965.

DAY, Martin S. *The Many Meanings of Myth.* Lanham: University Press of America, 1984.

ELLUL, Jacques. *The New Demons.* Trans. C. Edward Hopkin. New York: The Seabury Press, 1975.

GILKEY, Langdon. *Reaping the Whirlwind.* New York: The Seabury Press, 1976.

JENNINGS, Theodore W., Jr. *Introduction to Theology, An Invitation to Reflection upon the Christian Mythos.* Philadelphia: Fortress Press, 1976.

KOLAKOWSKI, Leszek. *The Presence of Myth.* Chicago: University of Chicago Press, 1989.

LÉVI-STRAUSS, Claude. *Myth and Meaning.* Toronto: University of Toronto Press, 1978.

McCOY, Charles S. *When Gods Change.* Nashville: Abingdon, 1980.

MOORE, Richard E. *Myth America 2001.* Philadelphia: Westminster Press, 1972.

"Mythology." *The Oxford Classical Dictionary.* Ed. N.G.L. Hammond and H.H. Sculland. Second Edition. Oxford: Clarendon Press, 1979.

OGDEN, Schubert. *The Reality of God and Other Essays.* San Francisco: Harper & Row, 1977.

OLSON, Alan M., ed. *Myth, Symbol and Reality.* Notre Dame: University of Notre Dame Press, 1980.

Panikkar, Raimundo. *Myth, Faith and Hermeneutics.* New York: Paulist Press, 1979.

Roszak, Theodore. *The Making of a Counter Culture.* New York: Doubleday Anchor Book, 1969.

Van Peursen, C.A. "Man and Reality—the History of Human Thought." *The Student World* 56/1 (1963).

SCIENCE

Barbour, Ian. *Myths, Models and Paradigms: A Comparative Study of Science and Religion.* New York: Harper & Row, 1976.

————. *Religion in an Age of Science.* San Francisco: Harper & Row, 1990.

Barrow, John D., and Frank J. Tipler. *The Anthropic Cosmological Principle.* Oxford and New York: Oxford University Press, 1986.

Carr, B.J. and M.J. Rees. "The Anthropic Principle and the Structure of the Physical World." *Nature.* 278 (12 Apr 1979).

Davies, Paul. *God and the New Physics.* New York: Simon and Schuster, 1983.

Dawkins, Richard. *The Selfish Gene.* London: Granada, A Paladin Book, 1978.

————. "Replicators and Vehicles," in *Current Problems in Sociobiology.* Ed. King's College Sociobiology Group. Cambridge: Cambridge University Press, 1982.

————. *The Blind Watchmaker.* Burnt Mill: Longman Scientific and Technical, 1986.

Gale, George. "The Anthropic Principle." *Scientific American.* 245 (Dec 1981).

Gribbin, John, and Martin Rees. "Cosmic Coincidences." *New Scientist.* 125/1699 (Jan 3, 1990).

Hawking, Stephen W. *A Brief History of Time.* New York: Bantam Books, 1988.

————. *Black Holes and Baby Universes, and Other Essays.* New York: Bantam Books, 1993.

Jastrow, Robert. *God and the Astronomers.* New York: W.W. Norton, 1978.

Kuhn, Thomas S. *The Structure of Scientific Revolutions.* Chicago: University of Chicago Press, 1970.

Lederman, Leon, with Dick Teresi. *The God Particle.* New York: A Delta Book, 1993.

Lindley, David. *The End of Physics, The Myth of a Unified Theory.* New York: Harper and Collins Basic Books, 1993.

Macquarrie, John. *The Scope of Demythologizing.* Gloucester, Mass: Peter Smith, 1969.

Margenau, Henry, and Roy Abraham Varghese, eds. *COSMOS, BIOS, THEOS.* LaSalle, Illinois: Open Court, 1992.

MIDGLEY, Mary. *Science as Salvation: A Modern Myth and Its Meaning.* London and New York: Routledge, 1992.

MONOD, Jacques. *Chance and Necessity.* Trans. Austryn Wainhouse. London: Collins Fount Books, 1977.

PEACOCKE, A.R., ed. *The Sciences and Theology in the Twentieth Century.* Notre Dame, Indiana: University of Notre Dame Press, 1981.

————. *God and the New Biology.* San Francisco: Harper & Row, 1986.

PLANCK, Max. *Scientific Autobiography and Other Papers.* New York: Philosophical Library, 1949.

POLANYI, Michael. *Personal Knowledge, Towards a Post-Critical Philosophy.* London: Routledge and Kegan Paul, 1962.

RUSSELL, Bertrand. *Why I Am Not a Christian.* New York: Simon and Schuster, 1957.

STEWART, Ian, and Martin GOLUBITSKY. *Fearful Symmetry, Is God a Geometer?* Oxford: Blackwell, 1992.

WEINBERG, Steven. *The First Three Minutes: A Modern View of the Origins of the Universe.* London: Andre Deutsch, 1977.

WILSON, E.O. *Sociobiology, The New Synthesis.* Cambridge, MA: Harvard University Press, 1975.

SPORTS

BAKER, William J., and James A. ROG, eds. *Sports and the Humanities: A Symposium.* Orono, MN: University of Maine at Orono Press, 1983.

FREEZELL, Randolph. "Sport, Character, and Virtue." *Philosophy Today* 33 (Fall 1989).

GALASSO, Pasquale J., ed. *Philosophy of Sport and Physical Activity.* Toronto: Canadian Scholars' Press, 1988.

GANTZ, W. "An Exploration of Viewing Motives and Behaviors Associated with Television Sports," *Journal of Broadcasting.* 25 (1981).

GARDNER, P. *Nice Guys Finish Last: Sport and American Life.* New York: Universe Books, 1975.

GUTTMAN, Allen. *From Ritual to Record, The Nature of Modern Sports.* New York: Columbia University Press, 1978.

HOCH, Paul. *Ripoff the Big Game.* New York: Doubleday Anchor Books, 1972.

JHALLY, Sut. "The Spectacle of Accumulation: Material and Cultural Factors in the Evolution of the Sports/Media Complex." *Insurgent Sociologist.* 3 (1984).

KEATING, James W. "Sportsmanship as a Moral Category." *Ethics.* 75 (1964).

KINSELLA, W.P. *Shoeless Joe.* New York: Ballentine Books, 1982.

LASCH, Christopher. *The Culture of Narcissism.* New York: Warner Books, 1979.

LIPSYTE, Robert. *SportsWorld: An American Dreamland.* New York: Quadrangle Books, 1975.

MACINTYRE, Alasdair. *After Virtue.* South Bend: University of Notre Dame Press, 1981.

MICHENER, James A. *Sports in America.* New York: Fawcett Crest, 1976.

PREBISH, Charles S. "Heavenly Father, Divine Goalie: Sport and Religion." *The Antioch Review.* 42 (Sum 84).

SIMON, Robert L. *Fair Play: Sports, Values and Society.* Boulder: Westview Press, 1991.

SKILLEN, Anthony. "Sport: An Historical Phenomenology." *Philosophy* 68 (1993).

VECSEY, George. "A Nation of Sports Fans." *New York Times.* 16 Mar, 1983, B11.

WENNER, Lawrence A., ed. *Media, Sports, and Society.* Newbury Park, Cal.: Sage Publications, 1989.

CONSUMER

BEAUCHAMP, Tom L., and Norman E. BOWIE, eds. *Ethical Theory and Business.* Second Edition. Englewood Cliffs, N.J.: Prentice Hall, 1983.

ELLUL, Jacques. *The New Demons.* Tr. C. Edward Hopkin. New York: Seabury Press, A Crossroad Book, 1975.

FROMM, Erich. *To Have or To Be?* London: Jonathan Cape, 1976.

FRYE, Northrop. *The Modern Century.* Toronto: Oxford University Press, 1967.

GALBRAITH, John Kenneth. *The Affluent Society.* Boston: Houghton Mifflin, 1968.

GLASSER, Ralph. *The New High Priesthood, The Social, Ethical and Political Implications of a Marketing-Orientated Society.* London: Macmillan, 1967.

GOODPASTER, K.E., and K.M. SAYRE, eds. *Ethics and Problems in the Twenty-first Century.* Notre Dame: University of Notre Dame Press, 1979.

GRAHAM, Fred W. "America's Other Religion." *Christian Century.* 17 Mar 1982.

GREELEY, Andrew M. *No Bigger than Necessary.* New York: New American Library, 1977.

JONES, Donald C., ed. *Business, Religion, and Ethics.* Cambridge, MA: Oelgeschlager, Gunn and Hain, 1982.

KAVANAUGH, John Francis. *Following Christ in a Consumer Society.* Maryknoll, NY: Orbis Books, 1982.

LEISS, William. *The Limits to Satisfaction, An Essay on the Problem of Needs and Commodities*. Kingston and Montreal: McGill-Queen's University Press, 1988.

LEVITT, Theodore. "Exploiting the Product Life Cycle." *Harvard Business Review*. Nov–Dec 1965.

MASLOW, Abraham. "A Theory of Human Motivation." *Psychological Review*. 50 (1943); *Toward a Psychology of Being*. Princeton: D. Van Nostrand, 1962.

MCCARTHY, E. Jerome, John F. GRASHOF, and Andrew A. BROGOWICZ, eds. *Readings and Cases in Basic Marketing*. Illinois: Richard D. Irwin, 1984.

MELAND, Bernard Eugene. *The Secularization of Modern Cultures*. New York: Oxford University Press, 1966.

POLAYNI, Karl. *The Great Transformation*. Boston: Beacon Press, reprint 1957.

RUBNER, Alex. *The Might of the Multinationals*. New York: Praeger, 1990.

SCHUDSON, Michael. *Advertising, The Uneasy Persuasion*. New York: Basic Books, 1984.

SCHUMACHER, E.F. *Good Work*. London: Abacus, 1980.

TOFFLER, Alvin. *Future Shock*. New York: Random House, A Bantam Book, 1971.

WALLIS, Jim. *The Call to Conversion*. San Francisco: Harper & Row, 1981.

WHITE, Lynn. "The Historical Roots of Our Ecological Crisis." *Science*. 155 (1967).

VALUES

BECK, Clive. *Learning to Live the Good Life, Values in Adulthood*. Toronto: OISE Press, 1993.

BELLAH, Robert N., Richard MADSEN, William M. SULLIVAN, Ann SWIDLER, and Steven M. TIPTON. *Habits of the Heart, Individualism and Commitment in American Life*. New York: Harper and Row, 1985.

DANNER, Peter C. *An Ethics for the Affluent*. Washington, DC: University Press of America, 1980.

EDWARDS, Paul, ed. *The Encyclopedia of Philosophy*. Vol. 8. New York: Macmillan, 1967.

HART, Samuel L. *Treatise on Values*. New York: Philosophical Library, 1949.

HUME, David. *A Treatise of Human Nature*. Ed. L.A. Selby-Bigge. Second Edition, revised by P.H. Nidditch. Oxford: Clarendon Press, 1978.

KILBY, Richard W. *The Study of Human Values*. Lanham, MD: University Press of America, 1993.

NIETZSCHE, Friedrich. *Beyond Good and Evil.* Trans. Marianne Cowan. Chicago: Henry Regnery Co., 1955.

Random House Dictionary of the English Language. New York: Random House, 1983.

RATHERS, Louis, M. HARMIN, and Sidney SIMON. *Values and Teaching.* Columbus, OH: Merrill, 1966, 1978

SAGOFF, Mark. *The Economy of the Earth.* Cambridge: Cambridge University Press, 1990.

SCHERER, Donald, and Thomas ATTIG, eds. *Ethics and the Environment.* Englewood Cliffs, NJ: Prentice-Hall, 1983.

SIMON, Sidney Sion, et al. *Values Clarification.* New York: Hart, 1972.

ECOLOGY

BERRY, Wendell. "A Secular Pilgrimage." *The Hudson Review.* 23 (Autumn 1970).

BRADLEY, Raymond, and Stephen DUGUID, eds. *Environmental Ethics.* Volume II. Burnaby, BC: Institute for the Humanities, Simon Fraser University, 1989.

BRINKHURST, Ralph O., and Donald O. CHANT. *This Good, Good Earth: Our Fight for Survival.* Toronto: Macmillan, 1971.

CAIRNCROSS, Frances. *Costing the Earth: The Challenge for Government, the Opportunities for Business.* Boston: Harvard Business School Press, 1992.

DAVIS, Elizabeth Gould. *The First Sex.* Baltimore: Penguin Books, 1971.

DONALDSON, Thomas, and Patricia H. WERHANE, eds. *Ethical Issues in Business.* Englewood Cliffs, NJ: Prentice-Hall, 1983.

EHRLICH, Paul R. *The Population Bomb.* New York: Ballantine Books, 1968.

EHRLICH, Paul and Anne. *The Population Explosion.* New York: Simon and Schuster, 1990.

EISLER, Riane. *The Chalice and the Blade.* San Francisco: Harper and Row, 1987.

JOHNSON, Lawrence E. *A Morally Deep World, An Essay on Moral Significance and Environmental Ethics.* Cambridge: Cambridge University Press, 1991.

LEOPOLD, Aldo. *A Sand County Almanac.* New York: Oxford University Press, 1949.

LEWIS, Martin W. *Green Delusions, An Environmentalist Critique of Radical Environmentalism.* Durham and London: Duke University Press, 1992.

LOVELOCK, James E. *GAIA: A New Look at Life on Earth.* Oxford: Oxford University Press, 1979.

MacNeil, Jim. "Strategies for Sustainable Economic Development." *Managing Planet Earth: Readings from Scientific American.* New York: W.H. Freeman, 1990.

Maurice, Charles, and Charles W. Smithson. *The Doomsday Myth.* Stanford: Hoover Institution Press, 1984.

Meadows, Donnela H., Dennis L. Meadows, Jørgens Randers, and William H. Behrens, III. *The Limits to Growth: A Report for the Club of Rome's Project on the Predicament of Mankind.* New York: Universe Books, 1972.

Naess, Arne. *Ecology, Community and Lifestyle.* Translated and revised by David Rothenberg. Cambridge: Cambridge University Press, 1989.

Nash, Roderick. *The Rights of Nature: A History of Environmental Ethics.* Madison: University of Wisconsin Press, 1989.

Parkinson, Thomas. "The Poetry of Gary Snyder." *Southern Review.* 4 (1968).

Piel, Gerard. *Only One World, Our Own to Make and to Keep.* New York: Freeman and Co., 1992.

Shea, Cynthia Pollock. "Protecting the Ozone Layer." *State of the World 1989: A Worldwatch Institute Report on Progress Toward a Sustainable Society.* New York: W. W. Norton, 1989.

Snyder, Gary. *Turtle Island.* New York: New Directions, 1974.

Spring, David, and Eileen Spring, eds. *Ecology and Religion in History.* New York: Harper and Row, 1974.

Stone, Merlin. *When God Was a Woman.* New York: Dial Press, 1976.

Taylor, Gordon Rattray. *The Doomsday Book.* London: Thames and Hudson, 1970.

Thompson, Donald M. *The Economics of Environmental Protection.* Cambridge, Mass.: Winthrop Publishers, 1973.

White, Lynn, Jr., "The Historical Roots of Our Ecological Crisis." *Science.* 155 (1967).

SEX

Christ, Carol P. *Laughter of Aphrodite, Reflections on a Journey to the Goddess.* San Francisco: Harper SanFrancisco, 1987.

Christ, Carol P., and Judith Plaskow, eds. *Womanspirit Rising.* Philadelphia: Fortress Press, 1987.

Daly, Mary. *Beyond God the Father.* Boston: Beacon Press, 1973.

Faludi, Susan. *BACKLASH, The Undeclared War Against American Women.* New York: Crown Publishers, 1991.

Friedan, Betty. *The Feminine Mystique.* New York: Dell, 1963.

GILLIGAN, Carol. *In a Different Voice: Psychological Theory and Women's Development.* Cambridge, MA: Harvard University Press, 1982.

————. "Reply." *Signs.* 11 (1986).

GILLIGAN, Carol, Janie Victoria WARD, and Jill McLEAN TAYLOR, with Betty Bardige, eds. *Mapping the Moral Domain.* Cambridge, MA: Center for the Study of Gender Education and Human Development, Harvard University Graduate School of Education, 1988.

GREER, Germaine. *The Female Eunuch.* New York: McGraw-Hill, 1971.

HAMPSON, Daphne. *Theology and Feminism.* Oxford: Basil Blackwell, 1990.

LEIDHOLDT, Dorchen, and Janice G. RAYMOND. *The Sexual Liberals and the Attack on Feminism.* New York: Pergamon Press, 1990.

McFAGUE, Sallie. *Models of God, Theology for an Ecological, Nuclear Age.* Philadelphia: Fortress Press, 1987.

SOMMERS, Christina Hoff. *Who Stole Feminism? How Women Have Betrayed Women.* New York: Simon and Schuster, 1994.

THISTLEWAITE, Susan Brooks. *Sex, Race, and God.* New York: Crossroad, 1989.

WOLF, Naomi. *The Beauty Myth.* Toronto: Vintage Books, 1991.

————. *Fire with Fire: The New Female Power and How to Use It.* Toronto: Vintage Books, 1994.

SOCIETY

ANTHONY, Dick, and Thomas ROBBINS. "From Symbolic Realism to Structuralism," "Review Symposium: Robert Bellah." *Journal for the Scientific Study of Religion.* 14 (1975).

BAUM, Gregory, ed. *Sociology and Human Destiny.* New York: Seabury Press, 1980.

BELLAH, Robert N. *Beyond Belief.* New York: Harper & Row, 1970.

————. "Christianity and Symbolic Realism." *Journal for the Scientific Study of Religion.* 9 (1970).

BELLAH, Robert N. "Response to Comments on 'Christianity and Symbolic Realism.'" *Journal for the Scientific Study of Religion.* 9 (1970).

BERGER, Peter L. *Facing Up to Modernity, Excursions in Society, Politics, and Religion.* New York: Basic Books, 1977.

BERGER, Peter L., and Thomas LUCKMANN. *The Social Construction of Reality, A Treatise in the Sociology of Knowledge.* Garden City, New York: Doubleday Anchor Books, 1967.

BUDD, Susan. *Sociologists and Religion.* London: Collier-Macmillan, 1973.

COLLINS, Randall. *Sociological Insight, An Introduction to Non-Obvious Sociology.* Oxford: Oxford University Press, 1982.

DALY, Mary. *Beyond God the Father.* Boston: Beacon Press, 1973.

DURKHEIM, Emile. *The Elementary Forms of Religious Life.* New York: Collier Books, 1961.

HADDEN, Jeffrey K. "The Sociology of Religion of Robert M. Bellah." "Review Symposium: Robert M. Bellah." *Journal for the Scientific Study of Religion.* 14 (1975).

HARTSHORNE, Charles. *Creativity in American Philosophy.* Albany: SUNY Press, 1984.

LUKES, Steven. *Emile Durkheim, His Life and Work.* Stanford, Cal.: Stanford University Press, 1985.

PARSONS, Talcott. *The Structure of Social Action.* Glencoe, IL: The Free Press, 1949.

POLANYI, Michael. *Personal Knowledge, Towards a Post Critical Philosophy.* London: Routledge and Kegan Paul, 1958.

SEGAL, Robert A. *Religion and the Social Sciences.* Atlanta: Scholars Press, 1989.

WILSON, Bryan. "The Return of the Sacred." *Journal for the Scientific Study of Religion.* 18 (1979).

RELIGION

BARTH, Karl. *Church Dogmatics.* Volume I, Part 2: *The Doctrine of the Word of God.* Ed. G.W. Bromiley and T.F. Torrance. New York: Charles Scribner's Sons, 1956.

BONHOEFFER, Dietrich. *Letters and Papers from Prison.* London: SCM Press, 1953.

BUBER, Martin. *I and Thou.* Trans. Ronald Gregor Smith. New York: Charles Scribner's Sons, 1958.

ELLUL, Jacques. *The New Demons.* Trans. C. Edward Hopkin. New York: The Seabury Press, 1975.

LASH, Nicholas. *The Beginning and the End of Religion.* Cambridge: Cambridge University Press, 1996.

SMITH, Wilfred Cantwell. *The Meaning and End of Religion.* Toronto: New American Library of Canada, Mentor Books, 1964.

TILLICH, Paul. *Dynamics of Faith.* New York: Harper Torchbooks, 1957.

The paper used in this publication meets the minimum requirements
of American National Standard for Information Sciences -
Permanence of Paper for Printed Library Materials, ANSI Z39.48-1992.

AGMV
MARQUIS
Québec, Canada
1998